# PERSPECTIVES

# ON

# EVANGELISM

Rom 1:16

To God be the glory!

To God be the glory!

# Perspectives

# on

# Evangelism

Encouraging Effective Evangelism

Gene Gurganus

Ambassador-Emerald International
Greenville, South Carolina●Belfast, Northern Ireland

Library of Congress Cataloging-in-Publication Data

Gurganus, Gene
      Perspectives on Evangelism: Encouraging Effective
      Evangelism / Willie Eugene Gurganus.
         p.cm.
      Includes bibliographical references, Scripture Index,
      Person Index, and Subject Index.
      ISBN 1-889893-37-4
      Historical, Biblical, Practical and Prophetical Study
      of Evangelism.
      9781889 893372

Ambassador-Emerald International
Emerald House Group, Inc.
427 Wade Hampton Blvd.
Greenville, SC 29609
Phone (864) 235-2434
Fax: (864) 235-2491
Toll-Free: 800-209-8570

and

Ambassador Productions, Ltd.
Providence House
Ardenlee Street
Belfast BT68QJ
Northern Ireland

www.emeraldhouse.com

First Printing, 2000
Printed in the United States of America

Cover design by Joseph Tyrpak

# Contents

## A Practical Perspective of Evangelism

## A Prophetical Perspective of Evangelism

## Appendices

## Indices

# Foreword

If there is a more thorough and exhaustive Biblical study of evangelism than this, I've never seen it. Dr. Gurganus, veteran missionary evangelist, has given birth to an epic work which comes forth from a lifetime of evangelistic enterprise. The ring of authenticity therefore reverberates from every page. As a qualified "tour leader," he shows us in detail from both Testaments of Scripture the wonders of God's loving plan from the fall of man to the redemption of man.

He shows us also the privilege and obligation of man to take this glorious message of grace to every creature. The wonder of it all is remarkable. The duty of it all is undeniable. The conviction of it all is inescapable.

This book is a wake-up call to the Bible-believing church which seems to have forgotten that the Saviour left us with a call to gather a bride for Him, even in this postmodern, secularistic society. So many church members are so busy trying to make a little bit of Heaven on earth for themselves that the reality of Hell and man's eternal soul that will live somewhere forever seems antiquated and uncompelling. In an effort to counteract that, I often have the students at Bob Jones University say the following words with me in Chapel: "The most sobering reality in the world today is that people are dying and going to hell today." Too many believers spend too much of their lives in forgetfulness and indifference toward the reality that man will not live forever on this planet. Rescuing men as brands from the burning is no longer our obsession.

One should not plan to read this book if he wants to live the rest of his life indulging his excuses for not being involved in evangelizing the lost. We can ignore what this book says; we can try to argue against what it says; but it makes it impossible to deny that the Bible says there is a mandate that God has "given to us the ministry of reconciliation; to wit, that God was in Christ, reconciling the world unto himself, not imputing their trespasses unto them; and hath committed unto us the word of reconciliation. Now then we are ambassadors for Christ" (II Cor. 5:18-20).

Dr. Bob Jones III
President, Bob Jones University

# Preface

President Dwight Eisenhower reportedly said, "Urgent things are seldom important; important things are seldom urgent." Yet, both urgency and importance mark the command of Christ to go into all the world and make disciples in all nations. Some separate missions and evangelism, but to do so is a grave error. Missions is evangelism over there, and evangelism is missions right here. Oftentimes evangelism and discipleship are treated as separate entities. To do so is to hinder the work of Christ.

> Go ye therefore, and teach all nations, baptizing them in the name of the Father, and of the Son, and of the Holy Ghost: teaching them to observe all things whatsoever I have commanded you: and, lo, I am with you alway, even unto the end of the world. Amen. (Matthew 28:19-20).

In these pivotal verses, our Lord lays out His will for the apostles and their followers. The goal is to teach, that is to disciple, the nations. The discipling process includes evangelism and edification. Our first duty is to evangelize the lost. In the Great Commission (Matthew 28:19), the first command is to baptize in the name of the Father, Son, and Holy Ghost. Only believers are to be baptized; therefore, baptizing presupposes preaching the gospel and persuading sinners to believe on the Lord Jesus Christ as Savior and Lord (Acts 16:31).

The observing student will notice that in verses 19 and 20 the command is to teach. In verse 19, the Greek verb for "teach" is *matheteuo,* which can be translated as "make disciples." The command is to disciple all nations or to make disciples in all nations. Dr. Roland Leavell clarifies the verb usage:

In this commission there is one dominant and controlling imperative, while all the other verb forms are participles. The central part of Jesus' commission is found in the imperative: 'Make disciples.' In the original Greek this verb is formed on the noun for 'disciple' and should be translated 'make disciples.' The other three verb forms of the Great Commission are participles: 'going,' 'baptizing,' 'teaching.'[1]

To make disciples is the goal; preaching, baptizing, and teaching are means to accomplish the goal. Discipling incorporates both evangelism and edification. The stated purpose of discipleship is to bring people from no faith to mature faith in the Lord Jesus Christ.

Evangelizing and discipling are not the only tasks to which the church is called, but these important duties are certainly foundational. Dr. Bob Jones, Sr., said, "The church that fails to evangelize will soon fossilize." He also said, "Orthodoxy cannot function without evangelistic unction." The greatest Bible exposition will soon grow cold and barren if it fails to encourage evangelism.

With fear, trepidation, and a deep sense of unworthiness I begin this treatise on evangelism and discipleship. Although I have been evangelizing and discipling for 45 years, I do not set myself up as an example or an expert. My colleague, Mel Lacock, and I conducted 54 Jerusalem Outreach Conferences from 1991 through 1995, with the stated purpose of mobilizing local churches to evangelize their Jerusalems. In these conferences, we have knocked on 6,773 doors and presented the gospel to thousands. I mention these facts to let the readers know that I am vitally interested in and involved in evangelism and discipleship. It would be great to think that I have found the secret. No, I have no secret formulas, but I have learned something along the journey both by practice and observation.

My desire is to share what I have learned with those who have a heart interest in reaching people for Christ and helping them mature in Christ. The Apostle Paul summed it up succinctly in Colossians 1:28: "Whom we preach, warning every man, and teaching every man in all wisdom; that we may present every man perfect in Christ Jesus."

Evangelism, soul-winning, and discipling are matters of great importance. Much controversy swirls around these subjects. Good men present differing and oftentimes clashing ideas. The controversy surrounding evangelism is not between those who do not believe the Bible. Sincere, earnest Bible-preaching and Bible-believing people find themselves in conflict as they purport to state what they believe the Bible teaches. Where good men differ, it is wise to tread cautiously, not dogmatically. I do not have the audacity to believe that this work will end the controversy. However, I have made an honest endeavor to stick with the Book. My motto has long been "what the Bible says is so; what the Bible says I will do."

In a study such as this, it is necessary to learn from others. Much research has gone into preparing this work. As I read what others have written, I find good teaching on evangelism and discipling from sources that in other areas, according to my limited judgment, may be mistaken. My agreement with a writer in the area under discussion does not mean that I approve of all he has written or done. It is not my purpose to take sides, to prove anyone right or wrong. My purpose is to go to the Bible, and, without fearing who may like it or not like it, let the Bible speak.

I am often asked why I write books. Let me tell you it is no fun. It is hard, hard work. To speak is to be misunderstood; to write is to be crucified. I am a fundamentalist Christian who believes the fundamental doctrines of the Christian faith. I am a separatist who believes it is wrong to join with and abet professed Christian teachers who deny the fundamentals of the faith. The Bible states plainly in II Corinthians 6:14-18 that we are not to infiltrate bastions of unbelief but rather to separate from them. Very little has been written by fundamentalists on evangelism and discipleship. For posterity's sake, it will be good to have on record what a fundamentalist had to say on this important subject.

Another reason caused me to undertake this taxing endeavor. Dr. John Sircar, president of the Bangladesh Theological Seminary, requested that I teach a course on evangelism and discipleship. Since the preparation for this course required significant effort, I thought the study should be shared with a larger group than the seminary students.

My aim is to look at this subject from four perspectives: the historical, the biblical, the practical, and the prophetical. Please join me in praying that God would be pleased to use this study to encourage His people to give attention to the main thing, making disciples.

Gene Gurganus
Taylors, South Carolina

---

1. Roland Q. Leavell, Evangelism: Christ's Imperative Commission (Broadman Press, Nashville, 1979) 15.

# Dedication

In dedicating this book, I wish to do so by making a particular and a general dedication.

First, the particular dedication. I dedicate this book on evangelism to the two men who were instrumental in bringing me to faith in the Lord Jesus Christ; Evangelist Oliver B. Greene, and Mr. Johnny Harper. The Spirit-filled preaching of Oliver Greene brought me under deep conviction of sin and the timely, scriptural counsel of Johnny Harper revealed to me salvation by personal faith in Jesus Christ. Praise God for the miracle of salvation and the human instruments He used to bring this sinful man to Christ.

Second, in general I dedicate this book to all those in the body of Christ who seek to do the work of an evangelist, who strive to bring sinful men and women to Christ the Lord and Savior. In these days of apostasy and compromise, may their number increase.

# Acknowledgments

Several key people have entered into my labors in producing this rather thorough book on evangelism. First, I acknowledge my great debt to all those who have written on the subject of evangelism from whom I have learned much. Second, I acknowledge my editors who have been a tremendous help in keeping me on track and in fine tuning the manuscript. Kim Reese Hall edited the first half of the book, and Wendy Rumminger took over the second half. I cannot thank them enough for their good work in helping me express in a correct way what I wanted to say. Bob Nestor, an English professor, and Paul Brown, retired chemistry professor of Bob Jones University, both carefully proofread the manuscript. My editor-in-chief, Robert Franklin, has been an encouragement from the very beginning. He has read and reread the manuscript and helped with the pagination, footnotes, bibliography, indexes, and all the technical aspects of preparing a book for publication. There is no way I can express my gratitude to Bob for his unselfish and untiring help. Dr. Edward Panosian gave good counsel on the section dealing with the historical perspective of evangelism. His knowledgeable suggestions made this portion of the book more accurate and understandable. My colleague, Melvin Lacock, helped me formulate many of the ideas found in the section on the practical perspective of evangelism. It has been a joy working in the harvest with my friend and brother in Christ. My wife, Elizabeth, has been very patient and understanding as great blocks of time were spent before the word processor. Finally, I thank the Lord of the Harvest who saved me and sent me to labor in His fields. During the writing of this book, I was conscious of His presence and His help. May it be a blessing to all who labor for Him.

We do not present our supplications before Thee for our righteousnesses, but for **THY GREAT MERCIES**

DANIEL 9:18

# Weekly Prayer Bulletin

Hampton Park Baptist Church

875 State Park Road, Greenville, SC  29609

Phone (864) 232-5691

# Wednesday, April 11, 2001

## Spiritual Requests

☐ Please keep praying for **Dawn Lennon's** family following the loss of her dad, Marshall Chapman. (233 Elaine Ave., Taylors 29687)

☐ **Daniel Ryerson**, grandson of the **Jim Ryersons** and nephew of Lisë Mizell and Margaret Polson, was killed in a car accident on Monday. His funeral will be in Louisiana. (Ryerson - 27 Prof's Place, Greenville 29609)

☐ **Evelyn McNeely's** sister in-law, Evelyn Foster passed away on Monday and her funeral is tomorrow. (3 Beverly Ave., Greenville 29605)

☐ **Shelley Johansen** asks prayer for the unsaved husband and children of a cousin who died suddenly in Michigan.

## Physical Requests

☐ **Barbara Counts** is improving and plans are to move her to Laurel Baye Nursing Home next week.

☐ **Darlene Bingham** was moved to the rehabilitation floor at St. Francis today and is making gradual progress since hip surgery.

☐ **Nona Patterson** will appreciate our prayers as she undergoes back surgery tomorrow.

☐ **Lester Wright** has been transferred to the Westside Nursing Home. (8 North Texas Ave., Greenville 29601)

☐ Continue to remember **Ron Tagliapiertra** in his recovery. Pray regarding a possible transfer to an Illinois hospital.

☐ **Gene Arnold** will be able to return to Greenville this weekend after emergency surgery in Georgia last week. (7 Ivanhoe Cr., Greenville 29615)

☐ **Edna Johnson** (121 Hilltop Drive, Travelers Rest 29690) had cataract surgery on Monday and **Joan Godwin** (157 Montague Road, #115 Greenville 29617) yesterday.

☐ **Sarah Larkin** had tests yesterday to determine the advisability of surgery for circulation in her foot. (704 Country Lane, Gray Court 29645)

☐ **Clarine Lovingood**, Audrey Bruce's mom, is now off the ventilator but still in intensive care. Others to remember are **Lewis Ziegler's mom** and **Betty Simons**, mother of Charles Simons, both of whom have cancer; **Diane Switzer's dad** who had knee replacement surgery; and **Dorcas Kinn**, Jackie Riebe's unsaved aunt, who has esophageal cancer. **Michael Larson**, grandson of the Eric Larsons, needs much prayer as he undergoes cancer treatment. Pray especially for insurance approval for a new type of bone marrow transplant.

## Others On Our Prayer List

| | | |
|---|---|---|
| John White | Julie Alexander | Mynette Eberline |
| Charlotte Bailey | Becka Loach | Allen Fretwell |
| Ron Channel | | |

## Shut-Ins to Remember

Carl Erikson, Rm 273, Brighton Gardens, 1306 Pelham Rd., Greenville 29615
Nellie Davis, 917 State Park Road, Greenville 29609

## Missionary Requests

☐ **Ken and Rhonda Johnson** (South Korea) and **Martha Jongewaard** (Austria) are missionaries for our prayer focus.

☐ **Don Morgan**, director of Lucerne Camp, remains hospitalized but is making slow progress. Continue praying for the family and the camp staff during this very busy time.

☐ **George and Marilyn Jensen** arrived home from Uruguay today, and **Ken and Joan Jensen** will be leaving Saturday for a missions conference in Wisconsin.

☐ Pray for the **Bill Masons** (Children's Gospel Clubs) as they prepare for two weeks of meetings in Carriacou, beginning April 26. Their summer revivals will be in Hendersonville, Piedmont, and Simpsonville. Pray for these revivals and for the telephone evangelism ministry in which cards are given to children with a number to call and hear the gospel. Last month there were more than 2,000 calls in South Carolina.

☐ **Dave and Donna Utter** (Marshall Islands) ask us to pray for the unsaved husbands of the ladies in their church. Dave has finished translation of Jeremiah through Malachi.

☐ Pray concerning our **missions conference**, June 24-28.

☐ The father of missionary **Eliseo Cuenca** passed away yesterday. (Apto. Postal 3, Zacualtipan, Hidalgo 43200, MEXICO)

☐ **Micah Moeller**, son of missionaries Brent and Sheila, is now on a second medication with no significant change in his condition.

☐ A two-week mission team to Haiti led by **Dennis Washer** with departure on April 22 has space for one more person to help with the continuing construction of **Dr. Anne Livingston's** medical clinic.

## Prayer for America

☐ Pray for **President Bush** and other diplomats who are dealing with China. Also pray for the safe arrival home of the 24 crew members of the airplane.

*PP.535-551*

*PP 556-575*

To have your prayer request listed in this bulletin, please phone it to the church office by 9:00 a.m. Wednesday morning. The office phone number is 232-5691.

## Local Hospital Addresses

**Allen Bennett Memorial Hospital**
313 Memorial Drive
Greer, SC  29651

**St. Francis Hospital**
One St. Francis Drive
Greenville, SC  29601

**St. Francis Women's &
Family Hospital**
125 Commonwealth Drive
Greenville, SC  29615

**Greenville Memorial Hospital**
701 Grove Road
Greenville, SC  29605

**W. J. Barge Memorial Hospital**
Bob Jones University
Greenville, SC  29614

**Hillcrest Hospital**
P. O. Box 279
Simpsonville, SC  29681

# Introduction

Armies do not move without orders. Can you envision an infantry division attacking and capturing an enemy position for the fun of it? Never. However, when orders come, military men are expected to move without regard to risks involved. As we were reminded on the 50th anniversary of D-Day, the discipline that enables men to go to their deaths in fierce combat is awesome.

The Bible uses the military metaphor to describe Christian service. The enemies are sin and Satan. The conflict is between good and evil, darkness and light. One of the great warriors of the Christian faith summed up his life in this statement: "I have fought a good fight, I have finished my course, I have kept the faith" (II Timothy 4:7). In Ephesians 6:11, we are admonished to put on the whole armor of God in order to withstand the wiles of the wicked one. This battle is not with flesh and blood (men), but against spiritual enemies, against spiritual wickedness in high places (the Devil).

To understand this conflict between God and Satan, we need to go back to the beginning. Satan, the implacable enemy of God, led our first parents into sin and rebellion against God (Genesis 3:4-5). In pronouncing punishment upon Satan for this dastardly deed, God gave the first promise of a coming Savior: "And I will put enmity between thee and the woman, and between thy seed and her seed; it shall bruise thy head, and thou shalt bruise his heel" (Genesis 3:15). Referred to by theologians as the *protevangelium* (first gospel), it describes the spiritual warfare that rages even today.

Since this verse is so important to our understanding of God's purposes, let us see what it means. *The Bible Knowledge Commentary* sums it up simply and accurately.

God said there would be a perpetual struggle
between Satanic forces and mankind. It would
be between Satan and the woman, and their
respective offspring or 'seeds.' The 'offspring'
of the woman was Cain, then all humanity
at large, and then Christ and those collectively
in Him. The 'offspring' of the serpent includes
demons and anyone . . . whose 'father' is the
devil (John 8:44). Satan would cripple mankind
(you will strike at his heel), but *the* seed, Christ,
would deliver the fatal blow (He will crush your
head).[1]

In Colossians, Paul shows the fulfillment of Christ's defeat
of Satan: "And having spoiled principalities and powers, he made
a shew of them openly, triumphing over them in it" (Colossians
2:15). Even though Satan is a defeated foe, he is still bruising
the heel of mankind. Satan is a deceiver, and his main work is
blinding the minds of men lest they believe on Christ and be saved
(II Corinthians 4:4).

Using the military metaphor helps us see the big picture.
The battle of the ages rages between God and Satan. The whole
race has been affected by Satan's lie and Adam's sin. "Wherefore,
as by one man sin entered into the world, and death by sin; and
so death passed upon all men, for that all have sinned" (Romans
5:12). The death mentioned here is twofold: physical and spiritual.
Death is not cessation of being, but separation. In physical death,
the soul separates from the body; in spiritual death, the soul
separates from God.

God tells us clearly His purposes for mankind: "For I have
created him; for my glory, I have formed him; yea, I have made
him" (Isaiah 43:7). God willed that man glorify Him in spirit,
soul, and body. He purposed that mankind would honor Him in
their attitudes and in their actions. He desired the voluntary,
unforced, unprogrammed love, honor, and worship of His
creatures because of who and what He is. Without the power to

choose, there is no power to love. Love cannot be forced or programmed. God gave man the freedom to choose good or evil. Unfortunately, man chose evil. By choice, man sided with the devil and rebelled against God. All the havoc, heartache, and decadence on planet Earth resulted from man's disobedience.

Of course, God was not caught by surprise. "Who [God] hath saved us, and called us with an holy calling, not according to our works, but according to his own purpose and grace, which was given us in Christ Jesus before the world began" (II Timothy 1:9). Before man sinned, God knew the result and purposed to save him and to make him holy, not by man's works, but by God's grace (Ephesians 2:8-10).

The Bible progressively reveals God at work to bring mankind back to Himself. In this drama of redemption, God has used various agencies. One of the first was Noah. "Noah found grace in the eyes of the LORD" (Genesis 6:8). Noah and his family were a believing remnant that God chose to fulfill His purposes when it was necessary to remove the unbelieving majority. "By faith Noah, being warned of God of things not seen as yet, moved with fear, prepared an ark to the saving of his house; by the which he condemned the world, and became heir of the righteousness which is by faith" (Hebrews 11:7).

However, Noah and his family failed to obey God, and in a few generations mankind was once again in open rebellion against God. This rebellion climaxed at Babel, at which time God intervened by confusing the languages and separating mankind into various nationalities (Genesis 11).

Next, God chose a particular nation to be a witness to the nations. The father of that nation was Abraham. The Bible tells us clearly the purpose of God's call to Abraham: "And I will make of thee a great nation, and I will bless thee, and make thy name great; and thou shalt be a blessing: And I will bless them that bless thee, and curse him that curseth thee: and in thee shall all families of the earth be blessed" (Genesis 12:2-3). George Peters' comments are helpful:

The central and significant fact is that the call of Abraham is not personal favoritism of a particularistic god to establish a local religion in practice and design . . . . Just as God does not call His minister for the minister's sake but for the sake of the congregation, the community and the world, so He did not call Abraham for Abraham's sake. The world was in view, and mankind was the goal . . . .[2]

Israel is God's continuing miracle. Although they failed God in their witness to the nations (Romans 2:24), their influence for God and good is inestimable. Through Israel came the Ten Commandments, which stand unparalleled in the history of mankind. Through Israel came the elaborate sacrificial system foreshadowing the ultimate sacrifice of Christ, the Lamb of God. Through Israel God revealed Himself and His will by the Holy Scriptures.

Presently God is using His church to be a witness to the nations. God has a special purpose for the church: "To the intent that now unto the principalities and powers in heavenly places might be known by the church the manifold wisdom of God" (Ephesians 3:10).

In Luke 24:47-48, Christ gave the Apostles and the embryonic church marching orders: "And that repentance and remission of sins should be preached in his name among all nations, beginning at Jerusalem. And ye are witnesses of these things."

As you read these words, the cosmic conflict rages. The battle for the souls, the minds, the worship of mankind continues. The devil covets the souls and minds of men, not that he might bless them, but that he might destroy them. He is Apollyon, the destroyer. Working for him are powerful forces: the lust of the flesh, the lust of the eyes, and the pride of life (I John 2:16).

On the other hand, God is seeking worshipers, too (John 4:23)—not that he might destroy them, but to endow them with eternal blessings. To reconcile fallen man and change him from rebel to willing servant there are three agencies at work: the Holy Spirit, the Word of God, and the servants of God.

Right results, right motivation, right approaches, and right methodologies depend, to a great extent, on a proper understanding of the battle. What are the objectives? What is success? And how do we measure it? What is our responsibility and what is God's? How do we know if we are winning or losing the battle? I trust these questions and many others will be answered from the Word of God as we study *Perspectives on Evangelism.*

---

1. John Walvoord and Roy Zuck, eds., *The Bible Knowledge Commentary* (USA: Victor Books, 1983) 33.

2. George W. Peters, *A Biblical Theology of Missions* (Chicago: Moody Press, 1972) 110.

# A
# Historical
# Perspective
# of
# Evangelism

"God, who at sundry times and in divers manners spake in time past unto the fathers by the prophets, Hath in these last days spoken unto us by his Son" (Hebrews 1:1-2).

# 1

# A Light
# to the Nations

God chose Israel to be a light to the nations. Israel, with its faith in the one true, Creator God, and its superb ethical and moral standards was an enigma to the pagans. This miracle nation has played and will play an important part in God's work of taking the good news of God to the nations of the world. Speaking through His prophet Isaiah, God declares, "Thou art my servant, O Israel, in whom I will be glorified" (Isaiah 49:3). A few verses later God promises that "I will also give thee for a light to the Gentiles [nations], that thou mayest be my salvation unto the end of the earth" (Isaiah 49:6). God has and will use Israel as a medium for blessing the whole world.

God identified Himself to Moses as *Yahweh (I Am That I Am)* and by delivering the Israelites from Egypt and bringing them into Canaan established a special relationship with the nation of Israel. He also revealed Himself as *Elohim*, the strong one, the Creator of the universe, and *El Elyon*, possessor of heaven and earth. Thus, He was God of the nations and had His servants among the nations.

In Genesis 14, after Abraham had rescued Lot and looted the five kings, he was met by Melchizedek, king of Salem, who also was priest of the most high God (*El Elyon*). "And he blessed him, and said, Blessed be Abram of the most high God, possessor of heaven and earth: And blessed be the most high God, which hath delivered thine enemies into thy hand. And he [Abraham] gave him tithes of all" (Genesis 14:19-20).

Melchizedek's priesthood which was outside the covenant was nevertheless honored by Abraham. In choosing Abraham, God did not reject the other nations. Be it forever remembered that the God of Israel is also the God of the nations.

To properly appreciate what God is doing now and will do in the future, it is essential to see how God worked in the past. Genesis 1-11 is the preface of the entire Bible and forms the foundation which undergirds all of Scripture.

In the first eleven chapters of Genesis God's focus was on the nations that were scattered by the events at Babel (Genesis 11). In Genesis 12, God changes His focus. He singles out one man, and through this man, Abraham, He purposes to bless all the families of the world.

> Now the LORD had said unto Abram, Get thee
> out of thy country, and from thy kindred, and
> from thy father's house, unto a land I will shew
> thee: And I will make of thee a great nation, and
> I will bless thee, and make thy name great; and
> thou shalt be a blessing: And I will bless them that
> bless thee, and curse him that curseth thee: and
> in thee shall all families of the earth be blessed
> (Genesis 12:1-3).

Although God changed His focus, He did not change His purpose. The verses above teach that God blessed Abraham and through his seed, Jesus Christ, blessed all the families of the world.

The religious history of Abraham's time (the period after the dispersion of the people at Babel) was characterized by idolatry, sensuality, and mental depravity. Due to universal apostasy, deep darkness settled upon the world. Only divine intervention could save mankind.

To accomplish His divine purposes, the sovereign LORD marched into the life of Abraham. Abraham did not seek God; God sought Abraham. Through this man, God began a counterculture, a culture designed both to arrest evil and to unfold God's gracious plan of salvation to the whole world. From Abraham stem the great monotheistic religions: Judaism, Christianity, and Islam.

The story of Abraham is not a myth. If it were a myth, how do we account for the Jewish nation and its tremendous impact upon history? Secular anthropologists would like for us to believe that religion is the result of ethical evolution. No, the revelation that came to Abraham was a supernatural act of God. This moving of God in the life of Abraham was not the result of ethical evolution. Furthermore, this work of God in Abraham was not due to his sensitive, religious nature. Rather, the call of Abraham was God's first step in implementing His grand plan of redeeming mankind.

## ISRAEL'S PREPARATION

God was not playing favorites with Israel. His plan was to use this nation to accomplish His redemptive work. Thus, special preparation was required. This preparation involved several factors.

First, Israel was conscious of a unique relationship with God. God was the God of Abraham, Isaac, and Jacob. He was bound to them in an unconditional covenant that their sin and failure could not break (II Samuel 7:14-16).

Second, to Israel had come a special revelation. The God of glory appeared to Abraham. God continued to reveal Himself to Isaac, Jacob, Moses, Joshua, Samuel, and the prophets. Israel was known as the "people of the book." Moses and others carefully wrote down and preserved the messages received from God, insisting that these words were the very words of God. Jesus Christ put His seal upon these inspired writings known as the Old Testament (Matthew 5:18).

Third, Israel had a deep consciousness of a true and unique knowledge of God and His purposes. They were light years ahead of their contemporaries in their concept of God. While their neighbors groveled before tribal deities, the Israelites worshiped the God of heaven and earth. J. Philip Hyatt says it well:

> The prophets were not systematic theologians [and this goes for Moses and the fathers—Abraham, Isaac, and Jacob—as well]. They were God-intoxicated men whose religion was God-centered. God was for them not primarily an object of thought and speculation but an object of intimately personal experience. Their teachings about deity do not constitute a carefully worked out system but are the result of insights that came to them in great moments of revelation.[1]

The God-concept of a people determines their quality and character of life, religion, and culture. Primitive tribes often endure horrible customs because of taboos. A people's concept of God influences morality, government, learning, commerce, art, and literature. I Peter 1:15 sums it up: "But as he which hath called you is holy, so be ye holy in all manner of conversation."

Fourth, God worked into the consciousness of Israel a relationship between sin and suffering. To them, disasters such as famine, drought, and pestilence did not just happen. Neither were they acts of nature or evil deities. These judgments came as a result of sin and disobedience, either individually or collectively. Yet unlike the idolaters that surrounded them, they rejected *karma*, which is the belief that penalty and suffering are inevitable and inescapable. The Jews served the moral Governor of the universe who justly meted out punishment tempered with mercy.

Fifth, they had a living hope of divine salvation from sin, the destruction of evil, and the final triumph of good. Unlike their heathen neighbors who believed in the "circle of life," or reincarnation, the Jews believed history is linear and time is moving toward a goal of salvation and glory. Salvation is of the Lord, not of man. God is able to save from sin and provide atonement as demonstrated by the continuing blood sacrifices.[2]

## ISRAEL'S POSITION

Through Abraham, Israel became the people of God; under Moses they became the priests and servants of God. God had great plans and purposes for Israel. Listen to the majestic promises God gives to them in Exodus 19:4-6:

> Ye have seen what I did unto the Egyptians, and how I bare you on eagles' wings, and brought you unto myself. Now therefore, if ye will obey my voice indeed, and keep my covenant, then ye shall be a peculiar treasure unto me above all people: for all the earth is mine: and ye shall be unto me a kingdom of priests, and an holy nation. These are the words which thou shalt speak unto the children of Israel.

God challenges His people to servanthood. Accepting this challenge would have given Israel meaning, purpose, and direction. Israel was to be a priest to the nations, a kingdom of priests mediating the blessings of God to the nations of the world.

This high calling put heavy responsibilities upon Israel. One of these responsibilities was a high moral and ethical standard as revealed in the Ten Commandments. Then the costly sacrifices and offerings tested their dedication. Israel unconditionally became the people of God in the sovereign call of Abraham. But to be servants of God and priests to the nations required voluntary commitment and implicit obedience.

Isaiah speaks of Israel as a servant and a witness. In chapters 40-55, there are eighteen references to Israel as the servant of Jehovah. Three times Isaiah refers to Israel as witnesses of Jehovah (not Jehovah's Witnesses) (Isaiah 43:10,12, and 44:8). As servants of God, Israel was to serve as priests and witnesses: "This people have I formed for myself; they shall shew forth my praise" (Isaiah 43:21). And to whom were they to shew forth this praise? Isaiah 43:9 gives the answer. "Let all the nations be gathered together, and let the people be assembled: who among them can declare this, and shew us former things?" Israel as a witness was to preach to the nations.[3]

Israel was also to function as a kingdom of priests. As priests they were to represent the nations before God. It was theirs to mediate the blessings of God to the world. Sad to say, Israel failed in these dual responsibilities as witnesses and priests. However, God is not through with Israel yet. In the book of Revelation, we learn that during the tribulation period, 144,000 of all the tribes of Israel will be sealed and used for the glory of God (Revelation 7:4-8 and 14:1-5).

To Israel was committed the moral and ceremonial law. The moral law (the Ten Commandments) codified what Israel's attitude should be toward God and man. The ceremonial laws regulated all facets of Jewish life. We learn in Galatians the real purpose of the Law:

> Wherefore then serveth the law? It was added because of transgressions, till the seed should come to whom the promise was made. . . . Is the law then against the promises of God? God forbid: for if there had been a law given which could have given life, verily righteousness should have been by the law. But the scripture hath concluded  all under sin, that the promise by faith of Jesus Christ might be given to them that believe. But before faith came, we were kept under the law. . . . Wherefore the law was our schoolmaster to bring us unto Christ, that we might be justified by faith (Galatians 3:19, 21-24).

God used the Law, which was misconstrued into a "works" religion by the Jews, to bring the Gentiles to Christ.

## GOD'S PROMISES TO ISRAEL

The Old Testament is filled with promises of a coming Messiah. The first promise speaks of His humanity: "And I will put enmity between thee and the woman, and between thy seed and her seed; it shall bruise thy head, and thou shalt bruise his heel" (Genesis 3:15). This promised Savior will be of Adam's race, as seed of the woman.

Genesis 9:26 indicates that the blessing would come through the line of Shem, son of Noah. Next, we learn that the promised Seed would come through Abraham (Genesis 12:1-3). Jacob, Abraham's grandson, prophesied, "The sceptre shall not depart from Judah, nor a lawgiver from between his feet, until Shiloh come; and unto him shall the gathering of the people be" (Genesis 49:10). Finally, Nathan, the prophet of God, revealed to David that Messiah would descend from his lineage (I Chronicles 17:12-15). Hence, Messiah would be the "Son of David."

The promises concerning the Messiah provide specific information relating to times, places, and details of His life and work. Daniel specifies the exact time of Messiah's coming. (Daniel 9:25-26). Micah delineates the place of Messiah's birth at Bethlehem (Micah 5:2). Many details of His life, work, death, resurrection, and ascension are recorded in the Old Testament. The most amazing prophecies are found in Isaiah 53. The Messiah was a man of sorrows, smitten of God, not for His own sins, but for the sins of man who had gone astray. He was killed with criminals, and He made His grave with the rich. His soul was made an offering for sin so that in bearing iniquity He could justify them that believe.

At the appropriate time in history Christ came to fulfill His mission.

> But when the fullness of the time was come, God sent forth his Son, made of a woman, made under the law, To redeem them that were under the law,

that we might receive the adoption of sons. And
because ye are sons, God hath sent forth the Spirit
of His Son into your hearts, crying, Abba, Father
(Galatians 4:4-6).

Godly Jews looked expectantly for the promised Messiah.
Jewish maidens cherished the hope of giving birth to the deliverer.
At long last, the message came to Mary of Nazareth:

And the angel said unto her, Fear not, Mary: for
thou hast found favour with God. And, behold,
thou shall conceive in thy womb, and bring forth
a Son, and shalt call his name JESUS. He shall
be great, and shall be called the Son of the
Highest: and the Lord God shall give unto him
the throne of his father David (Luke 1:30-32).

God illumined old Simeon to recognize the baby Jesus
as the Messiah.

For mine eyes have seen thy salvation, which thou
hast prepared before the face of all people; A light
to lighten the Gentiles (nations), and the glory
of thy people Israel (Luke 2:30-32).

Jesus was a Jew of the tribe of Judah, a son of David.
The presence of Jewish people should remind us that from their
nation came the greatest blessing of all time, the Lord Jesus Christ.
Indeed, Israel has been a light to the nations and a source of
innumerable blessings to mankind. Through Israel we have
received our Holy Bible; we have witnessed specific prophecies
concerning Israel fulfilled; and we have observed God working
out His plans for His chosen nation. Without her contribution,
we Gentiles would be spiritual paupers. Anti-Semitism displays
an abominable ignorance of the plans and purposes of God.

1. J. Philip Hyatt, *Prophetic Religion* (Nashville: Abingdon-Cokesbury Press, 1947) 149.

2. Peters, 99-106.

3. Ibid., 123-124.

# 2

# Evangelism
# in the
# Old Testament

The overarching theme of the Bible is redemption. Yet there is a stark contrast between God's method in the Old Testament and in the New Testament. Some have the mistaken idea that in the Old Testament God concerned Himself only with Israel. It is true that from Genesis 12 to Acts 2 God's primary interest is Israel. This interest is not to be interpreted as callousness toward the other nations. Rather, God was carefully preparing a people for the purpose of blessing all the nations of the world.

There never was a time when the nations did not have access to God. As we have seen, Melchizedek and later Balaam were men outside of Israel who had a relationship with God. The light of the knowledge of the glory of God was dimming. Idolatry was sweeping the world. God in His sovereign grace chose a man, a family, a tribe, and finally a nation through which He would rekindle the light and accomplish His redemptive purposes in the world.

## OLD TESTAMENT METHODOLOGY

As we study evangelism in the Old Testament, we never read that Israel was commanded to go into all the world to preach

the message of God. Instead, Israel was to be God's "showpiece."
In Deuteronomy 28:1-2, note how God promises to bless Israel:

> And it shall come to pass, if thou shalt hearken
> diligently unto the voice of the LORD thy God,
> to observe and to do all his commandments which
> I command thee this day, that the LORD thy God
> will set thee on high above all nations of the earth:
> And all these blessings shall come on thee, and
> overtake thee, if thou shalt hearken unto the voice
> of the LORD thy God.

Deuteronomy 28:10 tells the result of these blessings:
"And all people of the earth shall see that thou art called by the
name of the LORD; and they shall be afraid of thee." The shocking
disparity between the blessings of God upon Israel and the other
nations was designed to startle the nations, to arouse their inquiry,
to attract them, and to draw them like a magnet to Jerusalem,
to the temple, and ultimately to God.

Several examples illustrate this truth. Hearing of the fame
of Solomon, the Queen of Sheba came to him with questions in
her heart. "And Solomon told her all her questions: and there
was nothing hid from Solomon which he told her not" (II Chronicles
9:2). Her reaction to hearing and seeing the wisdom and glory
that God had bestowed on Solomon shows the effectiveness of
God's method:

> And she said to the king, It was a true report
> which I heard in mine own land of thine acts, and
> of thy wisdom: Howbeit I believed not their
> words, until I came, and mine eyes have seen it:
> and, behold, the one half of the greatness of thy
> wisdom was not told me: for thou exceedeth the
> fame that I heard. Happy are thy men, and happy
> are these thy servants, which stand continually
> before thee, and hear thy wisdom. Blessed be the

LORD thy God, which delighted in thee to set
thee on his throne, to be king for the LORD thy
God: because thy God loved Israel, to establish
them for ever, therefore made he thee king over
them, to do judgment and justice (II Chronicles
9:5-8).

Without a doubt, the Queen of Sheba experienced life
changes as a result of her visit with Solomon. Assuredly she told
to all her kingdom the greatness and the glory of the God of
Israel.

## FAITHFUL LITTLE WITNESS

Another interesting example is found in II Kings 5.
Naaman was the captain of the army of Syria. During a raid on
Israel, he captured an Israelite maiden and gave her to his wife.
Soon Naaman became a leper. It seemed a hopeless situation
until the little slave girl whispered some good news to Naaman's
wife: "Would God my lord were with the prophet that is in
Samaria! for he would recover him of his leprosy" (II Kings 5:3).
As a result of the simple, earnest, faithful witness of this
little slave girl, Naaman found his way to the prophet Elisha.
Reluctantly, he dipped seven times in the Jordan River, and he
was cleansed of his leprosy. We see the result in II Kings 5:15,17:

And he returned to the man of God, he and all
his company, and came, and stood before him:
and he said, Behold, now I know that there is no
God in all the earth, but in Israel: now therefore,
I pray thee, take a blessing of thy servant. . . .
And Naaman said, Shall there not then, I pray
thee, be given to thy servant two mules' burden
of earth? for thy servant will henceforth offer
neither burnt offering nor sacrifice unto other
gods, but unto the LORD.

Can you imagine the joy of Naaman's wife and servant girl on his return? Certainly, the king of Syria and all the army heard of the power and glory of the God of Israel.

## BEAUTY OUT OF ASHES

During the captivity of Judah when it seemed that the cause of God was suffering irreversible defeat, God made the wrath of man to praise Him. Daniel, Shadrach, Meshach, and Abednego were missionaries *par excellence*. By their godly character and devotion to their God, the glory and power of the God of heaven were spread to all the known world.

On four occasions God used these men to glorify His name: when Daniel recalled and interpreted Nebuchadnezzar's dream; when Shadrach, Meshach, and Abednego were delivered from the fiery furnace; when Daniel told Nebuchadnezzar the kingdom would be taken away and then returned to him; and when Daniel was put into the lion's den. Note the effect of Daniel's deliverance on the king:

> Then king Darius wrote unto all people, nations, and languages, that dwelt in all the earth; Peace be multiplied unto you. I make a decree, That in every dominion of my kingdom men tremble and fear before the God of Daniel: for he is the living God, and stedfast for ever, and his kingdom that which shall not be destroyed, and his dominion shall be even unto the end. He delivereth and rescueth, and he worketh signs and wonders in heaven and in earth, who hath delivered Daniel from the power of the lions (Daniel 6:25-27).

The king did not glorify Daniel, but he glorified the God of Daniel. By the faithfulness of Daniel to His God, the knowledge of the true God was heralded around the world.

## REVIVAL AT NINEVEH

From the book of Jonah we learn that God is not bound by any methodology but acts sovereignly as He wills. Generally speaking, God's evangelistic method in the Old Testament economy was not to send missionaries to other countries, but inquirers were to come to Jerusalem and to the temple. In the case of Nineveh, God acted sovereignly to save a wicked city. Jonah was less than enthusiastic about being a missionary to the Assyrians.

Evangelistically, Jonah's Nineveh campaign has never been equaled. First, there was straight preaching. God saw fit to restrict the message to eight words: "Yet forty days, and Nineveh shall be overthrown" (Jonah 3:4). Second, the message of coming destruction was heard and believed by everyone from the king to the peasant. It was a people's movement. "So the people of Nineveh believed God, and proclaimed a fast, and put on sackcloth, from the greatest of them even to the least of them" (Jonah 3:5). Third, there was genuine repentance. "But let man and beast be covered with sackcloth, and cry mightily unto God: yea, let them turn every one from his evil way, and from the violence that is in their hands. Who can tell if God will turn and repent, and turn away from his fierce anger, that we perish not?" (Jonah 3:8-9). Fourth, there was restitution: "And God saw their works, that they turned from their evil way; and God repented of the evil, that he had said that he would do unto them; and he did it not" (Jonah 3:10).

Everyone was happy except Jonah. "But it displeased Jonah exceedingly, and he was very angry" (Jonah 4:1). In chapter one we see Jonah's disobedience; in chapter two, God's discipline; in chapter three Nineveh's deliverance, and in chapter four, Jonah's disappointment. But why was he disappointed? He had just witnessed the greatest revival in the history of the world. A huge metropolis had believed, repented, turned from their sins, and had been saved. His disappointment came from a restricted love. Jonah loved God and Israel, but he could not force himself to love Israel's archenemy, Assyria. Could the church's lack of outreach today be a result of restricted love?

A humorous, yet sad incident occurs at the close of the book of Jonah. Awaiting further developments, Jonah went outside of the city and tried to make himself comfortable by building a booth. God caused a gourd to grow up and shade Jonah. This protection from the hot sun caused Jonah to rejoice. But God caused a worm to kill the plant, and it quickly withered. Jonah became vehemently angry over the loss of the shade tree. "And God said to Jonah, Doest thou well to be angry for the gourd? And he said, I do well to be angry, even unto death" (Jonah 4:9). Here we see Jonah's misdirected love. God asked Jonah which was more important—plants or humans?

> Then said the LORD, Thou hast had pity on the gourd, for the which thou hast not labored, neither madest it grow; which came up in a night, and perished in a night: And should not I spare Nineveh, that great city, wherein are more than sixscore thousand persons that cannot discern between their right hand and their left hand; and also much cattle? (Jonah 4:10-11).

In our day many people value whales and trees more than people. Sensible people certainly value a healthy environment and are against inhumane treatment of animals. Environmentalism has its roots in the New Age movement with its doctrine of monism, which elevates nature by teaching pantheism. Those who would deify nature, in the process denigrate man. God was teaching Jonah to get his priorities straight. People created in the image of God are of more value than trees. How current and relevant the Bible is!

## GOSPEL ACCORDING TO ISAIAH

The prophet Isaiah was a true evangelist who proclaimed the love God had not only for Israel, but for the whole world. A discussion of evangelism in the Old Testament necessitates that we look at the evangelistic message of Isaiah.

In his book, Isaiah deals with grand themes such as God, man, sin, grace, and deliverance. It is striking to note the similarities between the book of Isaiah and the Holy Bible.

J. Sidlow Baxter explains why the Book of Isaiah is a "mini-Bible":

> As there are sixty-six books in the Bible, so there are sixty-six chapters in this Book of Isaiah as it appears in our English version; and as the sixty-six books of the Bible are divided into the thirty-nine of the Old Testament and the twenty-seven of the New, so the sixty-six chapters of Isaiah are divided into thirty-nine and twenty-seven. Moreover, as the thirty-nine books of the Old Testament are mainly occupied with the Law, and the judgment which comes on those who disobey it, so the first thirty-nine chapters of Isaiah are mainly occupied with the thought of judgment on the covenant people because of their disobedience to the Law; and as the twenty-seven books of the New Testament are mainly occupied with the message of divine Grace, and the salvation which it brings, so the last twenty-seven chapters of Isaiah are a message of divine grace and comfort, and of coming salvation. Thus, the Book of Isaiah is a kind of Bible all in itself.[1]

It does not take Isaiah long to get to the point of human sin:

> Hear, O heavens, and give ear, O earth: for the LORD hath spoken, I have nourished and brought up children, and they have rebelled

against me. The ox knoweth his owner, and the ass his master's crib: but Israel doth not know, my people doth not consider. Ah sinful nation, a people laden with iniquity, a seed of evildoers, children that are corrupters: they have forsaken the LORD, they have provoked the Holy One of Israel unto anger, they are gone away backward (Isaiah 1:2-4).

Without mincing words, Isaiah pounds away at human pride:

The lofty looks of man shall be humbled, and the haughtiness of men shall be bowed down, and the LORD alone shall be exalted in that day (Isaiah 2:11).

Throughout his book, the fiery, silver-tongued prophet exposes sin and pronounces woe on those who continue in sin. Every true evangelist brings people face to face with sin. Only after the acknowledgment and confession of sin has taken place is the penitent ready for the good news of the gospel.

Isaiah's evangelistic burden came as he prayed in the temple. Chapter six describes Isaiah's vision and subsequent call. In the year that king Uzziah died, Isaiah saw the Lord and he saw himself (Isaiah 6:1). First, there was confrontation. The prophet met the Holy One of Israel. This confrontation resulted in confession of sin: "Woe is me! for I am undone; because I am a man of unclean lips, and I dwell in the midst of a people of unclean lips" (Isaiah 6:5). As always, true confession results in cleansing. The seraph took a coal from the altar and touched Isaiah's lips (Isaiah 6:6-7). It is interesting to note that the coals from the altar touched him on the mouth. Where would the coals touch us if we confessed our sins? Once the sin problem was settled, Isaiah heard God's call (Isaiah 6:8). In this call we see God's sovereignty and man's responsibility. "Whom shall I send?"

speaks of God's sovereignty. "Who will go for us?" reminds us of our human responsibility. Last, the commission to "Go, and tell this people" (Isaiah 6:9) comes to Isaiah.

Isaiah's first message is of sin and disobedience. He preaches to a religious but hard-hearted people. "Cry aloud, spare not, lift up thy voice like a trumpet, and shew my people their transgression, and the house of Jacob their sins" (Isaiah 58:1). He assures the people there is nothing wrong with God, but he warns them that their iniquities have separated them from God and caused him to hide His face from them (Isaiah 59:1-2).

As a bearer of good news, he brings to the people the eternal Word of God:

> The voice said, Cry. And he said, What shall I cry? All flesh is grass, and all the goodliness thereof is as the flower of the field: The grass withereth, the flower fadeth: because the spirit of the LORD bloweth upon it: surely the people is grass. The grass withereth, the flower fadeth: but the word of our God shall stand for ever (Isaiah 40:6-8).

Using the metaphors of grass and flower for flesh, Isaiah acknowledges the beauty and the pleasantness of life. Eloquently he contrasts the eternality of God's Word with the brevity of life.

Isaiah was far from provincial in his preaching and outlook. His message is all-inclusive: "Look unto me, and be ye saved, all the ends of the earth: for I am God, and there is none else" (Isaiah 45:22). The gospel shines brightly in Isaiah 53:6: "All we like sheep have gone astray; we have turned every one to his own way; and the LORD hath laid on him the iniquity of us all."

## PROOF OF INSPIRATION

Through the inspiration of the Holy Spirit, Isaiah preached

the crucifixion and resurrection of Christ 713 years before Christ came into the world. The Holy Spirit through the pen of Isaiah paints a word picture of the sacrificial death and the subsequent resurrection of our Lord Jesus Christ in Isaiah 53. That this passage refers to Christ, none but the willfully blind can fail to see. Again, J. Sidlow Baxter's comments are helpful:

> It has been truly said that 'the prolonged description of chapter liii. suits only one figure in all human history—the Man of Calvary.' The following twelve points absolutely confirm this, for in their totality they cannot possibly be applied to any other. (1) He comes in utter lowliness—'a root out of a dry ground', etc. (2) He is 'despised and rejected of men.' etc. (3) He suffered for the sins and in the place of others—'He was wounded for our transgressions,' etc. (4) It was God Himself who caused the suffering to be vicarious—'The Lord hath laid on Him the iniquity of us all.' (5) There was absolute resignation under the vicarious suffering—'He was afflicted, yet He opened not his mouth,' etc. (6) He died as a felon—'He was taken from prison and from judgment.' (7) He was cut off prematurely—'He was cut off out of the land of the living,' etc. (8) Yet He was personally guiltless—'He had done no violence, neither was any deceit in his mouth.' (9) And He was to live on after His sufferings—'He shall see His seed; He shall prolong His days.' (10) Jehovah's pleasure was then to prosper in His hand—'The pleasure of Jehovah shall prosper in his hand.'(11) He was to enter into mighty triumph after His suffering—'He shall divide the spoil with the strong', etc. (12) By all this, and by 'justifying many' through His death and living again, He was to

'see of the travail of His soul and be satisfied.'[2]

At the beginning of His ministry, Jesus following His custom went to the synagogue in Nazareth. When He stood up to read, they handed Him the Book of Isaiah and He read:

> The Spirit of the Lord is upon me, because he hath anointed me to preach the gospel to the poor; he hath sent me to heal the brokenhearted, To preach deliverance to the captives, and recovering of sight to the blind, to set at liberty them that are bruised, To preach the acceptable year of the Lord. And he closed the book. . . . And he began to say unto them, This day is this scripture fulfilled in your ears (Luke 4:18-21).

Many years before the Messiah came, Isaiah described His ministry of good news. In the synagogue at Nazareth, our Lord identified Himself with the prophecy of Isaiah.

Isaiah 61:3 capsulizes the outworking and final result of the gospel ministry:

> To appoint unto them that mourn in Zion, to give unto them beauty for ashes, the oil of joy for mourning, the garment of praise for the spirit of heaviness; that they might be called trees of righteousness, the planting of the LORD, that he might be glorified.

There it is, a divine summary of God's good news. The gospel blesses lives and heals relationships, resulting in a joyful righteousness in which God alone is glorified.

---

1. J. Sidlow Baxter, *Explore The Book*, Vol. 3 (London: Marshall, Morgan & Scott, Ltd., 1962) 239.
2. Ibid., 253-254.

# 3

# Evangelism
# in the
# Early Church

Winston Churchill, speaking before the House of Commons on August 20, 1940, spoke these words concerning the men and women of the Royal Air Force: "Never in the field of human conflict was so much owed by so many to so few."[1] Humanly speaking, these men and women saved the free world from Hitler and his hordes. The same tribute could be given to the men and women of the early church. Their enemies accused them of turning the world upside-down (Acts 17:6). Actually, they were turning it right side up! Michael Green's comments on these early Christians tell us why they turned the world right side up:

> The enthusiasm to evangelize which marked the early Christians is one of the most remarkable things in the history of religions. Here were men and women of every rank and station in life, of every country in the known world, so convinced that they had discovered the riddle of the universe, so sure of the one true God whom they had come to know, that nothing must stand in the way of their passing on this good news to others. As we have seen, they did it by preaching

and personal conversation, by formal discourse and informal testimony, by arguing in the synagogue and by chattering in the laundry. They might be slighted, laughed at, disenfranchised, robbed of their possessions, their homes, even their families, but this would not stop them. They might be reported to the authorities as dangerous atheists, and required to sacrifice to the imperial gods; but they refused to comply. In Christianity they had found something utterly new, authentic and satisfying. They were not prepared to deny Christ even in order to preserve their own lives; and in the manner of their dying they made converts to their faith.[2]

## THEIR MOTIVATION

What motivated these early Christians? What moved them to perform such great exploits for God and the gospel? What enabled them to overcome every difficulty and spread their message throughout the known world within the first two centuries of the Christian era? Without a doubt, discovering their motivation is vital to our study.

First, the church was motivated by the love factor. The love of Christ was their compelling force. In II Corinthians 5:14-15, Paul deals specifically with the matter of reconciling an alienated world: "For the love of Christ constraineth us; because we thus judge, that if one died for all, then were all dead: And that he died for all, that they which live should not henceforth live unto [for] themselves, but unto [for] him which died for them, and rose again." The demanding love experienced by these early Christians was not based on emotion. Their love had a theological base.

Three profound truths compelled the early Christians to live for Christ. First, the propitiation of the Savior moved them. "For Christ also hath once suffered for sins, the just for the unjust, that he might bring us to God" (I Peter 3:18). The fact that the Son of God loved them and gave Himself for them impacted their lives and service. (Galatians 2:20).

Second, the predicament of the sinner was fresh in their minds since they themselves had recently been delivered from the bonds of sin. They saw people as the Bible pictures them—children of disobedience, dead in sins, totally controlled by the god of this world (Satan) (Ephesians 2:1-2). The pitiful plight of sinful man fueled their desire to preach the gospel.

Third, their identification with Christ and their communion with Him clarified in their minds the purpose of the saints. The Christian life centers on Christ, not in self. They lived not for themselves, but for Christ, who loved them, died for them, and rose again for them. "Beloved, if God so loved us, we ought also to love one another" (I John 4:11).

The early Christians drank deeply of the love of Christ. Many of them sealed their testimony with their blood. In his remarkable *Foxe's Book of Martyrs,* John Foxe tells of the martyrdom of Polycarp, bishop of Smyrna. Just reading it should strengthen our resolve. Look at Polycarp's last words:

> The proconsul then urged him, saying, 'Swear, and I will release thee;—reproach Christ.'
> Polycarp answered, 'Eighty and six years have I served him, and he never once wronged me; how then shall I blaspheme my King, Who hath saved me?' The proconsul again urged him, 'Swear by the fortune of Caesar.'
> Polycarp replied, 'Since you still vainly strive to make me swear by the fortune of Caesar, as you express it, affecting ignorance of my real character, hear me frankly declaring what I am—I am a Christian—and if you desire to learn the Christian doctrine, assign me a day, and you shall hear from me. Hereupon the proconsul said, 'I have wild beasts; and I will expose you to them,

unless you repent.'

'Call for them,' replied Polycarp; 'for repentance with us is a wicked thing, if it is to be a change from the better to the worse, but a good thing if it is to change from evil to good.'

'I will tame thee with fire,' said the proconsul, 'since you despise the wild beasts, unless you repent.'

Then said Polycarp, 'You threaten me with fire, which burns for an hour, and is soon extinguished; but the fire of the future judgment, and of eternal punishment reserved for the ungodly, you are ignorant of. But why do you delay? Do whatever you please. . . .'

When they would have fastened him to the stake, he said, 'Leave me as I am; for he who giveth me strength to sustain the fire, will enable me also, without your securing me with nails, to remain without flinching in the pile.' So he said thus:—'O Father, I bless thee that thou hast counted me worthy to receive my portion among the number of martyrs.'[3]

Little wonder that the gospel of Christ won the day with men like Polycarp.

## THE LIGHT FACTOR

Second, the early church was motivated by the light factor. Try to fathom the darkness of the first century. II Corinthians 4:3-6 speaks to that light which motivated the early Christians to pierce and penetrate that darkness:

But if our gospel be hid, it is hid to them that are lost: In whom the god of this world hath blinded the minds of them which believe not, lest the light

of the glorious gospel of Christ, who is the image
of God, should shine unto them. For we preach
not ourselves, but Christ Jesus the Lord; and
ourselves your servants for Jesus' sake. For God,
who commanded the light to shine out of darkness, hath shined in our hearts, to give the light
of the knowledge of the glory of God in the face
of Jesus Christ.

In dispelling the darkness, the early Christians preached
to sinners and served the saints. Why did they preach? What
caused them to risk all to make Christ known? The only antidote
for darkness is light. They knew the power of the light of the
gospel for enlightening blinded minds. Satan blinds by ignorance;
the Holy Spirit enlightens by the preached gospel. "The entrance
of thy words giveth light; it giveth understanding unto the simple"
(Psalm 119:130). The glorious light of the gospel had shined in
their hearts making them eager to give the light of Jesus Christ
to all who would receive it. Annie Johnson Flint's poem, *His,*
catches the spirit of their shining:

His lamp am I, to shine where He shall say,
And lamps are not for sunny rooms,
Nor for the light of day;
But for dark places of the earth,
Where shame and crime and wrong have
    birth;
Or for the murky twilight gray
Where wandering sheep have gone astray;
Or where the lamp of faith grows dim,
And souls are groping after Him.

And as sometimes a flame we find,
Clear shining through the night,
So bright we do not see the lamp,
But only see the light:

So may I shine—His light the flame,
That men may glorify His name.[4]


Just what is the "light" that shines? The Holy Spirit through the Apostle Paul makes very clear the nature of the light. First, the light is the glorious gospel of Christ (II Corinthians 4:4). Second, the light refers to the knowledge of the glory of God as reflected in Jesus Christ (II Corinthians 4:6). Third, the light constitutes the treasure that God has been pleased to place in the bodies of the redeemed. "But we have this treasure in earthen vessels, that the excellency of the power may be of God, and not of us" (II Corinthians 4:7). The early church reveled in the treasure of the gospel.

> It was no ordinary good news that rocked Palestine around the year A.D. 30. It was no mere message about a carpenter-teacher who had been executed under the Roman procurator. It was nothing less than the joyful announcement of the long awaited Messianic salvation, when God had come to the rescue of a world in need. Small surprise, then, that the content of their message became known as *to euaggelion*, the good news.[5]

Along with preaching to sinners, the early Christians served one another. The love of the Christians for one another both amazed and attracted the heathen. Again the question may be asked: why did they serve one another? Because the light of God had shined in their hearts and now they served one another for Jesus' sake (II Corinthians 4:5).

The book of Acts records the spread of the gospel in Jerusalem, in the surrounding area of Judaea, then in Samaria, and finally reaching the uttermost parts of the earth. As the disciples of Christ were scattered, they went everywhere preaching the gospel (Acts 8:4). For the early Christians, witnessing was their *raison d'etre* (reason for being). As a result of their witness, the known world of that day was exposed to the good news of Christ (Colossians 1:5).

## THE LIFE FACTOR

This brings us to the third motivating factor that urged these Christians on to reach their world with the gospel of Christ: the life factor. The early Christians enjoyed a rich, vibrant, contagious spiritual life. Paul asks a rhetorical question. "What? know ye not that your body is the temple of the Holy Ghost which is in you, which ye have of God, and ye are not your own?" (I Corinthians 6:19). Imagine the impact of Spirit-filled Christians with a biblical, God-honoring life style infiltrating a heathen society.

I Corinthians 6:20 describes these believers as those who lived with a purpose: to glorify God. They glorified God in their bodies. Their bodies were temples of the Spirit of God and as such were not to be abused. The outworking of this principle produced clean, healthy living.

They also glorified God in their spirits. Their inward man as well as their outward man was to manifest the excellencies of their God. In a social atmosphere charged with hate, revenge, greed, and lust, is it any wonder their godly living attracted attention? This glorifying God in spirit and body equals sanctification. Peter connects holiness of life and witnessing when he writes, "But sanctify the Lord God in your hearts: and be ready always to give an answer to every man that asketh you a reason of the hope that is in you with meekness and fear" (I Peter 3:15).

Just prior to His ascension, the Lord emphasized to His disciples the relationship between the spiritual life and witnessing. "But ye shall receive power, after that the Holy Ghost is come upon you: and ye shall be witnesses unto me both in Jerusalem, and in all Judaea, and in Samaria, and unto the uttermost part of the earth" (Acts 1:8). This spiritual power enabled and motivated them to witness. Their Spirit empowered witness overcame all obstacles, and within 300 years of its founding the church of Jesus Christ had conquered the Roman empire.

## THEIR OBSTACLES

Can you imagine the audacity of twelve men believing that they could literally disciple all the nations of the world? How could they possibly impact the nations? Humanly speaking, everything was against them. Often we get discouraged because of obstacles hindering the spread of the gospel today. But as we consider the obstacles facing the early Christians, those we face pale in comparison.

Their message was offensive. The Apostle Paul did not deny the offense of the cross. "For the preaching of the cross is to them that perish foolishness; but unto us which are saved it is the power of God" (I Corinthians 1:18). The message offended Jew and Greek. "The Jews require a sign, and the Greeks seek after wisdom: But we preach Christ crucified, unto the Jews a stumbling block, and unto the Greeks foolishness" (I Corinthians 1:22-23).

The gist of Peter's sermon at Pentecost is found in Acts 2:36: "Therefore let all the house of Israel know assuredly, that God hath made that same Jesus, whom ye have crucified, both Lord and Christ." Many repented, but many more rejected the message. To the Jews (especially to the religious leaders) it was preposterous that an unordained rabbi who permitted himself to be crucified could possibly be the Messiah, the conqueror. The Old Testament made it clear that cursed is everyone that is hanged on a tree (Deuteronomy 21:23). Not only did Peter claim that Jesus was the Messiah, but he claimed Him to be Lord. The Jews understood "Lord" to mean deity (Psalm 110:1). This was too much for these champions of monotheism.

To the Greeks, the message of the gospel presented serious intellectual problems. Christianity was the new kid on the block, and to the Greeks nothing new could be true. To them it was not only untrue, but ridiculous. How could the wisdom of God be exhibited in the cross of Jesus? Platonic wisdom dealt in "universals" not in "particulars." They were not interested in a particular birth, a particular life, and especially not in a particular death. The whole idea was laughable to them. They were also offended with the cultural inferiority of the Christians. Paul confessed that most of the Christians were common folks. "Not many noble, are called" (I Corinthians 1:26).

Their manner of life offended both Jew and Gentile. The church replaced the temple as a center of worship. The law was replaced by grace. Circumcision became suspect. The Sabbath was replaced by Sunday (or the Lord's Day). The dietary laws were disregarded, and the Gentiles were given equal access to God. To the Jews, the Christians were discarding all that was holy and sacred.

The Christians also offended the Gentiles. As the Christian church multiplied, it ran head on into Rome. In a sense, Rome was experiencing a religious revival and was seeking to get back to her roots. To unite the empire and to promote patriotism, emperor worship was mandated. A state cult developed with the emperor being worshiped as a supreme being. Belief was a private matter, but emperor worship was to be public. Everyone was expected to do obeisance to the emperor.

The Christians' refusal to enter into emperor worship made it difficult for Christians to wholeheartedly participate in society. Their strong stand caused them to be accused of being atheists because they refused to worship the gods; to be accused of cannibalism because of eating and drinking the body and blood of Christ; and to be accused of immorality because of their love feasts.

In this context, the work of evangelism was a brave undertaking involving risk, social odium, and charges of political treachery. With so much against them, how could these early believers not only gain a foothold, but eventually rout the enemy?

## THEIR SUCCESS

Statistics in 1997 reveal a total of 1,955,229,000 persons

claimed allegiance to the Christian religion i.e., all who profess faith in the name of Christ, (35% of the world's 5.8 billion people)[6]—and it all began with 120 believers on the day of Pentecost. These early Christians overcame severe obstacles and by the process of multiplication of new believers spread their faith to all the known world. As far as the world was concerned they were uninfluential nobodies without credentials—"the offscouring of all things" (I Corinthians 4:13). How did these Christians do it?

## POWER OF THE GOSPEL

One of the greatest factors leading to their success was the gospel of Jesus Christ. Paul shows his pride in the gospel when he writes, "For I am not ashamed of the gospel of Christ: for it is the power of God unto salvation to everyone that believeth; to the Jew first, and also to the Greek" (Romans 1:16).

The early Christians shared Paul's enthusiasm for the gospel. They were proud of the gospel because of the people it served. The Christian gospel is meant for everyone. "For as many of you as have been baptized into Christ have put on Christ. There is neither Jew nor Greek, there is neither bond nor free, there is neither male nor female: for ye are all one in Christ Jesus" (Galatians 3:27-28). No race, nation, tribe, family, or person is excluded. The universality of the gospel gives it great appeal. It meets the heart needs of people in all circumstances of life: the intelligentsia or the man in the jungle.

The power of the gospel encouraged the early church to share it freely and boldly. Power equals energy; energy produces change. Simply yet powerfully their testimony sounded forth. In blindness and sin they were rushing toward eternal death. A power began to work—the power of the gospel. First, it stopped them, then it turned them around, and finally it launched them on to the path of eternal life. Multitudes were testifying to the power of the gospel to radically, instantaneously change an ungodly sinner into a worshiping saint. Sin and Satan are fearful foes, but their power is no match for the divine power manifested in the gospel of Christ.

The early Christians rejoiced in the gospel because of the problems it solved. A major social problem during the time of the early church was slavery. Slavery with all its devilish side effects presented the church a formidable challenge. However, without attacking slavery *per se*, the influence of the gospel ridded the world of that monstrous injustice. Most of the crippling, perplexing problems plaguing our world today can be traced to greed and pride, which are the essence of rebellion against God.

The message of the gospel struck a responsive chord in the hearts of the early Christians because of the pardon it secured. The gospel brings deliverance. It delivers those that believe from the penalty of sin, the power of sin, and one glad day from the very presence of sin. The message of the gospel swept across the world as a healing balm bringing peace and pardon to millions.

What exactly is the gospel of Christ that Paul, Peter, John, and the early Christians preached? In his scholarly work, *The Apostolic Preaching and Its Development,* C. H. Dodd claims that there existed a fixed pattern of preaching the gospel in the early church. From a study of I Corinthians, The Acts of the Apostles, and The Gospel According to Mark, Dodd came up with these six points:

> First, the age of fulfilment has dawned. . . . Secondly, this has taken place through the ministry, death, and resurrection of Jesus. . . . Thirdly, by virtue of the resurrection, Jesus has been exalted at the right hand of God, as Messianic head of the new Israel. . . . Fourthly, the Holy Spirit in the Church is the sign of Christ's present power and glory. . . . Fifthly, the Messianic Age will shortly reach its consummation in the return of Christ. . . . Finally, the *kerygma* (gospel) always closes with an appeal for repentance, the offer of forgiveness and of the Holy Spirit, and the promise

of 'salvation'. . . .[7]

The Holy Spirit gives us a glimpse of the gospel at work in the city of Thessalonica during the ministry of the Apostle Paul (I Thessalonians 1:5-10). The gospel message along with the power of the Holy Spirit wrought dynamic changes in the lives of people. What was the nature of these changes? These idolaters turned from their idols to serve the living God; they waited for His Son to return from heaven; and they experienced present deliverance from sin, expecting final deliverance from the wrath to come.

Behind every effect there is a cause. Two powerful forces wrought the changes: the gospel of Christ coupled with the Holy Spirit of God. "For our gospel came not unto you in word only, but also in power, and in the Holy Ghost, and in much assurance" (I Thessalonians 1:5). In spite of persecution, these that had been served by the gospel faithfully communicated their newly found faith and became exemplary Christians.

> And ye became followers of us, and of the Lord, having received the word in much affliction, with joy of the Holy Ghost: So that ye were ensamples to all that believe in Macedonia and Achaia. For from you sounded out the word of the Lord not only in Macedonia and Achaia, but also in every place your faith to God-ward is spread abroad; so that we need not to speak any thing (I Thessalonians 1:6-8).

Paul, the missionary *par excellence,* had worked himself out of a job in the regions of Macedonia and Achaia!

The second vital factor in the success of the early church was the presence and power of the Holy Spirit in their midst. Glancing through the Book of Acts, we are struck with the numerous mentionings of the Holy Spirit and His work. In Acts 1:8, the disciples were promised the power (enabling) of the Holy

Spirit who sent them forth to witness to a wicked world. This promise was fulfilled on the day of Pentecost when "They were all filled with the Holy Ghost, and began to speak with other tongues, as the Spirit gave them utterance" (Acts 2:4). Peter, preaching in the power of this anointing, gave a sterling witness as to who Christ was and what He came to accomplish. The result: 3000 men (probably an equal number of women) repented, gladly received the Word, were baptized, were added to the church, and "continued steadfastly in the apostles' doctrine, and fellowship, and in breaking of bread and in prayers" (Acts 2:41-42).

Some days later Peter healed the lame man at the Gate Beautiful (Acts 3:7) and used this opportunity to preach to a large multitude in the temple. Five thousand more men repented and joined with the apostles (Acts 4:4). The Sanhedrin took definite action by ordering Peter and John to be arrested and charged. In answering their charges, Peter shocked these learned men by the power, conviction, and authority with which he spoke. "Now when they saw the boldness of Peter and John, and perceived that they were unlearned and ignorant men, they marvelled; and they took knowledge of them, that they had been with Jesus" (Acts 4:13). They indeed had been with Jesus, but now Jesus was with them in a special way in the person of the Holy Spirit.

After warning Peter and John of dire consequences if they continued to witness of Jesus and the resurrection, the Sanhedrin released them. Rather than indulging in self-pity or praying for deliverance from the Sanhedrin, Peter and John prayed for boldness: "And now, Lord, behold their threatenings: and grant unto thy servants, that with all boldness they may speak thy word. . . . And when they had prayed, the place was shaken where they were assembled together; and they were all filled with the Holy Ghost, and they spake the word of God with boldness" (Acts 4:29, 31).

The power and presence of the Holy Spirit graced the church at Antioch. Indeed, during one of the church's prayer sessions, the Holy Spirit interrupted their prayers, issuing orders that Barnabas and Saul be dispatched for missionary work in the regions beyond (Acts 13:1-2). Without a doubt, the success of the early church can be credited to the presence and power of the Holy Spirit working in and through the churches. Likewise, the impotency of the modern church can be linked to its grieving and quenching of the Holy Spirit.

To this point we have discussed the divine factors affecting the growth of the church. But evangelism is a divine-human operation. God works, but He works through human instruments (Philippians 2:13). Notice some of the human factors involved in the success of the early church.

## THEIR OBEDIENCE

The obedience of the early believers affected the church's success. Just before the Lord Jesus ascended into heaven, He gave His disciples specific orders to wait. "And, behold, I send the promise of my Father upon you: but tarry ye in the city of Jerusalem, until ye be endued with power from on high" (Luke 24:49). They waited and they received the power. Once they received the power, they were to be witnesses for Christ (Acts 1:8). When challenged to give up witnessing of the resurrection of Christ, Peter gave a classic reply: "Whether it be right in the sight of God to hearken unto you more than unto God, judge ye. For we cannot but speak the things which we have seen and heard" (Acts 4:19). On another occasion, Peter rebuked those that forbad him to teach about Jesus by declaring pointedly, "We ought to obey God rather than men" (Acts 5:29).

Not only did obedience characterize the lives of the apostles, but it was also present in the other Christians also. Ananias, one of God's great, humble nobodies, provides a notable example. Saul of Tarsus, archenemy of the church, had come to work ruin in the church of Damascus. The Lord came to Ananias in a vision and said, "Ananias." His reply reflects his obedience: "Behold, I am here, Lord" (Acts 9:10). His going to meet Saul signified his expendability for the cause of Christ. By his obedience, Ananias became the human instrument in winning and discipling the greatest Christian of all time, the Apostle Paul. Loving obedience to the commands of Christ caused these early Christians to be unstoppable.

Let us think about the second human factor: the courage of these early Christians. Perpetua, the 22-year-old mother of an infant, illustrates this dedication and courage. She lived and suffered martyrdom in Carthage in 203 A.D.

> Her father tried everything to make her recant. First, he was rough with her, but found that he distressed her to no effect. Then he turned to appeals; his grey hairs, her mother, and supremely her own tiny son who would not be able to survive her, were all thrown in the scales to induce her to change her mind. But she remained firm, and went with dignity and courage to her death. The effect of such devotion to Christ can well be imagined.[8]

The third human factor affecting the growth of the church was its distinctive fellowship. Although all kinds of guilds, dining clubs, and associations met for communal activities in the Roman empire, the quality of the church's fellowship impressed the pagans. It transcended race, sex, class, and education. Master and slave, rich and poor, Jew and Gentile, provincial and Roman citizen met on equal terms—brothers and sisters in Christ—and enjoyed an intimacy of spirit unknown in pagan society.

We need to catch a glimpse of the depth and quality of the fellowship in the church at Antioch. The Jewish Christians broke out of the mold of preaching exclusively to the Jews when they preached to the Grecians (Acts 11:20). As a result, many within this community turned to the Lord (Acts 11:21). Those that turned to the Lord, both Jews and Greeks, were integrated into the church's doctrine and fellowship (Acts 11:26). They made disciples. The Christians at Antioch were not holed up in a Christian ghetto. As a result their lives and ministries did not go unnoticed by the locals. It was at Antioch that the disciples of Christ were first called Christians.

The pagans marveled at how the Christians loved one another. Upon hearing of the need of the suffering Christians in Jerusalem, there was an immediate and generous response: "Then the disciples, every man according to his ability, determined to send relief unto the brethren which dwelt in Judaea" (Acts 11:29). What an impact this church must have made on this great city.

## THEIR STRATEGY

Spontaneity characterized the growth of the early church. It is unlikely the apostles had a strategy. Yet as we observe their methods and operations, a definite strategy emerges. They had a goal. It was a grand goal: to preach the gospel to every living human being. On this point all agreed. Theirs was a universal mission. It was incumbent on them to reach Jerusalem first, next Judea, then Samaria, and finally the ends of the earth (Acts 1:8). Spreading the gospel was every Christian's responsibility. The gifted men evangelized and in so doing were an example to all. However, their chief work was preparing the rank and file for the work of the ministry (Ephesians 4:12).

Local churches served as training centers, sending out evangelists far and near. Churches sprang up everywhere. In Acts 14:21-23, Luke, through the guidance of the Holy Spirit, shares six steps used in organizing a New Testament church: the gospel is preached to the city (evangelism); the Word is taught to many (explanation); the disciples are established in the faith and exhorted to be faithful (exhortation); the local church is organized (establishment of the church); local leaders are enlisted as church leaders (enlistment); and the new leaders and the new church are committed to the Lord (entrustment).

Then the church planters leave for a new area to start the process again. Each local church was expected to start daughter churches in the surrounding territory. Churches increased and multiplied.

The astounding growth of the early church could not have been accomplished by adding members. It required a strategy of multiplication. II Timothy 2:2 sets forth this strategy: "And the things that thou hast heard of me [Paul, the first generation] among many witnesses, the same commit thou [Timothy, the second generation] to faithful men [the third generation], who shall be able to teach others [the fourth generation] also." The principle is for each one to win one and teach one to win and teach one. My colleague, Mel Lacock, emphasizes this with the following ditty:

> If each saved one, won one,
> And if each one won, won one,
> What hosts would be won
> If everyone won, won one.

Let me illustrate the effectiveness of the multiplication strategy from my own family. My wife and I got married, and we begat three daughters. All of our daughters are now married, and three of them have given us 19 grandchildren. So presently our number has increased from two to twenty-four. If our 19 grandchildren get married, follow our example and have at least three children, then the number of our great-grandchildren will have increased to 57. If all of these get married and have at least three children, there will be 171 great-great-grandchildren. In seven generations our family would number 5,631! However, if my wife and I had begotten three daughters, and had they failed to reproduce, there would have been but five of us. After two generations our family would have ceased.

Many other factors causing the amazing growth of the early church could be mentioned: their joy, their endurance, and their transformed lives. Now it is time to leave the early church with its great witness and unbelievable expansion to move on in our historical perspective.

---

1. John Bartlett, *Bartlett's Familiar Quotations* (Boston:

Little, Brown and Company, 1955) 744.

2. Michael Green, *Evangelism in the Early Church* (Grand Rapids: Wm. B. Eerdmans Publishing Company, 1991) 236.

3. John Foxe, *Foxe's Book of Martyrs* (Springdale, Pennsylvania: Whitaker House, 1981) 22-24.

4. Annie Johnson Flint, *Poems,* Vol. 1, Stanzas three and four (Toronto, Canada: Evangelical Publishers, 1944) 135-136.

5. Green, 48-49.

6. *The World Almanac and Book of Facts* (Mahwah, New Jersey: Funk and Wagnalls Publishing Company, 1997) 654.

7. C. H. Dodd, *The Apostolic Preaching and Its Development* (New York: Harper & Brothers Publishers, 1951) 21-23.

8. Green, 177.

# 4

# The Lights Go Off
# and Come On Again

The early church excelled in evangelism and discipleship. Their uncompromising faith coupled with inveterate zeal won against innumerable foes. Godly and gifted people gave themselves unstintingly to the tasks of preaching the gospel, persuading sinners, and planting churches. Their labors resulted in multitudes throughout the Roman empire embracing Christ as Lord and Savior.

By 300 A.D., the church had taken root throughout the Roman empire. The emperor Diocletian (284-305 A.D.) determined to restore the greatness of Rome. "To this end he reorganized the whole machinery of government."[1] An integral part of this reorganization was emperor worship. What a person believed was a private matter, but everyone was expected to profess to believe the emperor was God. It was the politically correct thing to do. When the Christians refused to perform the rituals required by the emperor cult, Diocletian declared war against them. He was the instigator of the Great Persecution, which lasted ten years. The number of martyrs that died during this time exceeded all who died for the faith from the beginning of the persecution until 300 A.D.[2]

But even while this terrible persecution was raging, Christianity's victory over paganism was about to culminate. In Britain, a young prince, Constantine, was growing to manhood under Christian influences. Inspired by a vision of a shining cross with the inscription *Hoc Vinces* (By this thou shalt conquer), Constantine gave his army a new banner emblazoned with a cross. In a dream, he was told to put the cross upon his banners. By 313 A.D., Constantine was emperor in the East. With his Western counterpart he signed the Edict of Milan, which recognized Christianity as a lawful religion. To demonstrate his sympathies toward the Christians, he required the state to restore all confiscated property and repay all financial losses due to persecution.[3]

## A HOLLOW VICTORY

What seemed like a great victory for the Christians and their thousands of churches turned into a curse. The conversion of Constantine to Christianity had far-reaching consequences. There was great numerical growth in the churches as the fear of persecution disappeared. Suddenly, being a Christian was popular and convenient, and it opened opportunities for material gain. Two generations later, the whole Roman empire was Christian in name. Unfortunately for the churches and the cause of Christ, many of these people never experienced the saving power of Christ. As a result, the spiritual life of the church suffered a near mortal blow.[4]

The organizational structure of the churches changed. The simple New Testament form of government was bypassed, and the new way was patterned after the Roman model. Strong leaders arose and gained power and prestige.[5]

The churches came under the empire's protection and soon were under its control. The people in the churches lost the freedom to govern themselves and chart their own course according to their consciences and the New Testament. In a short period of time, the Church had become the religious department of the state and thus a state church.[6]

The very nature and concept of the church began to change. Cyprian, bishop of Carthage, died a martyr's death in 258 A.D.[7] Before his death he wrote an important document, "On The Unity of the Catholic Church." In his writing, he was putting forth spiritual truths about the nature and organization of the Church. However, Rome later used his writings to champion the Church as a visible, temporal institution.

> Throughout the world there is but one Church of Jesus Christ; there may seem to be many churches, but it is only seeming, for 'there are many rays, but only one light; many branches of a tree, but only one strength; from one spring flow many streams.' To be a Christian, a man must be in this Church. 'They cannot dwell with God, who would not be of one mind in the Church'; 'he cannot have God for his Father, who will not have the Church for His mother.'[8]

As the preaching of the Word decreased, the power of the Church increased. Gradually, the traditions of the Church replaced the Word of God as the final authority.

The power and authority of the bishops continued to grow. Bishops in the New Testament led a local congregation, but now a bishop controlled a multitude of churches. Another insidious development hindering evangelism and discipleship was the division of the church into laity and clergy. The clergy became well-organized with various levels of authority. In some churches they even ordained grave diggers! Thus the work of the churches passed out of the hands of the members into the hands of paid professionals. The laity were the spectators; the clergy the actors. All of this had a chilling effect upon the spiritual life of the church.

In a short period of time, the Church underwent drastic changes. The Church replaced the churches; the Holy See replaced the Holy Ghost. If a member of the second-century church had visited the fourth-century church, he would have been shocked by the Church's political power, its wealth, its influence, its buildings, its liturgy, and its numbers. However, he would have been saddened by the lack of powerful preaching, soul-winning, making of disciples, exhilarating spiritual power, manifesting of divine love, and enriching Christian fellowship.

## HORRIBLE CONSEQUENCES

The leaders of the church could no longer say with Peter, "Silver and gold have I none; but such as I have I give thee" (Acts 3:6). Neither could they say, "In the name of Jesus Christ of Nazareth rise up and walk" (Acts 3:6). As the Church gained political power, it lost its divine dynamic. The Church had exchanged its spiritual and moral power for that power which was worldly, materialistic, and human. The life-giving, soul-saving, world-changing power was gone. Ichabod, the glory had departed.

Known as the Holy Catholic Church, it was far from holy. An influx of unconverted men and women eventuated in a loss of purity and power. Also, the politicizing of the clergy enabled unscrupulous, power-hungry men to seize positions of leadership. This corrupting of the Church caused great consternation among the godly. The more earnest Christians viewed these changes with alarm. Men who had fled to the church to get out of the world found the world pursuing them in the church. Eventually, these men left both the church and the world. In a new counterculture, they became known as "monks" and secluded themselves in monasteries. Their seclusion robbed both the world and the church of their light and salt. The abandoning of the church by these light-bearers quickened the world's and the church's entrance into the Dark Ages.

During the Dark Ages, the Church gained increasing control over the people. The common man looked to the Church for salvation. Salvation came through faith in what the Church taught. The Church replaced simple faith in the Lord Jesus Christ (Acts 16:31) with its seven sacraments. Along with the sacraments, good works were required. To lighten or escape the performance of good works, the Church sold indulgences.

For almost a thousand years the powers of darkness ruled. Although the light of the gospel flickered at times, it never went completely out in spite of the efforts of the Roman Catholic Church to suppress the dissent, which it labeled heresy. God has always had His light-bearers who somehow and somewhere preached the gospel.

## HOLY PROTEST

In the midst of spiritual declension in the Church, voices of protest rang out. As early as 251 A.D., the majority party led by Bishop Cornelius had become careless in applying the spiritual ideals of the Church. As a result, a minority group led by Bishop Novatian rose up in protest against the lax moral practices in the Church. Novatian precipitated the first schism in the history of the Church. This protest movement became known as Novatianism. These separatists believed that the Church, being the body of Christ, must be kept holy. According to them, the efficacy of the communion came not from the hand of the priest, but from the heart of the believer. They took sin seriously. In fact, they took it so seriously they denied the possibility of confession that resulted in forgiveness and restoration. Hence, terms like "second chance," "restoration," and "a new start" evaded them. The moral looseness and the Church's failure to deal with it caused the Novatians to overreact.[9]

During the periods of persecution, especially the Great Persecution, not all Christians stood firm. Many compromised and came to terms with their persecutors. For example, Bishop Felix allegedly had surrendered copies of the Scriptures to the Roman officers. According to Donatus, this defection disqualified him and rendered all of his official acts invalid. In 311 A.D., Bishop Donatus spearheaded a movement that contended that the Church did not have the authority to forgive and restore defectors. His contentions caused a sharp division in the African Church. The Donatists, as his followers were called, stressed holy living and refused to tolerate evil. Even though they were condemned by one synod after another, they refused rapprochement with the Roman Church. Considering themselves to be the true Church, they argued that a church which condones evil ceases to be the Church. After 411 A.D., Donatism was repressed by law, but did not finally disappear until the Vandal invasion of Africa (429-430).[10]

Between 500 A.D. and 1200 A.D., the Church's power over the people was almost complete. Few, if any, viable protest movements calling for a return to the fervency and purity of the New Testament surfaced. The truth can be suppressed, but not forever. Two main groups arose to oppose the Roman Catholic Church: the Cathari and the Waldensians. Both groups condemned and criticized the Church. The Cathari were not orthodox Christians but Manichaeans who held the doctrine of dualism. In contrast, the Waldensians, followers of Peter Waldo, believed it was their duty "to return to the simple teachings of the Bible" and to stand against the prevalent ritualism and corruption of the Church. With the help of the king of France, Pope Innocent III crushed both the Cathari and the Waldensians.[11]

About 1213 A.D., as more and more incidents of "heresy" surfaced, the popes demanded that the kings declare "heresy a capital offense." An infamous institution, the Inquisition, was organized to root out and destroy all heretics. The numbers of those executed was "appallingly large."[12]

In spite of the terrible persecution, truth-bearers continued to surface. It is not possible to mention all of them, but John Wyclif, the leader of the English Lollards, is a good representative. In 1377, Wyclif was tried in absentia for heresy contained in 45 of his written statements. Miraculously, the trial came to nothing. Along with protesting against the Church, John Wyclif and two of his associates translated the Scriptures from Latin to English.[13]

"Among the new discoveries of the fifteenth century none was more revolutionary in its effect upon human thought and life than John Gutenberg's printing press with movable type." "The first book that came from his press was a Bible, printed about 1453. . . ." By 1500 all the major cities had presses which provided the means of disseminating ideas far and wide.[14]

## HOPE REBORN

Like a caterpillar coming out of its cocoon, the world was slowly shedding the rags of darkness. The influx of ideas resulted in the R*enaissance,* a rebirth or transformation, which affected every field of thought and endeavor in European life. The ideas spawned by the Renaissance were pagan, giving vent to self-expression and self-discovery.

Desiderius Erasmus, the scholarly Dutch reformer, paved the way for the Reformation. "He was not only the greatest Christian scholar of his generation, but also the most popular author.... In his books, he exposed the corruption, the superstition, the divorce between religion and morals, and he specifically flayed the Church. His Greek New Testament (1516) was the first publication of the entire New Testament in its original language. However, he never left the Church. The Reformation demanded greater men, greater in insight, courage."[15]

One of these great, courageous men was Martin Luther (1483-1546). Turning his back on a career as a lawyer, he became a monk and later a professor at the University of Wittenberg. For many years he was a true son of the Church of Rome. After years of spiritual struggle, the truth of justification by faith freed him from the bondage of sin. As early as 1513 his convictions differed from those of the Church. By 1517 his convictions had matured and led him to publish 95 theses regarding indulgences. His protests against the Church and his denial of papal infallibility resulted in his excommunication. Luther made many contributions, but one of the greatest was the translation of the Bible into the vernacular of the German people.[16]

Time and space forbid to tell of Zwingli of Switzerland, Calvin of France, and Knox of Scotland and many others. Each one of these reformers championed a return to the Bible. Zwingli summed it up in his statement in The First Zurich Disputation, "All who say that the Gospel is nothing unless it have the support and approval of the Church are in error and blaspheme against God."[17] Through these brave men and their followers, the Word was preached and the lights came on again. How true the words of the psalmist: "The entrance of thy words giveth **light;** it giveth understanding unto the simple" (Psalm 119:130).

---

1. Charles M. Jacobs, *The Story of the Church* (Philadelphia: The United Lutheran Publishing House, 1925) 29.

2. Ibid., 29-30.

3. Ibid., 31.

4. Ibid., 32.

5. Ibid., 31.

6. Ibid., 33.

7. Ibid.

8. Mendell Taylor, *Exploring Evangelism* (Kansas City, Missouri: Beacon Hill Press,1964) 77.

9. Jacobs, 61-62.

10. Ibid., 146.

11. Ibid., 147.

12. Ibid., 156-157.

13. Ibid., 166-167.

14. Ibid., 190.

15. Ibid., 193-195.

16. Ibid., 219-220.

17. Ibid., 219-220.

# 5

# Evangelists–God's Gift to the Church

God gave gifts to His church in the persons of gifted men. Ephesians 4:11-12 lists the offices and the overall purposes of these offices or gifts. The offices are apostles, prophets, evangelists, pastors, and teachers. Their specific purpose is to perfect the saints to minister to the body of Christ. In so doing, the body will be both edified and increased, indicated by spiritual and numerical growth. Since the evangelist's responsibilities relate to evangelism, it is necessary to take a close look at this office or gift.

The anglicized Greek word for the gospel is *evangel*. From the word evangel comes the office of evangelist. Evangelizing (spreading the good news of Christ) appears 55 times in the New Testament. Surprisingly, the word evangelist occurs only three times. However, this infrequency does not belie its significance.

The writings of the church father, Eusebius, indicate that the early evangelists functioned much like our present-day missionaries. He writes:

> They preached the gospel more and more widely and scattered the saving seeds of the Kingdom of Heaven broadly throughout the whole world . . . . Then setting out on long journeys they performed the duty of evangelists, being eager to preach Christ to those who had

never yet heard anything of the word of faith, and to pass on to them Scripture of the Divine Gospels. These men were content with simply laying the foundations of the faith in foreign places, and then appointing others as pastors, entrusting them with the husbandry of those, newly reclaimed, while they themselves went on again to other countries and nations, with the grace and cooperation of God.[1]

In his *Theological Dictionary of the New Testament*, Kittel concludes that the evangelists were assistants to the apostles and were their rightful successors. They performed a comparable task without the dignity and authority of an apostle. Thus, their major task was to preach the gospel in unevangelized areas, congregate believers into assemblies, and establish them in faith, doctrine, and life (Acts 14:21-23).[2]

Evidently, the perception of an evangelist in our day differs from that of the early church. In our thinking, an evangelist is a revivalist, an itinerant preacher who stirs the church to holy living and soul-winning. God has graced the church with great evangelists. An historical review of evangelism would be incomplete without remembering some of the most outstanding evangelists of the past several hundred years.

## JOHN WESLEY
### (1703-1791)

John Wesley was the fifteenth of nineteen children born to Samuel and Susanna Wesley, Samuel being a Church of England minister at Epworth, England.[3] Although raised in a Christian home, John was not truly converted until after serving as a missionary to the Indians in the state of Georgia. In his journal he wrote,

'I went to America, to convert the Indians; but

O! who [sic] shall convert me? who, [sic] what
is he that will deliver me from this evil heart of
mischief? I have a fair summer religion. I can talk
well; nay, and believe myself, while no danger
is near; but let death look me in the face, and my
spirit is troubled.'[4]

Ceaseless searching of the Scriptures along with the
witness of Peter Bohler, a Moravian missionary, led to Wesley's
conversion at Aldersgate in Bristol, England. At a meeting at
Aldersgate-street in Bristol while listening to the reading of the
preface to Luther's Epistle to the Romans, Wesley was converted.
He again wrote in his journal:

About a quarter before nine, while he was
describing the change which God works in the
heart through faith in Christ, I felt my heart
strangely warmed. I felt I did trust in Christ,
Christ alone, for salvation; and an assurance was
given me that He had taken away my sins, even
mine, and saved me from the law of sin and
death.[5]

The society in which he lived was at its lowest depth of
depravity–morally, spiritually, and politically. J. Wesley Bready
in his book, *England: Before and After Wesley,* also describes
that day:

The English episcopate of the eighteenth century,
though still purporting to be the exclusive
mediators of Apostolic Grace, by the pride,
arrogance and venality of their lives, and by
compromising Christianity to the idolatry of
wealth, class, 'reason' and Constitution, caused
the light that was in them to turn to darkness: and
how great was that darkness is nowhere more

clearly revealed than in the fact that these sol-
emnly ordained ecclesiastical 'guides' failed
utterly to recognise [sic] either the importance
or the majesty of the most selfless, most heroic,
and most truly amazing life's work ever spent for
the salvation of England or, through England,
of the world. The episcopal bench of Wesley's
day, with but few and notable exceptions, was
spiritually unbaptised [sic].[6]

The theme of his early peaching was salvation by faith
in which he defined the nature of justifying faith. Wesley's message
and method, being too radical for the Church of England, caused
him to be unwelcome in their churches.[7] Denied this privilege,
he took to preaching literally everywhere people would listen.
Under the tutelage of George Whitefield, Wesley became an "open
air" preacher and took England by storm.[8] His tireless travels
took him to all parts of the British Isles.

In his journals, Wesley relates many instances of beatings,
stonings, riotings and of divine protection. One example will
suffice. From his journal dated August 26, 1748 he writes:

Sir,—Yesterday, between twelve and one o'clock,
while I was speaking to some quiet people,
without any noise or tumult, a drunken rabble
came, with clubs and staves, in a tumultuous and
riotous manner, the captain of whom, Richard
B., by name, said, he . . . was come to bring me
to you. I went with him; but I had scarce gone
ten yards, when a man of his company struck me
with his fist in the face with all his might; quickly
after, another threw his stick at my head: I then
made a little stand; but another of your champions, cursing and swearing in the most shocking
manner, and flourishing his club over his head,
cried out, 'Bring him away!'[9]

Wesley excelled in the gift of administration. Societies were formed, preachers were trained and assigned, and class meetings were organized. "Rules for the Societies" was published and became the basis for governing what later was known as the Methodist Church.[10] The influence of John Wesley was felt not only in England, but also in America. He and his followers evangelized and transformed England. Their outreach spanned the Atlantic Ocean and resulted in the formation of the large denomination, the Methodist Church of America.

What kind of man was John Wesley? Fred Barlow after researching his life and ministry described him this way:

> Wesley was a unique, many-faceted man. He was an evangelist, a musician… a genius at organization, a scholar. In his theology, Wesley was an Arminian as contrasted with Calvinism. He was a disciplinarian and indefatigable. Slight of build (*he was five feet, five inches tall*), never weighing over one hundred and twenty pounds, was tubercular in his early life. Yet, he was a giant for God in his ministry. His travels took him over a quarter of a million miles on horseback! He preached 42,000 messages. He wrote over 200 books. A few days before he died, at eighty-eight, he preached to sinners to get saved, '*Seek ye the Lord while he may be found.*'[11]

## ADONIRAM JUDSON
### (1788-1850)

Since missions is evangelism over there, it is right and proper to include this missionary to Burma. Judson suffered for the cause of Christ as few men or women have ever suffered. At the age of 37, he endured a "horrible seventeen months of imprisonment" and survived because "his heroic wife brought little bits of food to him."[12]

Judson was born in the home of Pastor Adoniram and Abigail Judson of Malden, Massachusetts. Being a precocious child, he learned to read at three and was proficient in Greek by his twelfth birthday. His brilliance led him into skepticism, causing him to seek escape from the faith and convictions of his parents.[13]

Spending the night at an inn, his sleep was disturbed by the cries of a dying man. The next day he learned that the man who died a horrible death in the next room was Jacob Eames, a well-known agnostic who had led Judson from his faith. Shortly thereafter, Judson was saved at the age of twenty.[14]

While a student at Andover Theological Seminary, Judson got a burden for the Orient. He and several others implored the Congregational Church to form a mission society to send them out. As a result, the American Board of Commissioners for Foreign Missions was formed, and they sent Judson and his new wife, Ann Hazeltine, to India as missionaries.[15] Mr. and Mrs. Samuel Newell went with the Judsons and on the way to India the four saw the truth of baptism by immersion and were convinced they should become Baptists. On arrival in Calcutta, William Carey baptized them by immersion.[16]

The Judsons labored together until Ann died at the age of 37.[17] Several years after her death, Judson led a Karen tribesman to the Lord. This tribesman was slave to a Burmese Christian and had been a robber and murderer. Judson trained him in the Word, and he became an evangelist to his own people. In 1837 there were 1,144 Karens baptized. Thirty years after Judson's death, the work he initiated had grown to 7,000 converts, 63 churches, many schools, and a publishing house.[18]

Judson took one furlough in 37 years of missionary service in Burma. In America, his heroic work was known because his wife, Ann, had written and published a book describing it. People flocked to hear him. However, like Livingston, he shunned the public gaze. When asked if the prospects were bright for the conversion of the world, Judson gave his now famous reply: "As bright, Sirs, as the promises of God!"[19]

Before Judson went to Burma, there were no Burmese

Bibles and no Burmese Christians. One hundred years after his death in 1850, Burma had a Bible in its own language and 200,000 Christians.[20]

## DWIGHT L. MOODY
## (1837-1899)

In his interesting and challenging book, *With Christ After The Lost,* L. R. Scarborough shares vignettes of several great evangelists. His insights into the evangelists' lives and ministries are most perceptive. The following is what he writes about D.L. Moody:

He was born at Northfield, Massachusetts, in 1837, and died in 1899. He stands out today as America's greatest evangelist, probably excepting Billie [sic] Sunday. He was greater than Sunday in his constructive evangelism. He founded and fostered some educational institutions on the evangelistic basis which will carry on for generations the work for which he stood. . . . His evangelistic work in winning souls in many centers in America and England, Scotland and other places was far-reaching. He swept large communities into the evangelistic atmosphere and won hundreds of thousands to Christ. Probably his most lasting influence aside from his educational institutions lies in the direction of his influence over preachers and laymen in creating and stimulating the soul-winning spirit and method. He, like Wesley, turned formal and unspiritual preachers and churches into soul-winning agencies. Moody will live forever in a class with Spurgeon, Wesley, Finney, and W. A. Sunday, the world's greatest soul-winners.[21]

## CHARLES HADDON SPURGEON
## (1834-1892)

Again, Dr. L. R. Scarborough captures the genius and power of Charles Haddon Spurgeon:

He was born in Kelveton, Essex, in 1834, and died at Mentone, France, 1892. He was the greatest pastor-evangelist in the world. At the age of twenty he was called to the New Park Street Baptist Chapel in London. He developed this church into the world-famed 'Metropolitan Tabernacle,' where he preached the Gospel of saving grace and wrought wonders in constructive Kingdom work until he died in 1892, thirty-eight years. He made it in many respects the greatest church and preaching place in all the world. He was a constructive soul-winner. He built a great orphanage, a pastoral college, a sort of Moody Bible Institute, from which Moody obtained his ideas, a school for workers, preachers, missionaries, etc. Thousands of God-called, Spirit-filled men have gone out from this place of Bible teaching and evangelistic inspiration to bless the world and win souls. He was a great preacher. For thirty-eight years multiplied thousands hung on his words from Sunday to Sunday. His sermons have been more widely published and read than those of any other preacher save the Apostle Paul. His ministry was a pastoral one with the evangelistic spirit, power and method. He rarely ever preached that he did not seek to turn the Gospel to the salvation of the lost in his congregation, and rarely ever did he preach that some one or more was not saved. The strongest emphasis of his great ministry was on constructive evangelism. His crown at Christ's coronation day will shine with myriads of the diadems of glory because of the multitudes he led to Christ.[22]

## WILLIAM A. SUNDAY
## (1862-1935)

Billy Sunday, as he was called, was America's most colorful, enthusiastic evangelist. Born to a civil war widow in Ames, Iowa, Sunday was led to Christ by the street preaching of the Pacific Garden Rescue Mission in Chicago and the personal work of Mrs. Clark, wife of the superintendent. At the time, Billy Sunday was at the height of his fame as a baseball player.[23] His personality, popularity, and physical prowess came under Christ's control and focused on soul-winning. Dr. L. R. Scarborough, a contemporary of Billy Sunday, comments on his effective ministry:

> His record for many years in soul-winning and in carrying communities, cities, and states for the abandonment of the saloon, is probably the most remarkable since John Wesley and probably far beyond John Wesley as an evangelist. His city campaigns for souls have resulted in the turning of many thousands to Christ and back to a renewed Christian life. He has a great soul-winning organization. He is a great preacher, sound on the fundamentals of the plan of salvation and mighty in his grip on the common heart of man, tremendous in faith and spiritual power. He adds to all this a great organization. He hits sin hard, direct blows. He compromises with none, preaches Christ and Him crucified, exalts God's Word and depends mightily upon prayer and the power of God. He will likely go down in history as America's greatest single winner of men to

Christ. His work is not constructive. He is a winner, not a builder.[24]

## BOB JONES, SR.
### (1883-1968)

One of the spiritual giants of the twentieth century, Dr. Bob (as he was called) was born near Dothan, Alabama, on October 30, 1883. Born in a godly home, he was converted at age eleven, and by the time he was thirteen he preached his first sermon. With the help of his father, Alex Jones, this aspiring young evangelist built a brush arbor in which he conducted his first revival and continued preaching for seventy years.[25]

Dr. Bob was the last "old time evangelist" in the tradition of Finney, Moody, Sunday, and Torrey. Dr. Fred Barlow describes the immense scope and success of his ministry:

> It is estimated that Bob Jones preached face to face to more people than any person living. When he was only forty, Jones had delivered more than 12,000 sermons, had preached to over fifteen million people and had seen over 300,000 come forward in his crusades to confess Christ. The mighty impact his ministry made for Christ is surely seen in this one campaign that could be multiplied manyfold—Montgomery, Alabama, his home when an evangelist. In that city of 40,000 population, the campaign averaged over 10,000 in attendance nightly, and many nights over one thousand came forward to make decisions for Christ. Recently the Montgomery ADVERTISER, in its 125th Anniversary edition, cited Jones' campaign in Montgomery over thirty-five years before 'as the historical religious event of the 125 year history of Montgomery.'[26]

Dr. Bob was more than an evangelist. Seeing the need for a Christian college to train Christian servants in all areas of life, he founded Bob Jones College in Panama City, Florida, in 1927.[27]

When I was a student at Bob Jones University in the early 1950's, there were 1,400 eager "preacher boys" in Dr. Bob's preachers class. Our theme song was "Souls for Jesus Is Our Battle Cry." For five years I had the privilege of sitting at Dr. Bob's feet. His ministry was Christ-exalting and Bible-honoring. Several of his sayings illustrate this: "I would support a hound dog that barked for Jesus," and "Whatever the Bible says is so." Condemning sin and preaching righteousness, Dr. Bob drilled a distinct philosophy into the hearts of his students: "Do right till the stars fall." His life manifested great compassion in and out of the pulpit and made an indelible imprint upon me. Literally thousands of preachers trained at Bob Jones University serve around the world. Many college presidents, evangelists, pastors, and missionaries can thank Dr. Bob for his sound teaching coupled with a great evangelistic burden that helped them in their ministries.

An enthusiasm for world missions led him to journey in 1952 and 1959 on round-the-world preaching trips. In 1964, when he was eighty years of age, Dr. and Mrs. Jones were sent on a good will tour and visited 14 countries. By this time, 850 missionaries ministering in 90 countries had received training at Bob Jones University.[28]

Dr. Bob had a simple but profound philosophy of life: "Do right." The outworking of this philosophy embroiled him in a controversy with those who insisted on joining with unbelievers to conduct evangelistic campaigns. Believing ecumenical evangelism was wrong, anti-biblical, and hurtful to the cause of Christ, Dr. Bob took his stand. For his stand, he was vilified and accused of jealousy, but he never wavered from his philosophy of doing right. R. K. Johnson, Dr. Bob's friend, long-time University business manager, and biographer sheds light on how much this controversy hurt Dr. Bob:

Some thought that this issue was *a personality clash between Dr. Bob and Billy Graham.* That is not true. Dr. Bob *loved* Billy Graham, and until Billy started hobnobbing with liberals, Dr. Bob promoted him. It was when Billy adopted unorthodox methods that Dr. Bob took issue with him. To be scriptural himself, Dr. Bob had no alternative. No one will ever know how earnestly Dr. Bob prayed that Billy would see that the liberals, the enemies of God, were not interested in promoting God's Word or Cause but were seeking to control Billy and hold back what good he might do. It seemed that Billy had come under the spell of the wrong crowd, and his warped conceptions were becoming more and more apparent as he accepted invitations to speak in such places as Union Theological Seminary and as he began to mention with favor men who were rank modernists.[29]

This policy crossed Dr. Bob's lifetime philosophy: "It is never right to do wrong in order to get a chance to do right." II John 9-11 teaches against recognizing and fellowshipping with any who deny the doctrine of Christ.

The last two years of his life were spent in the University hospital. His last words heard by his wife were, "Mary Gaston, get my shoes. I must go to preach." So ended the battle of one of the great warriors of the faith.[30]

## JOHN R. RICE
## (1895-1980)

Dr. Rice was a champion of evangelism and soul-winning during our generation. He was instrumental in promoting soul-winning and revival throughout America. For fifty years without interruption, he conducted successful evangelistic campaigns, established soul-winning churches, and promoted evangelism through soul-winning conferences.

Along with his great preaching, he wielded a mighty pen. In 1934, he founded the *Sword of the Lord*, a 16-page weekly featuring a sermon from a great preacher of the past and one from a preacher of the present. It included numerous articles on current issues, answers to questions, illustrations, and much more. At the time of Dr. Rice's death, 300,000 issues were going weekly to every state in the union and to many foreign countries. This paper lit soul-winning fires around the world.[31]

What a prolific pen was his! Over 47 million copies of his books and pamphlets have been distributed by the Sword of the Lord publishers. This includes over 150 full-length books, the most famous being *Prayer—Asking and Receiving,* "the world's best seller on prayer." Over 17,000 people have written to report being saved through Sword of the Lord literature.[32]

His pamphlet, "What Must I Do To Be Saved?" has been translated into many languages, including Bengali. Our literature center in Bangladesh translated and published one million copies of this booklet in Bengali. We included this booklet in packets of literature that we distributed in the market place. A young lad purchased one of these packets from me. On returning home, he became fearful of his father's reaction to his buying Christian literature. He threw the packet behind a piece of furniture. For ten years it stayed there. When the furniture was moved, the same young man saw the packet, opened it, and read it. He read the booklet over and over and wanted to be saved, but he did not know how. Eventually, he met some Bengali Christian workers who led him to the Lord. This former Muslim man is now a fine Christian husband, a father, a deacon, and a Christian worker.

Another of Dr. Rices's contributions to rekindling evangelism in America was Conferences on Evangelism. These conferences were begun in the 1940's when evangelism was at a low ebb. Dr. Rice committed "himself to God to bring back mass evangelism and city-wide campaigns." For many years Dr. Rice and his associates encouraged pastors and people to win souls.

It was these conferences that spurred the growth of the independent Baptist movement in the 1950's and 1960's. I personally attended many of these conferences and was stirred to the depth of my soul.[33]

As with all the great evangelists, people either loved or hated Dr. Rice. Looking and talking like Will Rogers, he was sometimes called, "the Will Rogers of the pulpit." John R. Rice was controversial since he was never afraid of a fight and dared to take on even the tobacco industry of Winston-Salem, North Carolina! He waged a continual battle against modernism, the World Council of Churches, unbelief in seminaries and colleges, the Revised Standard Version of the Bible, and well known liberals of his day. [34]

Dr. Rice joined Dr. Bob Jones and many other evangelists in condemning the ecumenical and inclusivistic evangelism of Billy Graham and others. Though he was a man of intense convictions, he was also a man of deep compassion and he preached with tears. In referring to Dr. Rice, Dr. Bob Jones said, "I regard Dr. Rice as one of the greatest spiritual assets this nation has."[35]

## OLIVER B. GREENE
## (1915-1976)

Several reasons cause me to include Oliver B. Greene in this chapter on great evangelists: he is my spiritual father and his ministry has had great spiritual impact on me.

Born in a respectable South Carolina family, Oliver soon became the black sheep. According to his testimony, from an early age he loved sin, mocked God, and broke his godly mother's heart. The prayers of a godly sister and mother saved him from certain death many times as he ran with bootleggers. At age twenty he was gloriously saved at the Laurel Creek Baptist Church near Greenville, South Carolina. Five months later came the call to preach. After studying several years in a local Bible college, Oliver bought a tent and launched an outstanding tent ministry.[36]

It was through his powerful, Spirit-filled preaching that I came under the conviction of sin. Preacher Greene (as he was called) brought his big green tent to my hometown, Rocky Mount, North Carolina, in May, 1950. His preaching made everyone who heard him either angry or glad. Being a sinful, pleasure-seeking young man of 21 years of age, it was my intention not to hear him. However, during his final week, my parents persuaded me and my brother to attend the tent meeting. I cannot tell what he preached on that hot night in July, but I remember what happened to me. Preacher Greene had a unique style of giving an invitation. After concluding his message, he requested everyone in the tent to stand with heads bowed and eyes closed. Then he asked everyone who knew for sure they were saved and on their way to heaven to sit down. Those left standing were requested to look up at the preacher while those seated were instructed to pray. My brother and I were among those who kept standing. The Word of God, the Spirit of God, and the man of God had been speaking to me as I sat under that tent. Preacher Greene spoke to those standing and invited us to come to the prayer room and receive Christ as Savior. I went to the prayer room but was met by an old gentleman who was unskilled in leading a person to faith in Christ, and I did not find Christ that night.

My Dad asked me if I was saved and I said no. But the Spirit was convicting me, showing me my lost estate, and creating in me a strong desire to know Christ and to have the assurance of salvation. For the next several nights I returned to hear the preaching. On July 6, 1950 I left my seat to once again visit the prayer room. I knelt at the back of the room earnestly talking to God. Without realizing it, I repented of my sins by telling God I was sorry for my sins and that with His help I would turn from them. Still there was no peace in my troubled heart. Then Mr. Johnny Harper, a humble Christian man, touched me on the shoulder, and asked if I needed help. I told him I wanted to be saved but did not know how. Opening his huge Bible, he explained Ephesians 2:8-9, and that night I was completely, instantaneously, and everlastingly saved! Praise His name! So Evangelist Oliver B. Greene and Mr. Johnny Harper have a special place in my heart.

Quoting from his autobiography, *From Disgrace to Grace,* Preacher Greene mentions his Rocky Mount campaign of 1950.

> Our greatest meeting was in Rocky Mount, North Carolina . . . IN SEVEN WEEKS we recorded seven thousand professions of faith. One Baptist church baptized nearly two hundred out of that meeting. Other churches baptized scores of others. Many fine Christians who live at present in Rocky Mount were saved in that meeting.[37]

My wife, Elizabeth English, offered her life for missionary service during that meeting. Our city was deeply touched and at least seven churches can trace their beginnings to its influence.

Along with his tent preaching, he was the founder of The Gospel Hour. This radio ministry grew until it was being heard on 180 stations. In my travels I find people all across this land who were converted listening to the Gospel Hour.[38]

Realizing the power of the printed Word, Oliver Greene involved himself in gospel literature. His son, David, explains his father's burden:

> As The Gospel Hour ministry grew, Dr. Greene saw a need for a new form of literature to help reach the lost. He felt that something larger than a tract but smaller than an entire book was needed to adequately grab and hold an unsaved person's attention. He developed this form, which he called the soul-winning booklet. He wrote forty-four of these before his death. . . . We have mailed out literally millions of these booklets to people all over the world to use in their personal witnessing ministry. It would be impossible to count the

letters which have been received at The Gospel Hour telling how the reader was saved after reading one of the soul-winning booklets.[39]

The Gospel Hour ministry also published 26 of Dr. Greene's commentaries and "thirty-three hardback study and sermon books."[40]

Oliver Greene literally preached himself to death. At the relatively young age of 61, he suffered an aneurysm of the heart and died a few hours later. He being dead yet speaks as The Gospel Hour is still being heard and Gospel Hour literature is still being read.[41]

If we had the time and space, we could glimpse into the lives of more of God's great evangelists such as William Carey, Gypsy Smith, Mordecai Ham, R. A. Torrey, William Booth, and many, many more. Reading the biographies of great evangelists will enrich the spiritual life.

---

1. Eusebius (HE iii.37), *Dictionary of the Apostolic Church*, ed. James Hastings (New York: Charles Scribner's Sons, 1922) 379.

2. Gerhard Kittel, editor, *Theological Dictionary of the New Testament* (Grand Rapids: Wm. B. Eerdmans Publishing Company, 1964) 737.

3. C. T. Winchester, *The Life of John Wesley* (New York: The Macmillan Company, 1938) 11.

4. Percy Livingstone Parker, ed., *The Heart of John Wesley's Journal* (Cincinnati, Ohio: Jennings and Graham, n.d.) 29.

5. Ibid., 43.

6. J. Wesley Bready, *England: Before and After Wesley* (London, England: Hodder and Stoughton, 1939) 63.

7. Winchester, 64.

8. Ibid., 68-70.

9. Parker, 162.

10. Bready, 215.

11. Fred Barlow, *Profiles in Evangelism* (Mufreesboro, Tennessee: Sword of the Lord Foundation, 1976) 210.

12. Ed Reese, *The Life and Ministry of Adoniram Judson* (Glenwood, Illinois: Fundamental Publishers, 1975) 4.

13. Edward Judson, *The Life of Adoniram Judson* (Philadelphia: American Baptist Publication Society, 1883) 1-2.

14. Ibid., 12-13.

15. Courtney Anderson, *To The Golden Shore* (Grand Rapids: Zondervan Publishing House, 1977) 106.

16. Julia H. Johnston, *Missionary Annals: The Life of Adoniram Judson* (Chicago: Fleming H. Revell Company, 1887) 17.

17. Reese, 11.

18. Ibid., 2-13.

19. Reese, 12.

20. Ibid., 13.

21. L. R. Scarborough, *With Christ After the Lost, A Search for Souls* (Nashville, Tennessee: Sunday School Board, Southern Baptist Convention, 1919) 77-78.

22. Ibid., 78-79.

23. William T. Ellis, *"Billy" Sunday: The Man and His Message* (Swarthmore, Pennsylvania: L. T. Myers, 1914) 25, 39-41.

24. Scarborough, 79-80.

25. R. K. Johnson, *Builder of Bridges* (Mufreesboro, Tennessee: Sword of the Lord, 1969) 6, 22.

26. Barrow, 93-94.

27. Johnson, 174.

28. Ibid., 338-343.

29. Ibid., 273-274.

30. Ibid., 351.

31. Barlow, 147-148.

32. Ibid., 149.

33. Ibid., 148.

34. Ibid., 149.

35.  Ibid.

36.  Oliver B. Greene, *From Disgrace to Grace* (Greenville, South Carolina: The Gospel Hour, Inc., 1991) 33, 38, 54.

37.  Ibid., 60.

38.  David Greene, Part 2, *From Disgrace to Grace* (Greenville, South Carolina: The Gospel Hour, Inc., 1991) 69.

39.  Ibid., 70.

40.  Ibid.

41.  Ibid., 73.

# A
# Biblical
# Perspective
# of
# Evangelism

"To wit, that God was in Christ, reconciling the world unto himself, not imputing their trespasses unto them; and hath committed unto us the word of reconciliation" (II Corinthians 5:19).

# 6

# Man's Plight

Sin is written in bold letters upon the pages of the Bible. Only four chapters of the Bible are free of sin. Genesis 1 and 2 describe man and the world before sin entered. Revelation 21 and 22 record the scene when sin has been put away. From Genesis 3 to Revelation 20, the Bible deals with man's sin and God's intervention.

Man is the crown of God's creation. Created in the image of God, a vast gulf separates man from all other living creatures. Being created in the image of God, man is an intelligent, volitional, emotional personality endowed with capabilities and authorities which defy our present comprehension in this life.

## THE FALL

The entrance of sin radically changed man. When put to the test, man chose knowledge over obedience. In the very beginning, Satan used all three of his weapons to trap Eve: "And when the woman saw that the tree was good for food, [lust of the flesh] and that it was pleasant to the eyes, [lust of the eyes] and a tree to be desired to make one wise, [pride of life] she took of the fruit thereof, and did eat, and gave also unto her husband with her, and he did eat" (Genesis 3:6).

In this original sin, our first parents willfully rejected God and replaced Him with a satanic substitute, human wisdom. True, their eyes were opened to know good and evil. But they no longer had the power or the will to do good. They entered a permanent state of disobedience, enslaved to evil, separated from God, and destitute of divine purpose and plan. As a result, although he does not admit it, man is lost and his life is meaningless and empty. His existence is a living death since he has fallen prey to death. What a tragic story! History is but a sad repeat of Genesis chapter 3.

Modern theologians and psychologists tell us that man is sick. Robert Schuller tells us that sin is low self-esteem. They have been studying the psychology book instead of the Holy Book. Sin is sinful because of what it does to man. And sin with its inherent evil continues to wreck havoc and turmoil upon a fallen race and a cursed world. But sin is sinful supremely because it is committed against God. The enormity of sin, the evil of sin, and the everlasting punishment of sin derive from whom sin is committed against.

Today there is an abysmal lack of the hatred of sin. Sin, to many, is a joke to be laughed at. Sin is not a joke. Sin put the angels out of heaven; sin put Jesus Christ on a cross; and sin will put unforgiven sinners in an eternal hell. Sin is not the absence of good; it is moral perversity. Sin is man confronting God in brazen disobedience. Sin is self-love, self-rule, self-redemption, self-reliance, and self-worship.[1]

John Champion gives an excellent and a very realistic description of sin:

> Sin is pre-eminently a wrong to God. . . . The Apostle John well describes it as lawlessness, anarchy. It turns the heart into a dark chamber of treacherous plotting against the government of God. It is the ceaseless attempt to undermine the dominion of the Divine. . . . It is not merely assault upon the throne of God; it is the blow struck full at the face of the Father. Sin is the unsheathed sword and the straight thrust at the heart of God.[2]

## RESULT OF THE FALL

In this study, it is necessary to find out what God says about man. The two great master ideas of God's Holy Word are sin and redemption. Ignorance of man's desperate condition leads to faulty solutions to his problems. A casual view of sin always brings about a false view of God. "Alexander McLaren of Manchester [England] stated that 'ninety percent of all doctrinal errors have grown up around defective views of sin.' "[3] Any teaching that minimizes sin at the same time minimizes the redemptive work of Christ and the regenerating work of the Holy Spirit.

We have learned that man is a fallen creature, inherently selfish, cherishing his own autonomy. In Genesis 6:5, God gives us a divine commentary on Noah's generation: "And God saw that the wickedness of man was great in the earth, and that every imagination of the thoughts of his heart was only evil continually." This persistent, unrestrained evil necessitated the purging of that sinful society.

The seeds of sin were in Noah and his family. In only a few generations, their descendants were in open defiance against the God of heaven. We read of this rebellion in Genesis 11:4: "And they said, Go to, let us build us a city and a tower, whose top may reach unto heaven and let us make us a name, lest we be scattered abroad upon the face of the whole earth." First, they went about to invent their own religious system. This building of a tower certainly refers to the Zodiac and the ancient religion of Babylon. Nimrod was a "shaker and mover" in Babylon, and "from secular sources we gather that she [his wife] was the infamous Semiramis, the woman who first introduced idolatry on the earth and who made Babylon the eternal home of the 'mysteries'. The vast system of pagan religion, which thereafter swiftly inundated the globe, stemmed from Babylon."[4] Thus their making a name for themselves speaks of glorifying themselves, or humanism. And their refusal to obey God's command to disperse indicates the "one worlders" were at work.

Next, we see sin in all its perversity. In Genesis 19, angels came to Sodom to escort Lot and his family from sin city. The men of the city, young and old, descended on Lot's house demanding the right to have sex with his guests. This whole incident is so current, so relevant. The perverts of Sodom no longer practiced their sin in secret; in their thinking, they had a constitutional right to indulge their passions how, when, where, and with whom they pleased. Anyone who dared to stop them would incur their wrath.

Social scientists would have us believe that man's biggest problem is his environment: poverty, poor education, lack of employment, and a host of other villains. In Mark 7:15, our Lord refutes this erroneous social theory. He says, "There is nothing **without** a man, that entering into him can defile him." In other words, environment is not the cause of our social ills. Then our Lord teaches the real source of crime and sin: "But the things which come **out of** him, those are they that defile the man." The master teacher gave His disciples a lesson on anthropology as He lists what defiles a man: "For from **within,** out of the heart of men, proceed evil thoughts, adulteries, fornications, murders, Thefts, covetousness, wickedness, deceit, lasciviousness, an evil eye, blasphemy, pride, foolishness: All these evil things come from **within,** and defile the man" (Mark 7:21-23).(Author's emphasis).

In this Epistle to the Romans, Paul begins with sin. He lays the premise for his epistle in Romans 1:18: "For the wrath of God is revealed from heaven against all ungodliness and unrighteousness of men, who hold the truth in unrighteousness." This ungodliness resulted from an unwillingness to see and to understand the power and wisdom of God. Then Paul, in logical sequence, describes man's departure from God: "Because that, when they knew God, they glorified him not as God, neither were thankful; but became vain in their imaginations, and their foolish heart was darkened. Professing themselves to be wise, they became fools, And changed the glory of the uncorruptible God into an image made like to corruptible man, and to birds, and fourfooted beasts, and creeping things" (Romans1:21-23).

Before launching into the great doctrine of justification by faith, Paul drives home the sinfulness of man. He proves both Jew and Gentile under sin and guilty before God. Paul gives a fearful description of man. Throats are likened to an uncovered grave spewing out corruption, tongues full of deceit, mouths bitterly cursing God and man, feet running to violence, leading to paths of miser ʼand destruction, minds and hearts without peace and the fear of God (Romans 3:13-18)

In contrasting saint and sinner, believer and unbeliever, Paul once again paints an ugly picture. After affirming that the unrighteous shall not inherit the kingdom of God, he characterizes the unrighteous. "Be not deceived: neither fornicators, nor idolaters, nor adulterers, nor effeminate [homosexual], nor abusers of themselves with mankind, Nor thieves, nor covetous, nor drunkards, nor revilers, nor extortioners, shall inherit the kingdom of God" (I Corinthians 6:9-10).

In the Epistle to the Galatians, Paul lists the works of the flesh and the fruit of the spirit, which are the two diverse principles governing human behavior:

> Now the works of the flesh are manifest, which are these; Adultery, fornication, uncleanness, lasciviousness, Idolatry, witchcraft, hatred, variance, emulations, wrath, strife, seditions, heresies, Envyings, murders, drunkenness, revellings, and such like: of the which I tell you before, as I have also told you in time past, that they which do such things shall not inherit the kingdom of God (Galatians 5:19-21).

In Ephesians, Paul deals with man's condition. Instead of listing man's sin, he tells us several fundamental realities about people. People are dead in trespasses and sins (Ephesians 2:1). This, of course, refers to spiritual death. Dead men are unresponsive. The spiritually dead are unresponsive to the things of God. However, these same people are physically very much alive. In fact, most people are extremely busy and, without knowing it, are controlled by the prince of the air, Satan. Their days and nights are consumed with activities as they fulfill the desires of their minds and flesh. Paul characterizes them as the children of disobedience and the children of wrath.

In his last epistle, Paul gives twenty characteristics of unsaved people: "For men shall be lovers of their own selves, covetous, boasters, proud, blasphemers, disobedient to parents, unthankful, unholy, Without natural affection, trucebreakers, false accusers, incontinent, fierce, despisers of those that are good, Traitors, heady, highminded, lovers of pleasures more than lovers of God; Having a form of godliness, but denying the power thereof: from such turn away" (II Timothy 3:2-5).

The last list which describes man without God comes from The Revelation. One last time the Holy Spirit warns by telling what kind of people are destined for the lake of fire, which is the second death: "But the fearful, and unbelieving, and the abominable, and murderers, and whoremongers, and sorcerers, and idolaters, and all liars, shall have their part in the lake which burneth with fire and brimstone: which is the second death" (Revelation 21:8).

## AWESOME TASK

We have taken the time and effort to see God's appraisal of mankind to remind ourselves of the awesome task to which we have been called. Education, psychology, human efforts, church programs, and seminars cannot effect the change. The task of winning people to Christ and integrating into their lives a godly lifestyle requires the work of God.

The gospel of Christ, the power of God (Romans 1:16), is the only solution to the problem of sin. But God ordained that this power flow through a medium. Just as electricity flows through wires to release tremendous power, the power of God must have a channel. God has chosen to use saved men and women to reach unsaved men and women with the soul-saving, life-changing message of the gospel of the Lord Jesus Christ.

The following pages will discuss the great matters of evangelizing and discipling. The herculean task of confronting rebels and by the Word of God reconciling them to their rightful King and Sovereign demands our human best combined with the power of the Holy Spirit. Let me encourage prayerful reading as we look into these matters of ultimate importance. "For what shall it profit a man, if he shall gain the whole world, and lose his own soul?" (Mark 8:36).

---

1. Peters, 17.

2. John B. Champion, *The Living Atonement*, Quoting McLaren of Manchester (Philadelphia: The Griffith & Rowland Press, n.d.) 149-150.

3. A. B. Winchester, Foreword, *True Evangelism or Winning Souls By Prayer,* by Lewis Sperry Chafer (Chicago: The Bible Institute Colportage Ass'n., 1938) x.

4. John Phillips, *Exploring Genesis* (Chicago: Moody Press, 1980) 99-101.

# 7

# God's Purpose

In the previous chapter, a careful effort was made to give a biblical portrait of man. The sordid picture, however humbling to our human natures, squares with human history and present reality. Just as a faulty view of sin leads into doctrinal error, so a faulty view of God's purposes for man will lead inevitably to defective evangelism.

Success to a great extent, depends on focusing on a goal. Without a destination, a traveler will never know when he has arrived. Great achievements demand great planning. Success in evangelizing and discipling depends on both recognizing the purposes of God and seeking to fulfill these purposes.

## GOD'S ORIGINAL PURPOSE

Undoubtedly, God had great plans for man, His viceroy on planet earth. God created man in His own image and desired that man reflect His image through loving, obedient service. Our imaginations fail when we contemplate what a standard of living, what spiritual, social, and physical blessings would have been enjoyed in a society untainted by the fall. The present insurmountable obstacles and unsolvable problems plaguing our planet would be conspicuously absent.

According to Genesis 2:15, God entrusted to man the task of developing a garden. To be sure, Adam set about his task with great gusto. Never again will flowers so beautiful, fruits so luscious, and such physical harmony between all living beings be seen. Along with this physical harmony, man enjoyed unbroken fellowship with God.

In our effort to bring men to Christ and to Christ-likeness, a thorough knowledge of man is essential. In order to properly relate to the realities of life, God endowed man with a threefold consciousness: a consciousness of himself, a consciousness of the world, and a consciousness of God. Man relates to the world around him through his physical senses and organs. The *ego,* or self-consciousness, constitutes a person as an individual. Man is much more than flesh and blood; he is a distinct self, possessing volition and personality. The entity that gives to man an inner consciousness and a self-awareness is the soul. God endued man with spirit, the divine part of man, that separates him from all other creatures. Through the spirit man gains God-consciousness. In contrasting the two invisible parts of man, soul and spirit, the soul relates to the sensual and the earthly while the spirit relates to God and heaven.

The soul connects the spirit with the body and only through its mediation can the spirit act on the body. Eric Sauer in his tremendous book, *The Dawn of World Redemption,* clarifies the issue with these words: "Hence the soul is the bond between both these [body and spirit]; it is, as it were, a 'body' for the spirit, even as it is itself enclosed by the body as its own material frame."[1]

In creating man in His own image, God is the prototype; man is the copy. Spirituality, liberty, and blessedness characterize the nature of God. God infused into man intellect (spirituality), will (liberty), and feeling (blessedness). By these endowments, God made it possible for man to glorify his Creator by knowing Him, loving Him, and enjoying Him.

God gave man a cultural mandate: "Be fruitful, and multiply, and replenish the earth, and subdue it" (Genesis 1:28). God crowned Adam in three ways. First, He bestowed upon him a *posterity*: "Be fruitful, and multiply." From Adam and Eve the whole human race became sinners. Romans 5:12 bears this out. "Wherefore, as by one man sin entered into the world, and death by sin; and so death passed upon all men, for that all have sinned."[2]

Next, "God crowned Adam with a *position* (Genesis 1:28), giving him dominion over the fish of the sea, the fowl of the air, and over every living thing." In spite of the fall, man has been amazingly successful in dominating planet earth with unimaginable scientific and technological advances.[3]

"Finally, God crowned Adam with a *possession* (Genesis 1:29-31)." To Adam was given a "paradise to enjoy." Try to envision life unspoiled by the ravages of sin. Each day must have been an exciting adventure for Adam. Over all of this Adam was given dominion.[4]

An understanding of this cultural mandate is pivotal to a correct understanding of God's original purposes for man. George Peters helps us understand the importance and scope of God's command:

> The first mandate was spoken to Adam as representative of the race and involves the whole realm of human culture. In its widest sense it includes religion. It serves man in his need as a socio-religio-cultural creature. It includes the natural and social aspects of man such as habitat, agriculture, industrialization, commerce, politics, social and moral order, academic and scientific advancement, health, education, and physical care. . . . Here are the basic concepts and directives for an ordered and progressive society based on principles of sound morality and ethical monotheism. The Bible does concern itself with social and cultural welfare.[5]

If Adam had not fallen, he would undoubtedly have built a society that in every respect would have glorified God and benefitted man.

## GOD'S PRESENT PURPOSE

With the Fall, everything changed. Man went from a state of innocence to guilt. To deal with these changed conditions, new principles were required. Eric Sauer makes some interesting comments:

> Without a fall human progress would have been a gradual ascent. It might well have been a history of ever increasing blessing but not a history of redemption. All would have been an uninterrupted upward development. But now in place of the capacity for the developing of man there entered the possibility and necessity of his redemption. Henceforth it was no more a matter of the *evolution* of his slumbering powers but of the *revolution* of the spirit by acts of divine love and a new creation.[6]

The fall of man was great, but the love and mercy of God was greater (Romans 5:20). Man had indeed fallen, but his fall was not beyond hope. He remained redeemable and God became his Redeemer. Two important facts make this so. First, man himself had not invented sin. In his sin, he had not acted from within but was acted upon from without. Otherwise, he would have become a self-originator of sin and thereby a devil. Second, after he fell he did not identify with sin and the devil, but felt sin to be something foreign to him and distanced himself from it. Feeling the shame of nakedness, he made a failed effort to cover himself with fig leaves (Genesis 3:7,10). This first attempt of overcoming evil was vain, but it was a sign that man was not willing to succumb to shamelessness and baseness. Though he had acted against his conscience, he refused to kill it.[7]

God responded to man's feeble faith by covering his nakedness with skins of animals. "Unto Adam also and to his wife did the LORD GOD make coats of skins, and clothed them"

(Genesis 3:21). For the first time in paradise, blood was shed. God, as it were, removed man's own attempt to cover his sin and by divine initiative clothed man with skins of innocent animals. This action introduced the principle of sacrifice. The animal (presumably a lamb) that was slain in that first sacrifice looked toward the Lamb of God that takes away the sins of the world (John 1:29).

"All men have not faith" (II Thessalonians 3:2). Cain was one of these men. He was the first child born in this world. In spite of having God-fearing parents, Cain chose not to follow God but the devil (I John 3:12). It was not that Cain was irreligious. Indeed he offered an offering, but not the offering God required. Jude 11 speaks of the "way of Cain." His worship is a type of the natural religious man who believes in God and in "religion," but after his own will and on his own terms. Just as Abraham is the father of the faithful, Cain is the father of the people of this world. He founded the first city (Genesis 4:17) and began a godless society which was destroyed in the flood.

Abel in contrast, was a man of faith. He humbly acknowledged that sin demands death which he demonstrated by offering an animal (presumably a lamb) as a sacrifice for sin. God's acceptance of Abel's sacrifice and the rejection of Cain's resulted in the first murder. Cain slew his godly brother who died in faith looking for redemption through the woman's seed (Genesis 3:15).

Through the course of history, God has been working out His purposes. He is past finding out. But as we move into the New Testament, His purposes are revealed. The angelic messenger broke the centuries-old silence with these words: "Fear not: for behold, I bring you good tidings of great joy, which shall be to all people. For unto you is born this day in the city of David a Saviour, which is Christ the Lord" (Luke 2:10-11). The key word is "Saviour." Another angel echoed the same message to Joseph: "And she shall bring forth a son, and thou shalt call his name JESUS: for he shall save his people from their sins" (Matthew 1:21).

Albert Barnes elaborates on the phrase "from their sins" emphasizing the importance of being saved from sin:

> **From their sins.** This is the great business of Jesus in coming and dying. It is not to save men IN their sins, but FROM their sins. Sinners could not be happy in heaven. It would be a place of wretchedness to the guilty. . . . We have no evidence that we are his people, unless we are saved from the power and dominion of sin. A mere profession of being his people will not answer. Unless we give up our sins; unless we renounce the pride, pomp, and pleasure of the world, and all our lusts and crimes, we have no evidence that we are the children of God.[8]

## GOD'S FUTURE PURPOSE

In Romans 8:28-30, Paul speaks specifically to the purpose of God:

> And we know that all things work together for good to them that love God, to them who are the called according to his purpose. For whom he did foreknow, he also did predestinate to be conformed to the image of his Son . . . . Moreover whom he did predestinate, them he also called: and whom he called, them he also justified: and whom he justified, them he also glorified.

God's working in the past, present, and future is seen in this majestic statement. God's call precedes the beginning of the world (II Timothy 1:9). Presently, God is justifying those He has called: "And such were some of you: but ye are washed, but ye are sanctified, but ye are justified in the name of the Lord Jesus, by the Spirit of our God" (I Corinthians 6:11).

In the future, God's final purpose will be fulfilled: "That in the dispensation of the fullness of times he might gather together in one all things in Christ, both which are in heaven, and which are on earth; even in him. . . .That we should be to the praise of his glory" (Ephesians 1:10,12). The work of redemption transcends time extending from eternity to eternity.

The Holy Spirit, using the pen of the Apostle Paul, grants us an insight into God's redemptive purpose:

> Even when we were dead in sins, hath quickened us together with Christ, (by grace ye are saved;) And hath raised us up together, and made us sit together in heavenly places in Christ Jesus: That in the ages to come he might shew the exceeding riches of his grace in his kindness toward us through Christ Jesus. . . . For we are his workmanship, created in Christ Jesus unto good works, which God hath before ordained that we should walk in them (Ephesians 2:5-7,10).

God designed His people to be filled with good works. In fact, their very purpose for being called is to "shew forth the praises of him who hath called you out of darkness into his marvelous light" (I Peter 2:9). Many texts could be quoted to show God's concern for godly living, but Titus 2:12, 14 will serve as a good example:

> Teaching us that, denying ungodliness and worldly lusts, we should live soberly, righteously, and godly, in this present world . . . . Who gave himself for us, that he might redeem us from all iniquity, and purify unto himself a peculiar people, zealous of good works.

Just as Israel in the Old Testament was to be a light to the nations, God intends for His church to "be blameless and harmless, the sons of God, without rebuke, in the midst of a crooked and perverse nation, among whom ye shine as lights in the world" (Philippians 2:15). God's people are on display, for good or bad.

However, a day is coming when God will be on display. Throughout eternity He will be showing His people how exceedingly rich is his glory and kindness. "When he shall come to be glorified in his saints, and to be admired in all them that believe [because our testimony among you was believed] in that day" (II Thessalonians 1:10). Albert Barnes gives a beautiful comment on this verse:

> The general idea is, that Christ in that day will be manifested in a glorious manner, and that the source of his highest triumphs will be what is seen in the saints. His main honour, when He returns to the world, will not be the outward splendours which will attend his coming, nor the angels that will accompany him, nor the manifestation of his power over the elements, but the church which he has redeemed. It will then be seen that He is worthy of universal admiration, for having redeemed that church.[9]

Perhaps at the same time "the four and twenty elders [representatives of the redeemed from all ages] fall down before him that sat on the throne, and worship him that liveth for ever and ever, and cast their crowns before the throne, saying, Thou art worthy, O Lord, to receive glory and honour and power: for thou hast created all things, and for thy pleasure, they are and were created" (Revelation 4:10-11).

## MINISTRY OF RECONCILIATION

"Salvation is of the LORD" (Jonah 2:9). Yet God has been pleased to include man in His work of reconciliation. The Apostle

Paul speaks expressly to this point:

> All things are of God, who hath reconciled us to himself by Jesus Christ, and hath given to us the ministry of reconciliation; To wit, that God was in Christ, reconciling the world unto himself, not imputing their trespasses unto them, and hath committed unto us the word of reconciliation (II Corinthians 5:18-19).

God has given us a ministry of reconciliation (bringing man into a right relationship with God). II Corinthians 5:20 describes this ministry of reconciliation: "Now then we are ambassadors for Christ, as though God did beseech you by us: we pray you in Christ's stead, be ye reconciled to God." The reconciled are commissioned to become reconcilers. The task of reconciling willful, rebellious men is thrust upon those who know and love the Lord Jesus Christ.

To accomplish this task, God has given us the message of reconciliation. II Corinthians 5:21 declares the marvelous message: "For he hath made him [Christ] to be sin for us, who knew no sin; that we might be made the righteousness of God in him." Christ took our sins that we might by faith receive His righteousness.

During this age of grace (the church age), the tasks of preaching the gospel, persuading sinners, and planting churches have been committed to the church (Matthew 28:19). Thankfully, God does not expect the church to act alone in these great endeavors. Revelation 22:17 assures us that the Holy Spirit engages along with the church in evangelism: "And the Spirit and the bride [church] say, Come. And let him that heareth say, Come. And whosoever will, let him take the water of life freely."

---

1.    Eric H. Sauer, *The Dawn of World Redemption* (Grand Rapids: Wm. B. Eerdmans Publishing Company, 1962) 40.

2. Phillips, 45.

3. Ibid, 46.

4. Ibid.

5. Peters, 166-167.

6. Sauer, 49.

7. Ibid.

8. Albert Barnes, *Barnes' Notes on the New Testament* (Grand Rapids: Kregel Publications, 1962) 4.

9. Ibid, 1109.

# 8

# The Primacy
# of Evangelism
# in the Synoptic Gospels

What has gone wrong with the harvest? Any honest student of the church must confess that something is dead wrong in American churches. Eighty-five percent of churches are plateaued or are in decline. Only five percent of Christians witness to their faith in Christ. A mere fifteen percent read their Bible on a daily basis. Our theological seminaries skirt around the subject of evangelism and church growth. The salt has lost its savor and is being trodden under the feet of men as our society continues to sink into a morass of evil and violence.

Could it be that we have majored in the minors and overlooked the primacy of evangelism in the New Testament? New Testament evangelism changes lives, and in changing lives has a positive impact on society. The emphasis on anti-crime legislation, gun control, values, etc., misses the point. Guns are not the problem; people that use the gun to kill and maim are the culprits. Violent people terrorize; regenerated people evangelize by bringing the message that saves from sin and destructive behavior.

It will be profitable to survey the New Testament and note the mentions of the work of evangelism. A testimony to the primacy of evangelism shows itself in that the first and the last chapters of the New Testament speak about the subject of evangelism. In Matthew 1:21 we read, "Thou shalt call his name JESUS: for he shall save his people from their sins." The Apostle John in the closing verses of The Revelation gives the last invitation to salvation: "And the Spirit and the bride [church] say, Come. And let him that heareth say, Come. And let him that is athirst come. And whosoever will, let him take the water of life freely" (Revelation 22:17).

In Matthew 3 and Luke 1, John the Baptist appears on the scene. His father, Zacharias, prophesying by the Holy Spirit, says, "And thou, child, shalt be called the prophet of the Highest: for thou shalt go before the face of the Lord to prepare his ways; To give knowledge of salvation unto his people by the remission of their sins" (Luke 1:76-77). The Lord used John the Baptist to prepare a people who would be receptive to the ministry of the Lord Jesus. God used this prophet to call the nation of Israel to repentance and remission of sins. Although the nation officially rejected his message, some repented and came to a knowledge of salvation. John had a strong message that was predictive, invective, and convictive. John the Baptist was indeed a shining light, a faithful witness to his Lord.

Jesus' teaching was filled with metaphors. One of His most famous metaphors is "fishers of men." Peter and John received their call as they were casting their nets: "And he saith unto them, Follow me, and I will make you fishers of men" (Matthew 4:19). Later, Jesus reinforced that promise by explaining that from now on their occupation would be to "catch" men. (Luke 5:10). The grand metaphor, fishing for men, speaks straightforwardly of soul-winning. Salvation is of the Lord, but the Lord chooses to use people to "catch" people for Christ. Christ's statement, "Follow me, and I will make you fishers of men" should cause us great concern. If we claim to be followers of Christ but are not fishers of men, we contradict the words of Christ.

## EVANGELISTIC TECHNIQUES

Many people have been won to faith in Christ through

cottage prayer meetings or house meetings. Presently they are called home Bible studies. As a young preacher I developed my preaching skills at Saturday night cottage prayer meetings. As well as evangelizing the unbelievers, these meetings also edified the believers. Our Lord Jesus used this method in Capernaum. Mark 2:1-13 describes one of these meetings. As our Lord, the Living Word, was expounding the written Word, the ceiling opened up and four determined men lowered their sick, lost friend in front of the Lord. How fortunate for this paralyzed man that he had friends who loved him and brought him to Jesus! The man had physical and spiritual needs. Jesus said to the man, "Thy sins be forgiven thee. . . . Arise, and take up thy bed, and walk" (Mark 2:9). Significantly, Christ met first the spiritual need and then the physical.

In evangelism, three inevitables are always present: saints (those four determined, compassionate workers), a lost sinner in need of forgiveness, and the Savior who is able to save unto the uttermost all that trust Him.

Immediately following the saving and healing of the paralyzed man, another example of Jesus' evangelizing techniques comes to our attention. After calling Levi, also known as Matthew, to be His apostle, Christ used another proven method to evangelize: an evangelistic dinner. "And Levi made him a great feast in his own house: and there was a great company of publicans and of others that sat down with them" (Luke 5:29).

When Christ was queried by the Pharisees as to why He ate with publicans and sinners, He gave a forthright answer: "They that are whole need not a physician; but they that are sick. I came not to call the righteous, but sinners to repentance" (Luke 5:31-32). Can you imagine the impact that gathering had on Levi's friends? The great feast and the numerous friends indicate the affluence of Levi. His testimony of forsaking all to follow his new Master no doubt sent shock waves through the crowd.

We used this method effectively in Bangladesh when a high ranking police officer was converted. He gave a spiritual birthday party and announced his entrance into Christ and his exit from the Masons! Through the centuries, multitudes have been won to Christ at testimonial dinners where new believers invite their friends to hear what Christ has done for them.

## THREE SERIOUS WARNINGS

At the end of the Sermon on the Mount, our Lord gives three serious warnings related to evangelism. First, He contrasts two ways: the straight gate with the wide gate, and the narrow way with the broad way. I used to think of those on the broad way as people outside the church who never trusted Christ, and those on the narrow way as those in the church who had trusted Christ and were on the path of life. But in studying the context of false prophets, false professions, and false foundations, it seems that the people entering the wide gate and traveling the broad way are under the impression they are on the right way, the way to heaven.

Present day evangelism, in many places, widens the gate and broadens the way. Its aim is to be like the world in order to win the world. It sounds good, but many who think they are on the way leading to life will too late find they are on the road to destruction.

The second warning contrasts real and false faith. Not everyone who claims faith in the Lord Jesus and calls Him Lord will be saved. "Not everyone that saith unto me, Lord, Lord, shall enter into the kingdom of heaven; but he that doeth the will of my Father which is in heaven." (Matthew 7:21). To make matters more frightening, our Lord goes on to tell us that many who preach, heal, exorcize demons, and do other wonderful works enter the wide gate and travel the broad way that leads to destruction.

Our Lord gives two evidences that contrast mere professors from real possessors: they do not the will of His Father, and they are workers of iniquity. James in his epistle teaches that there is a dead faith, which is a professed faith, and it fails to produce (James 2:26). Saving faith produces a changed life. Where there is no change, there is no faith.

Jesus' last warning concerns foundations. Once a house is completed, the foundation is usually covered and forgotten. In this parable (Matthew 7:24-27) our Lord compares life to a house and the foundation to the principles upon which life is founded. He tells us that wise men build their lives upon rock, and foolish men build upon sand. Sooner or later everyone's foundation will be tested. The Master Teacher explains the difference between the two foundations. Those who build on sand hear, but they do not obey. They have been sold a false bill of goods by smooth talking false teachers who scream about legalism and salvation by works. The apostle John summed it up succinctly: "If ye know that he is righteous, ye know that every one that doeth righteousness is born of him" (I John 2:29).

Biblical evangelism results in converts who have a heart for God and a hatred for the pit from which they have been dug. Hordes of people who are obviously ungodly and are living wicked lifestyles are under the impression that all is right with them and God because long ago they asked Jesus to come into their hearts or they went forward in a church service. Sad will be their bitter wail. Evangelism that results in people becoming new creatures in Christ is the need of the hour (II Corinthians 5:17).

## JESUS' PRAYER REQUEST

In Matthew 9:35-38, vital teaching concerning evangelism confronts us. Jesus is our tremendous example: "And Jesus went about all the cities and villages, teaching . . . and healing . . . the people" (Matthew 9:35). Oh, how we need to fan out in our communities witnessing and working for Christ and His church.

In Matthew 9:36, we see His tender empathy: "When He saw the multitudes, he was moved with compassion." The best way to get a burden for lost people is to go and see them. Seeing that great multitude, He made a true evaluation: "The harvest truly is plenteous, but the laborers are few" ( Matthew

9:37). Not only is the harvest plenteous, but it is white (ripe). Nothing is wrong with the harvest; the trouble is with the laborers. In America, there are over 500,000 Christian workers. The great majority are church workers that never get into the harvest. How few are the laborers, those who strive to win souls, who exert themselves to get people reconciled with God!

"Pray ye therefore the Lord of the harvest, that he will send forth labourers into his harvest" (Matthew 9:38). Here we see Jesus' terrific exhortation. In this verse are four keys that open the possibility of local church and world evangelism. First, the key priority is prayer. All hinges upon prayer. A prayerless endeavor is a powerless endeavor doomed to failure and disappointment. Prayer is the nuclear bomb in our spiritual arsenal. Lord, teach us to pray!

Second, the key person is the Holy Spirit, the Lord of the harvest. Only He can call saints to the work of evangelism (Acts 13:2), and only He can convict sinners of sin (John 16:8). We dare not neglect the Holy Spirit and insult Him in our efforts to work without His presence and power.

Third, the key people are laborers; those who will venture into the whitened harvest fields to give themselves to the task of reaching people for Christ.

Fourth, the key program is the harvest. Regrettably, the harvest is low on the church's priority list. A host of good programs consume the time, energy, and resources of the church while the key program flounders. The church has two legitimate programs: edification of the saints and evangelism of sinners. Generally speaking, ninety percent of time, talent, and treasure edifies the saints while ten percent evangelizes the sinners. Then we ask, "What went wrong with the harvest?"

Two important traits characterize the harvest: urgency and importance. Ripened harvests do not wait. A golden harvest whitens; a whitened harvest soon perishes. Why would a farmer permit his harvest to perish? Only two reasons can be given: lack of laborers or laziness of laborers! A whitened harvest cries for urgent measures. The harvest's importance leaps out of the gospels. Jesus wept over the harvest, He died for the harvest, He rose for the harvest, He intercedes for the harvest, and one glad day He will return for the harvest.

## PARABLE OF THE SOILS

The parable of the sower gives us insight as to Jesus' thinking about evangelism. The Master Teacher talks about four types of soils and compares the soil to people who hear the Word of God. He gave three pieces of data about each type of soil or hearer: a description of the hearer, an identification of the enemy, and a tabulation of the results.

"Those by the way side [footpath] are they that hear; then cometh the devil, and taketh away the word out of their hearts, lest they should believe and be saved" (Luke 8:12) First, the hearer is described as a calloused, hardhearted hearer in whose life the Word fails to gain access. Second, the enemy is identified as the devil who steals away the Word lest it be believed and the hearer be saved. Third, an honest report indicates the hearer has no faith due to the absence of the Word resulting in a lifeless condition.

"They on the rock are they, which, when they hear, receive the word with joy; and these have no root, which for a while believe, and in time of temptation fall away" (Luke 8:13). First, the hearer is described as a careless, superficial, and emotional hearer. Second, the enemy is identified as fleshly temptation, testings, and persecution. Third, an honest report indicates the hearer makes a pretense of faith. His faith is spurious, without conviction, resulting in a rootless condition.

"And that which fell among thorns are they, which, when they have heard, go forth, and are choked with cares and riches and pleasures of this life, and bring no fruit to perfection" (Luke 8:14). First, the hearer is described as a crowded, choked, and cluttered hearer. Second, the enemy is identified as worldly interests, the pursuit of wealth, and devotion to having a good time. Third, an honest report indicates the hearer has faith, but a defective faith without perspective. The hearer, after receiving the Word, turns around and lives for the here and now, resulting in a fruitless condition.

"But that on the good ground are they, which in an honest and good heart, having heard the word, keep it, and bring forth fruit with patience" (Luke 8:5). First, the hearer is described as a cultivated and conditioned hearer. Second, the enemies are all present: the flesh, the world, and the devil. An honest report indicates an entrance of the Word in the heart of the hearer which takes root in his life resulting in a fruitful condition.

What do we learn from this data? There are two constants and one variable: the sower and the seed are the constants, and the hearer is the variable. As we look at these four hearers, we note that only the last hearer evidenced the fruit of salvation. The first hearer failed to hear, and the word was quickly stolen away by the devil. The next two professed to believe, and all indications were that they were true believers. But the test of time proved their professions spurious. "But the word preached did not profit them, not being mixed with faith in them that heard it" (Hebrews 4:2).

The word entered the hearts of the three hearers, but only one exercised saving faith. This parable corroborates Jesus' statement, "Many will say. . . . Lord, Lord . . . . And then will I profess unto them, I never knew you: depart from me, ye that work iniquity" (Matthew 7:22-23).

## FRIEND OF SINNERS

Jesus earned the reputation of being a friend of sinners. "Then drew near unto him all the publicans and sinners for to hear him" (Luke 15:1). In replying to the Pharisees' murmuring about his association with sinners, our Lord answered with three parables: the lost sheep, the lost coin, and the lost son.

Several common denominators run through these parables. First, the parables emphasize the value of that which was lost. The shepherd, the woman, and the father exercised themselves to find that which they had lost. The lost sheep, the lost coin, and the lost son represent sinners that were alienated from God.

Second, the return of that which was lost caused great rejoicing. Jesus likened the finding of that which was lost to a sinner repenting and being saved. There is joy in heaven when a sinner humbles himself, confesses and forsakes his sin, and by faith receives Christ as Lord and Savior. New Testament evangelism both glorifies God and rejoices His great heart of love.

In the gospels, the Divine Historian shares with us Jesus dealing with inquirers. The most enigmatic interview occurs between a rich young ruler and Jesus. "And when he was gone forth into the way, there came one running, and kneeled to him, and asked him, Good Master, what shall I do that I may inherit eternal life?" (Mark 10:17). This young man came in the right way—running; he came in the right spirit—kneeling; and he asked the right question—what must I do to inherit eternal life? Jesus brought the man back to the ten commandments. The ten commandments are in two sections: the first five relate to God, and the last five relate to man. Our Lord brought to his attention the last five commandments, and the young man confessed to keeping them from his youth. Then a strange statement comes out of our Lord's mouth: "One thing thou lackest" (Mark 10:21). In telling this rich young man to go and sell his belongings, give to the poor, and come take up the cross and follow Him, the Lord touched this man where it hurt. Mammon—money and all the creature comforts money can buy—had captured the affection of this young man. Christ put his finger on his sin, and the young man loved his possessions more than eternal life. A man cannot have two masters; neither can he have two gods. "Thou shalt have no other gods before me" (Exodus 20:3).

This brings us to an interesting and oft debated question: does one have to give up one's sin to be saved? To correctly answer the question we must determine what "giving up" sin means. Solomon said, "There is not a just man upon earth, that doeth good, and sinneth not" (Ecclesiastes 7:20). Sinlessness is not a requirement for salvation. If so, no one would be saved. From a personal point of view, I knew when the Holy Spirit was convicting me of sin, and in the process of my receiving Christ as my Lord and Savior, my sin—specific wrong doing in which I was engaged—was clearly brought to my attention. I repented and turned from that sin and was subsequently, instantaneously, completely, and everlastingly saved. Hallelujah! Without being willing to quit that sin, I would have walked sorrowfully away from Christ just as the rich young ruler did centuries before.

## EVANGELISTIC PRINCIPLES

The story of Zacchaeus has always been a favorite of children. From this amusing incident, important evangelistic principles emerge. Zacchaeus' great desire to see Jesus undoubtedly was the work of the Holy Spirit. His joy in receiving Jesus at his house indicates keen spiritual hunger.

In our comings and goings, we need to be on the lookout for people who are spiritually hungry and willing to discuss spiritual matters. Going to Zacchaeus' home enabled Jesus to have an in depth meeting instead of a fleeting, superficial contact. Much present day evangelism is too fleeting and superficial to ensure lasting results.

The oft overlooked principle of restitution presents itself. Zacchaeus probably was convicted of his unjust extortion of taxes. His willingness to make wrong things right is commendable. Immediately, following Zacchaeus' willingness to restitute, Jesus declared, "This day is salvation come to this house" (Luke 19:9).

The salvation of this tax collector elicited a statement from Christ proving the primacy of evangelism: "For the Son of man is come to seek and to save that which was lost" (Luke 19:10). With sixteen monosyllabic words our Lord stated His ultimate purpose for coming: to seek and save the lost. Our Lord never veered from this purpose of seeking and saving sinners. Most organizations have a policy statement stating their purpose of ministry. Hampton Park Baptist Church, of which I am a member, simply and eloquently states its purpose: "Our purpose is to glorify the Lord Jesus Christ by bringing the saints into a closer fellowship with God and with one another through the study of His Word and obedience to its precepts and by seeking every opportunity to evangelize the lost both in the Greenville area and around the world."[1]

## CHRIST'S FINAL DEED

The primacy of evangelism asserts itself as our Lord Jesus Christ suffers on the cross. Just before dismissing His spirit and giving up the ghost, He saved one who was lost. At one juncture, both thieves were accusing Christ and blaspheming. Luke records the conversion of one of the malefactors. What caused this man to turn from rejection to become a humble, repentant supplicant is not shown. But change he did. First, he rebuked the thief that continued to badger Christ (Luke 23: 40). Second, he confessed his own sin and admitted he was getting what he deserved (Luke 23:41). Third, he testified to the innocence of Christ saying, "this man hath done nothing amiss" (Luke 23:41). Then he called on the Lord: "Lord, remember me when thou comest into thy kingdom" (Luke 23: 42). Here we see faith. He believed that this was not the end of Christ, but just the beginning of His glorious kingdom. Christ responded to that faith and gave this man a word of assurance: "To day thou shalt be with me in paradise" (Luke 23:43). Is it not significant that Christ's last deed was that of saving a poor lost sinner?

## THE GREAT COMMISSION

In bringing to a close this survey of evangelism in the synoptic gospels, we must look at the command to evangelize the world, known as the Great Commission. Matthew emphasizes the method. He reminds us that the goal is not just preaching the gospel, nor just teaching those who are baptized. Both of these are means to achieving the purpose: making disciples of

Jesus Christ in all nations.

In Mark, the emphasis is preaching the gospel to the masses and giving every individual the privilege of hearing the good news of a sinless, crucified, risen Lord and Savior. The preaching of the gospel is the means by which the world will be evangelized and discipled. No nation, tribe, family, or individual is to be neglected. All nations, every creature needs discipling.

Luke emphasizes the message. The risen Lord commanded His disciples to preach in His name among all nations, and then He spelled out what was to be preached: the sufferings of Christ, the resurrection of Christ, repentance, and remission for sins. I am not happy with evangelists, theologians, Bible colleges, or any others who delete repentance from their preaching and teaching. I am sure that their motives are mostly honorable. Still, no one has the right to change the message.

Christ said repentance and remission for sins must be preached. Paul obeyed and preached "repentance toward God and faith toward our Lord Jesus Christ" (Acts 20:21). Peter preached it as he wrote "The Lord is. . . .not willing that any should perish, but that all should come to repentance" (II Peter 3:9). Those taking liberties with the message need to consider these words of Christ: "For whosoever shall be ashamed of me and of my words, of him shall the Son of man be ashamed, when he shall come in his own glory, and in his Father's, and of the holy angels" (Luke 9:26).

---

1. *Bylaws*, as amended, October 29, 1997 (Greenville: South Carolina: Hampton Park Baptist Church) 1.

# 9

# The Primacy
# of Evangelism
# in the Gospel of John

The author of the Gospel of John unabashedly states his purpose: "And many other signs truly did Jesus in the presence of his disciples, which are not written in this book: But these are written, that ye might believe that Jesus is the Christ, the Son of God and that believing ye might have life through his name" (John 20:30-31). Without a doubt, the Gospel of John is one of the most important books ever written. What greater theme can be imagined? The book promises not only life, but eternal life!

This book assumes people are important. Gaines Dobbins said it so well:

> It assumes that each individual represents a universe about which all values gather and that this universe of personality is the measure of supreme value. The person may be an eminent Nicodemus or a despised Samaritan woman; the measure of value remains the same. The individual is never dealt with apart from his or her relationships, the first and most important of which is with God. Of all the amazing qualities of the mind of Christ, none seems to have impressed John so much as his person-minded-

ness. This remains the basis of all successful disciple winning.[1]

The success of books, stories and sermons depend largely upon their introductions. The Prologue, the first eighteen verses of John, startle the mind and captivate the spirit. "In the beginning was the Word [Logos], and the Word was with God, and the Word was God. The same was in the beginning with God" (John 1:1-2). John immediately identifies the Word as God. In verse 14, the Word becomes flesh (incarnate) and dwells among us. Very quickly John established the deity of the Lord Jesus Christ.

In using *Logos,* John was not seeking to impress the Greeks. His audience would know little of Greek philosophy. He was simply saying that Jesus was a true representation of God. "No man hath seen God at any time; the only begotten Son, which is in the bosom of the Father, he hath declared him" (John 1:18). Logos means "word" and a word is a symbol, spoken or written to identify an object or idea. Jesus Christ is God and He reveals to us what God is really like.

To further cement the truth that Jesus Christ is God, John tells us that He is also the Creator. "All things were made by him; and without him was not any thing made that was made" (John 1:3). In an awesome, solemn fashion the credentials of Jesus Christ the Son of God are unfolded. As the Creator, He is the source of all life and light. "In him was life; and the life was the light of men" (John 1:4). Jesus Christ is the source of all life and light both physical and spiritual.

Next, we are sobered by the fact that the awful curse of sin cuts off the light. "And the light shineth in darkness; and the darkness comprehended it not" (John 1:5). In short order, John has introduced several great themes: deity, life, light, and darkness.

## MAN SENT FROM GOD

John the Baptist, a man sent from God came to bear

witness of that light. John was sent, as it were, to run interference, to clear the way, and to prepare a people for the Lord's coming. He bore witness to that light (Jesus Christ) that men might believe. John was ably successful as two of his disciples, Andrew and John, became disciples of Jesus. With obvious enthusiasm both these men brought their brothers to Christ. Andrew brought Peter and John brought James. Then through the influence of these four, Philip and Nathaniel came to the Lord.

In reference to world evangelism, John 1:9 speaks volumes. "That was the true Light, which lighteth every man that cometh into the world." All men, Jew and Gentile, cultured and uncultured, rich and poor, have been in some way touched by Jesus Christ. By this we do not mean that every man has an inner light or a spark of divinity. Yet every man has been given a conscience, a law written in his heart (Romans 2:15) and is responsible before God. This truth assures us that all men have the potential of responding to God.

In his introduction, John was a faithful reporter, an interpretive reporter. He was writing for a verdict. Modern newspaper reporting uses the five "W's" and the "H": (1) the who, (2) the what, (3) the why, (4) the where, (5) the when, (6) the how. Interestingly, the divine reporter follows this method. Gaines Dobbins points this out in his excellent book, *Evangelism According to Christ:*

> The first eighteen verses of John's Gospel constitute an unsurpassed example of the 'lead' in a classic interpretive reporting. He begins with 'who'—the Word and his forerunner, John; then he explains 'why'—that those who receive him might be given the right to become children of God; next he tells 'what'—the Word became flesh; to this he adds 'where'—and lived among us; he then informs us as to 'when'—a contemporary event known to eye witnesses; finally he asserts 'how'—by means of divine begetting and

birth. If a headline writer had given John's account a caption, it might well have read: 'THE MOST WONDERFUL THING HAS HAPPENED!'[2]

In religion, men seek God; in Christianity, Christ seeks men. The Creator came to His own world, and to His own people. The Jews, failing to recognize Him, rejected Him (John 1:11). Their rejection opened the doors to all who will receive and believe. John gives one of the great salvation verses of the Bible: "But as many as received him, to them gave he power to become the sons of God, even to them that believe on his name" (John 1:12).

John 1:12 gives the human side; John 1:13 gives the divine. Verse 12 tells us how to become children of God and verse 13 tells us three ways no one becomes God's child. "Which were born, not of blood, nor of the will of the flesh, nor of the will of man, but of God" (John 1:13). To become a child one must be born. "Not of blood" speaks of heredity. Christian parents do not give birth to "Christian" children. Regeneration is not in the veins. "Nor of the will of the flesh" refers to fleshly desire or ability. That which is flesh is flesh and will remain flesh. No one can birth himself. "Nor of the will of man" removes all human saviors. Only God can regenerate and give spiritual life.

## FOUNDATION FOR EVANGELISM

John lays a foundation for his entire book in his preface. For that reason I am taking time to deal with important issues involving evangelism. The basis of our faith rests on three important truths: the incarnation, the death, and the resurrection of Christ. John 1:14 declares authoritatively, without hesitation or equivocation, "The Word [Logos] was made flesh [human], and dwelt among us. . . ." Jesus Christ is God, and at the same time He is man. The writer of the book of Hebrews points out the necessity of the incarnation: "Forasmuch then as the children are partakers of flesh and blood, he also himself likewise took part of the same;

that through death he might destroy him that had the power of death, that is, the devil" (Hebrews 2:14). Without the incarnation, the death and resurrection would be meaningless and incomprehensible.

Another major issue meets us in John 1:17: the matter of law and grace. "For the law was given by Moses, but grace and truth came by Jesus Christ." The law had its purpose in the old dispensation and still has its purpose today. Without law there is no need for grace. Law is to grace what thirst is to water. "Now we know that what things soever the law saith, it saith to them who are under the law: that every mouth may be stopped, and all the world may become guilty before God" (Romans 3:19). Failure to preach the law emasculates present day evangelism. The holiness of God, hatred for sin, and a confession of guilt must grip the heart of the sinner before he is in a state of mind to receive grace, truth and forgiveness.

With John 1:18 John closes the prologue. "No man hath seen God at any time; the only begotten Son, which is in the bosom of the Father, he hath declared him." The incarnation of Jesus Christ was unique, a once and forever happening. Hindus believe in at least fourteen incarnations. John tells us it never happened before, and by the nature of the event it will not happen again. Then the endearing relationship of Jesus Christ the Son of God with God the Father vindicates the purpose of the incarnation: to declare the Father. Since no man hath seen God, no man knows what God is like. The Son, who came from the bosom of the Father, knows Him intimately and shows us what God is like. "He that hath seen me hath seen the Father" (John 14:9).

Put yourself in the place of a person who knows little or nothing about Jesus Christ. Into your hands comes the Gospel of John. Could you read these first eighteen verses and put the book down and forget it. Never! The whole book presents Jesus Christ as the Son of God, the Savior of the world, the suffering servant, and finally as the resurrected Lord. It demands a verdict. Is Jesus Christ who He claimed to be or not? John, under the inspiration of the Holy Spirit, wrote this treatise as a gospel tract to prove to all who receive it that Jesus Christ was the Son of God, and that believing they might have eternal life through His name.

Shortly after baptizing Jesus, John the Baptist gave testimony concerning the person and work of Christ. "Behold the Lamb of God which taketh away the sin of the world" (John 1:29). Christ is portrayed as the Suffering Servant who by His death shall justify many (Isaiah 53:11). This testimony impressed two of John's disciples. One is named Andrew and the other unnamed is probably John. They turned from John the Baptist and began following Jesus. They believed what John had said, and now they wanted to know more about this One who was the Lamb of God. At His invitation, they went with Jesus to the place where He was staying. What they talked about we do not know. We are told the outcome—the two men were convinced, and with irrepressible enthusiasm each set out to bring another to Jesus. In commenting on this passage, Gaines Dobbins shares some insightful words:

> 'Watch the beginning of things!' Observe the slow unfolding of the redemptive plan: two thousand years of preparation for Christ's coming; a preacher, divinely called and prepared for his mission; two men, as the fruit of a lifetime of preaching, who followed Jesus; then two men, from personal experiences, convinced of the claims of Christ; each of the two bearing successful witness to his brother; two of the brothers influencing a fifth man whom Christ won; the fifth man finding a sixth, who was convinced and converted. Before long the six have grown to twelve in number. A little later there are 'seventy also,' and beyond these an undesignated number to whom the twelve and the seventy have borne effective witness. With divine patience, the pattern of disciple winning was thus established. Dare

we hope to improve upon it?[3]

From John chapter two we learn that evangelism is inseparably joined to two fundamental concerns: the home and the place of worship. Is it not significant that Jesus chose at the beginning of His ministry to grace a wedding with His presence and then went to Jerusalem to cleanse the temple? John saw that effective evange ism has two centers: the home and the church. Christ must be welcomed in the home and worshipped in the church.

The last three verses of chapter two need careful reading. "Many believed in his name, when they saw the miracles which he did" (John 2:23). Instead of rejoicing in their faith and welcoming them to Himself we see Jesus acting in an opposite manner. "But Jesus did not commit himself unto them, because he knew all men" (John 2:24). John 2:25 tells us that He knew what was in every man. In our previous chapter we dealt with true faith and false faith or real faith and spurious faith. Obviously, Jesus was not interested in superficial professions, but instead was looking for men and women of commitment. The reason He did not commit Himself to the believing crowd in Jerusalem was their lack of commitment. As mortals we do not know what is in man, but we need to pray for discernment as we deal with people lest we commit ourselves and the truth of God to undeserving and uncommitted people.

## JESUS THE EVANGELIST

The meeting between Nicodemus and Jesus brings valuable lessons on the subject of evangelism. Nicodemus, an excellent product of Judaistic moral culture, was man at his best. He was a member of the Sanhedrin, a Pharisee, a distinguished teacher, and a man of wealth and influence. Here he is seeking a private, uninterrupted interview with a young, impressive rabbi. G. Campbell Morgan points out the progressive movement of the conversation in the following verses from John chapter three.

If we examine this conversation we find very distinctly that there are three movements; and in order to follow them we may state them thus. In the first we see Jesus and Nicodemus face to face (John 3:2–3). Then we see them mind to mind (John 3:4–8). Finally we see them heart to heart (John 3:9–21).[4]

Nicodemus probably thought he was complimenting Jesus, the young rabbi, by addressing him as a teacher come from God. No, this falls far short. Before the interview ended Nicodemus was aware that he was talking to more than a teacher come from God, but with the Son of God. Hailing Jesus as a great teacher will not pass muster.

Nicodemus had religion and culture but he did not have spiritual life. Rather brusquely Jesus presents Nicodemus with his real need: a new birth. In answer to Nicodemus' question, "How?", Jesus responded, "Except a man be born of water and of the Spirit, he cannot enter into the kingdom of God" (John 3:5). Born of water speaks of being born by the Word of God. The Word of God is the seed. In spiritual birth, the Spirit uses the Word to beget a new creation in Christ. "Being born again, not of corruptible seed, but of incorruptible [seed], by the word of God, which liveth and abideth forever" (I Peter 1:23).

Having shown Nicodemus his problem, our Lord now shows him the solution. To this man schooled in the Old Testament Scriptures, Jesus refers him to the brazen serpent lifted up by Moses in the wilderness (Numbers 21:9). In this incident we see the plight of the sinner—dying. The love and grace of God provide a way for escape—by looking. The sinner' responsibility is to look and live—by believing. Then Jesus relates all of this to Himself as He says "even so must the Son of man be lifted up" (John 3:14). It was to Nicodemus Jesus spoke the words so dear to the hearts of millions: "For God so loved the world, that he gave his only begotten Son, that whosoever believeth in him should not perish, but have everlasting life" (John 3:16).

Toward the end of the interview, Jesus talks about lovers of darkness and lovers of light. "And this is the condemnation, that light is come into the world, and men loved darkness rather than light, because their deeds were evil" (John 3:19). In all our evangelistic work an important truth must be in our minds: men are responsible. Those who love darkness perish; those who love light will be enlightened. Evil men hate the light because it condemns them. Those who repent, that is, who hate their sins, and want the truth will come to the light. The Holy Spirit did not see fit to reveal the results of this conversation, but the fact that Nicodemus defended Jesus before the Sanhedrin and helped in his burial gives evidence that he received Christ as Lord and Savior.

In the Gospel of John, the word "must" keeps appearing. We point them out because each imperative accentuates the primacy of evangelism in the Gospel of John. The first "must" appears in Jesus' reply to Nicodemus' question, "How can these things be?" "Marvel not that I said unto thee, Ye **must** be born again" (John 3:7). This is the imperative of the new birth.

As Jesus and His disciples planned their trip from Judea to Galilee, Jesus found it necessary to go through Samaria. "And he **must** needs go through Samaria" (John 4:4). We will call this the imperative of soul-winning.

As Jesus discoursed with the woman of Samaria, he instructed her in the imperative of true worship. "God is a Spirit: and they that worship him **must** worship him in spirit and in truth" (John 4:24).

When confronted with the man born blind and queried concerning the cause of his affliction, Jesus gave another imperative: "I **must** work the works of him that sent me, while it is day: the night cometh, when no man can work" (John 9:4). Is this not the imperative of urgency?

In John 10:16 another divine imperative meets our eyes. "And other sheep I have, which are not of this fold: them also I **must** bring". What could this be than the imperative for world evangelism, bringing people of all races to own Christ as their

Shepherd?

As Jesus approaches the close of His ministry, the cross looms constantly before Him ". . .and how sayest thou, The Son of man **must** be lifted up" (John 12:34)? This signifies the imperative of the cross. The last imperative crowns and completes all the others ". . .he **must** rise again from the dead" (John 20:9). The imperative of the resurrection validates His claim to be the Son of God with power (Romans 1:4).

Jesus met people where they were and as they were. As we come to the fourth chapter, John gives us another case study of Christ dealing with an individual. In personal work, there is no one method that will work with every one. The Gospel of John does not give an analysis of the techniques of Jesus in disciple-winning. Rather he gives us examples of Christ meeting people in their particular area of need. In dealing with Nicodemus, a moral, religious leader, He disarmed him by necessitating a spiritual birth. Jesus was just as skillful in talking with the woman of Samaria who was from the bottom rung of the social ladder. He used that basic commodity, water, and that universal need, thirst, to introduce this woman to the "water of life."

## LESSON IN SOUL-WINNING

Jesus' encounter with this sinful woman demonstrates soul-winning at its best. There are so many lessons to be learned. Let us try to grasp a few of them. First, we cannot but note a **heavy burden**. Jesus did not use the normal way of going to Galilee by crossing the Jordan River and thus by passing Samaria. "And he must needs go through Samaria" (John 4:4). He came to Samaria because He had a burden for these "unreachables."

Second, the **holy zeal** of Jesus evidences itself. He was weary, thirsty, and hungry. In such circumstances, most of us avoid social involvement. However, on seeing this desperate woman, Jesus came to attention and engaged her in conversation with the avowed purpose of bringing her to know Him as both Lord and Savior. Third, as Jesus deals with this woman we are aware of His **heavenly wisdom**.

Making the right approach is essential in gaining the confidence of the person with whom we meet. What could have been more natural than for a thirsty man to ask for water? When Jesus asked for a drink of water, the woman reminded Him of the social and religious problems that existed between Jews and the Samaritans and that she was a woman of Samaria. Without being deterred, our Lord masterfully brings the spiritual into a mundane conversation. "If thou knewest the gift of God, and who it is that saith to thee, Give me to drink: thou wouldest have asked of him, and he would have given thee living water" (John 4:10). Not only did He deter her sidestep, but kindles her curiosity. She is intrigued as to how He can give her "living" water since He had no bucket. Again she tries to get away from the issue by bringing up religious difficulties. Who is right anyway, the Jews or the Samaritans? Ignoring the question, Jesus tells her that the water He gives is unique. They that drink His water shall never thirst again, and it springs up into everlasting life. Naturally, she wanted this kind of water. Who would not? On hearing her request for the water of life, the master Soul-Winner told the woman to call her husband. In doing this, He was bringing her face to face with her sin.

Present day evangelism fails to confront people with personal sin. Nearly every one will confess sin in the abstract. But notice that Jesus personalized sin. At the crucial moment Jesus confronted the woman with her sin of immorality. Shrewdly, she sought to divert Him in a religious argument, but Jesus kept on track. He spoke to her of love, of worship, of salvation, of spirit, and of truth. He revealed Himself as Messiah, and she believed. The woman was changed, born anew, born of God. Immediately, she raced into the city, bore witness of the Savior which eventually led many to believe and become disciples.

The glorious Gospel specializes in remaking ruined lives. This Samaritan woman who had been relegated to the trash-heap of society and considered scarcely worth saving, exhibited in the presence of Jesus remarkable intelligence, insight, and spiritual sensitivity. Only Jesus could see her capacity for greatness and believed in her and the possibility of her recovery. In a great moment of faith, her life was transformed. All who have experienced deliverance from a life of sin know the exhilaration of being set free.

All around us are people like the Samaritan woman who are missing both the way and the meaning of life. They may be people in our own families, or in our circle of friends and acquaintances, or those who are deep in the mire of sin. Whatever their condition, they can be saved.

From Jesus' example we learn how to approach them and be the human instrument in bringing them to Christ: Gaines Dobbins notes seven important factors in leading people to Christ:

> (1) Believe that they are worth saving; (2) Win their confidence; (3) Arouse their interest and curiosity; (4) Deepen their concern into spiritual desire; (5) Face them firmly and inescapably with the question of sin; (6) Lead them to turn from sin to simple trust in Christ as Savior; (7) Get them to share their salvation with others at once. Not always may we be as successful as Jesus was with the Samaritan woman—even He sometimes failed—but we shall often succeed, and our joy will be like His when He said to the wondering disciples, 'My food (satisfying portion) is to do the will of him that sent me, and to finish his work' (John 4:34).[5]

## COSMIC CONFLICTS

As we read the Gospel of John, we sense the reality of a vast, all-embracing struggle, the conflict between light and darkness, between good and evil, between God and the devil. In chapter nine the battle intensifies. In the previous chapter, Jesus saved the adulterous woman from the stones of a blood-thirsty mob of religious hucksters. As the chapter ends, the Pharisees took up stones to stone Him, but Jesus hid Himself (John 8:59).

Then another evil pops up. A man born blind stands before Jesus and His disciples. "His disciples asked him, saying, Master, who did sin, this man, or his parents, that he was born blind?" (John 9:2). Christ chose not to philosophize but rather to heal this man to prove the power of light over darkness and of goodness over evil.

Blindness has symbolical significance. In II Corinthians 4:4, we read: "In whom the god of this world hath blinded the minds of them which believe not." In this incident there are truths concerning evangelism that need our attention. First, Christ used means to heal the blind man. He could have spoken the word, and the man's eyes would have opened. Maybe for preparing the man for the miracle or for teaching spiritual lessons, He chose to use means. The making of mud from spittle and anointing the blind man's eyes emphasized his blindness (John 9:6). The command to go and wash in the pool of Siloam tested the man's obedience and faith.

Salvation is of God. The greatest soul-winner that ever lived never saved a soul. Yes, that is true. However, God has been pleased to use men and women in the work of reconciliation. God has been pleased to use tracts, music, drama, audio cassettes, video cassettes, radio, television, tent meetings, door-to-door visitation, personal work, public preaching, etc., to bring men to Christ.

Second, we learn something about faith. The going and the washing validated the blind man's faith. Real faith responds to the commands of Christ. Intellectual faith, i.e., just agreeing that something is true, does not save. James teaches us that the devils believe and tremble (James 2:19). The Bible is very clear to differentiate between real faith and false faith, and a live faith from a dead faith. Live faith moves, acts, repents, changes. Dead, intellectual faith leaves the possessor helpless in his sins.

Third, the spiritual progress of the blind man staggers the mind. He boldly told what Christ did for him (John 9:11).

Many who think they are Christians are unable to testify because nothing has happened in them or to them. His knowledge of Christ, though limited, increased rapidly. In John 9:11, he said a man called Jesus opened his eyes; in John 9:17, he asserts that Jesus is a prophet; and in John 9:24, he refutes the Pharisees claim that Jesus is a sinner and insists Jesus is a man sent from God. For his bold testimony the Jews excommunicated the man.

Christ, in love and mercy, revealed Himself to the man as the Son of God. The man's response typifies those who are saved: "he said, Lord, I believe, And he worshipped him" (John 9:38). People who profess faith in Christ and consequently resist or half-heartedly respond to follow-up, cause those who measure all things by the Bible grave concern.

Fourth, we see tradition and prejudice as the deadly foes of evangelism. The soul-winner is all but helpless when confronted with a person who will not believe because he does not want to believe. When faced with undeniable evidence, the prejudiced traditionalist will shift his arguments from point to point, not in accordance with facts but in accordance with whatever bolsters his position. These people will resort to vituperation, threats of violence, and even murder to stifle the voice of truth.

The Pharisees here symbolize the most helpless kind of darkness. In the presence of light, they shut their eyes tight and refused to see. Like words of doom came the pronouncement of Jesus upon them: "For judgment I am come into this world, that they which see not might see; and that they which see might be made blind" (John 9:39). The unseeing believing man was made to see, the seeing unbelieving men were made blind.

Fifth, what is our attitude to be toward the willful blind? We must warn them of their danger, we must appeal to them to open their eyes before it is too late, and we must never give them up. Christ died for these Pharisees and possibly on the day of Pentecost some, by His grace, opened their eyes and believed. There may be "hopeless cases," but we do not know who they are. We do know that Christ is the light of the world and that

He said: "He that followeth me shall not walk in darkness, but shall have the light of life" (John 8:12).

## JESUS THE PASTOR

A change of emphasis, a new direction begins with chapter ten. In the first nine chapters Jesus has been portrayed as the evangelist and John has shown us how the Lord Jesus dealt with varying individuals. Beginning at chapter ten, Jesus takes the role of pastor, shepherd. This does not mean that Jesus discontinued His interest in evangelism, i.e., winning the lost to the Savior, but there is a complementary aspect of evangelism—training the saved so they in turn might be soul- winners who will also disciple those who have been won to Christ. Jesus turned away from the multitudes and devoted Himself to the training of the twelve.

In this book, evangelism means not only winning the lost, but also ministering to the saved. All too often evangelism and discipleship are truncated. To do so is to leave the teaching of Jesus, the teaching of Paul, Peter, James, and John. Too many consider the object of evangelism achieved when an individual makes a commitment to Christ and the church.

Leading people to faith in Christ is the first step and an essential and important step, but it is only one step in evangelism. All thinking Christian workers feel a keen sense of disappointment when so many who make professions of faith—seemingly sincere professions–fall by the wayside. Many on our church rolls are nowhere to be found. Others never attend a service, take no part in its activities, give nothing to its support, and their Christian witness proves detrimental instead of beneficial to the cause of Christ. This problem needs attention today, and it needed attention when Christ and His disciples were facing storm clouds of persecution. During His last months, our Lord gave great attention to the matter of assurance and perseverance.

Another of Jesus' great metaphors likens followers of Christ to sheep. From all the animals, Christ chose sheep to represent His people. This comparison does not speak well of

Christ's followers. Sheep are stupid animals with a tendency to self-destruct. Since they are highly imitative, they are easily misled. They have no weapons for offense and no protection for defense. Almost all carnivorous animals are their enemies and seek their life. The similarities between sheep and Christians are evident: we behave with a strange lack of intelligence; we follow leaders with little thought of the consequence; and we are no match for the devil. But there is a more complimentary aspect to the comparison. Sheep are among the most valuable of animals, providing both clothing and food. The comparison holds good: human life is our common measure of all values. Man, rebel that he is, remains God's most prized possession.

Using this metaphor, Jesus highlighted the primacy of world evangelism. "And other sheep I have, which are not of this fold: them also I must bring, and they shall hear my voice; and there shall be one fold, and one shepherd" (John 10:16). In speaking of the "other sheep" which were not of this fold (Jewish), Christ is referring to Gentile sheep.

In this verse, our Lord makes three outstanding statements: "them also [the other sheep] I must bring" speaks of a **divine priority** of world evangelism; "and they shall hear my voice" gives evangelists a **divine promise** of success; "and there shall be one fold [the Church], and one shepherd" comforts a divided Church with a **divine prophecy** of final accord.

Sheep, unlike other domesticated animals, require a shepherd. They simply cannot survive without one. Christ claims to be the good shepherd and as such renders invaluable services to His sheep.

In John chapter 10, we learn much about the Good Shepherd and also about His sheep. First, He calls His sheep, and they hear His voice, and they know Him. This speaks of relationship and fellowship. Second, He saves His sheep. "I am the good shepherd: the good shepherd giveth his life for the sheep" (John 10:11). Third, He protects His sheep. Unlike the hireling who flees in fear of wolf, lion, or bear, the Good Shepherd flings Himself between His sheep and their enemies. Fourth, He keeps His sheep. "My sheep hear my voice, and I know them, and they follow me: And I give unto them eternal life; and they shall never perish, neither shall any man pluck them out of my hand" (John 10:27-28).

The question of "once saved, always saved?" continues to divide churches, families, and friends. Let us look at this matter sanely and scripturally. The promise of eternal life cannot be claimed by virtue of being a member of a church, or having once made a profession of faith, or signing a card, or asking Jesus to come into one's heart. In verse 27, Jesus restricted the promise of eternal life (often called eternal security) to those who hear (obey) His voice, and follow Him. "And hereby we do know that we know him, if we keep his commandments" (I John 2:3).

The promise of security cannot be claimed by those who are flaunting His Word, neglecting their duties, and living more like a goat than a sheep. The luxury of the assurance of eternal life can be enjoyed by those who are obeying and following the Good Shepherd. By no means can one live a life of sin and at the same time console oneself with "once saved, always saved." Gaines Dobbins speaks wisely concerning this subject:

> The evangelist, in public proclamation and in individual interviews, should use boldly and wisely this great assurance of the believer's safety. To the objection, 'I am afraid that I won't hold out,' the obvious reply is: 'You do not have to hold out; Jesus holds out while you hold on.' The real issue is not that of the 'perseverance of the saints,' but of the power of divine preservation on the part of Christ. The saved sinner is still a sinner, but he has had an experience with Christ which will forever make sin loathsome to him. He may confidently claim the benediction of Jude: 'Now to him who is able to keep you from falling and to present you without blemish before the presence of his glory with rejoicing, to the only God, our

Saviour through Jesus Christ our Lord, be glory,
majesty, dominion, and authority, before all time
and now and forever. Amen' (Jude 24-25).[6]

## HARD QUESTIONS

Questions, large and small, significant and insignificant,
plague the minds of people. The questions of God, evil, death,
and resurrection all find answers in the Gospel of John. "And
the Word [God] was made flesh, and dwelt among us, (and we
beheld his glory, the glory as of the only begotten of the Father,)
full of grace and truth" (John 1:14). Jesus Christ perfectly
reveals God.

When confronted with evil manifested in a man born
blind, Christ used that evil to manifest the works of God by
restoring sight to the man. Now in Chapter 11 the enemy of
death crosses the path of Christ. Lazarus, one who loved Christ,
and was loved by Christ had died. "If a man die, shall he live
again?" (Job 14:14). His answer to this question was the raising
of Lazarus.

The truth of the resurrection appears in the Old Testament, but the light of the Old Testament teaching is dim. Job
saw it! David saw it! But many did not see it. Martha had faith
in a general resurrection, but it was not offering her much hope
in the present situation. Then Jesus forever ended the mystery
with these words: "I am the resurrection, and the life: he that
believeth in me, though he were dead, yet shall he live: And
whosoever liveth and believeth in me shall never die" (John
11:25-26). In these verses Christ gives two sets of promises: one
to those who have died and await His coming and the resurrection (I Thessalonians 4:16); the other to those who will be living
when Christ comes. They shall never taste death, but will go
without dying (I Thessalonians 4:17).

Evangelism reaches its high point as "good news" in its
affirmation of the resurrection power of Jesus Christ. Because
He lives, we also shall live. This is not "pie in the sky by and

by", but the true evangelist presents life as a continuum, with death as a stream to be crossed only momentarily separating between time and eternity. The answers to life's hard questions are answered in the Bible. "And ye shall know the truth, and the truth shall make you free" (John 8:32).

Previously in this chapter, allusion was made to the disappointing results of professed believers in the Lord Jesus Christ. In our eagerness for people to respond to the gospel, we emphasize the freeness of the gospel, and great emphasis is placed on the wealth of the rewards. It cannot be denied that the salvation of Christ is free; it is all of grace and not of works. But do we make it plain that salvation is not cheap or easy? Jesus made it clear that to follow Him is the most expensive undertaking imaginable. In our eagerness to protect grace and preach an unsullied gospel, have we formulated a gospel that is foreign to the teachings of Christ?

There is a key question that needs to be asked: can a person receive Jesus Christ as Savior, receive eternal life, and refuse to accept the responsibilities of discipleship? Is it true that every disciple is a believer, but every believer is not a disciple? Can we divorce salvation from the Christian life? How can we know for sure the answer to these vital questions? We must come to the scriptures and compare Scripture with Scripture. What men say is not important unless they back up what they say with "thus saith the Lord."

John chapter twelve speaks pointedly to the root cause of failure in the Christian life. In John 12:24-25 Jesus presents one of life's greatest principles in the form of an apparent contradiction: "Except a corn of wheat fall into the ground and die, it abideth alone: but if it die, it bringeth forth much fruit. He that loveth his life shall lose it; and he that hateth his life in this world shall keep it unto life eternal." To gain life, one must lose it. Life will be lost by the one who seeks to find it. To keep life, it must be hated. Life springs from death. The "getting" life is the losing life, and the "giving" life is the winning life. Self-seeking culminates in emptiness; self-giving in fullness.

This principle of gaining by losing, and living by dying, is the simplest and yet the most profound philosophy of creative living ever enunciated. Violating this principle wreaks ruin. Of course, this principle runs counter to human reasoning. "Get all you can and keep all you get." This humanistic philosophy so contrary to Christ's robs Christians of the fullness and the blessings of an unselfish life.

## HOLY SPIRIT IN EVANGELISM

In Chapter 16 the work of the Holy Spirit in evangelism is addressed. Christ seeks to prepare his disciples for His departure and in doing so promises the coming of a Comforter (Paraclete). As a result of the Spirit's coming into the believers, the work of convicting the world of sin, righteousness, and judgment will begin. The Holy Spirit indwelling the believer, convicts the world of sin.

What Jesus prophesied here, happened on the day of Pentecost. Peter, filled with the Holy Spirit, preached the Word. Those that heard the Word were convicted and 3,000 were saved. As we go with the gospel message, we need to be conscious of our need for dependence upon the Holy Spirit to convict, convince, and convert.

As we enter the seventeenth chapter of John, it is like walking into the Holy of Holies. Our Great High Priest communes with and petitions His heavenly Father. Christ is coming close to the end of His earthly ministry. As He contemplates His demise, resurrection, and ascension, His focus is on a small group of men upon whom the accomplishing of His Father's work (the reconciling of the world unto Himself) depends.

Keep in mind that God's sovereignty does not negate man's responsibility. Here as well as everywhere else in the Bible both God's sovereignty and man's responsibility appear side by side with no effort to explain or reconcile them.

Our Lord is praising His Father for those who have responded to and have kept God's Word. Realizing the key role these men will play in the evangelization of the world, Christ prays passionately on behalf of them and for all those through the centuries who will believe on Him. "I pray for them: I pray not for the world, but for them which thou hast given me; for they are thine. . . .Neither pray I for these alone, but for them also which shall believe on me through their word" (John 17:9, 20). It is comforting to know that our Lord continues to pray for His own: "Who is even at the right hand of God, who also maketh intercession for us" (Romans 8:34).

## THE GREAT COMMISSION

The Great Commission appears in all four Gospels and the Book of Acts. The commission in John 20:21 inspires awe and humility. "Then said Jesus to them again, Peace be unto you: as my Father hath sent me, even so send I you." As the Father sent the Son, so the Son sends His servants. **Authority** characterized the ministry of our Lord Jesus Christ. "All power [authority] is given unto me in heaven and in earth" (Matthew 28:18). "For he taught them as one having authority" (Matthew 7:29).

In our pluralistic society, a babble of voices clamors to be heard. With humility, yet without deference, Christ's servants must herald the truth of an exclusive Savior. Incarnating and proclaiming such a message often will lead to **agony**. "It is enough for the disciple that he be as his master, and the servant as his lord. If they have called the master of the house Beelzebub, how much more shall they call them of his household?" (Matthew 10:25). Through the centuries to this very day, men and women have suffered untold agonies for bearing faithful witness for Christ.

When God the Father sent God the Son, He equipped Him with the fullness of God the Holy Spirit. "For God giveth not the Spirit by measure unto him" (John 3:34). "And when he had said this, he breathed on them, and said unto them, Receive ye the Holy Ghost" (John 20:22). Christ's "sent ones" are to be marked by an **affluence**, a fullness of the Spirit. Throughout this study, we have emphasized the utmost necessity of the fullness and power of the Holy Spirit as a criteria for effective and biblical evangelism.

In His commission to His disciples in John's Gospel, our Lord connects several eminent aspects of ministry. He gives them authority. He breathes on them an affluence; and now He instills in them an **awareness** of the nature of their task. "Whose soever sins ye remit, they are remitted unto them; and whose soever sins ye retain, they are retained" (John 20:23). Ours is a spiritual task dealing specifically with the sin problem. No apostle, pope, preacher, evangelist, no one, in and of himself, has the authority or the power to "remit" (forgive) sins.

Repentance and remission of sin are to be preached in His name (Luke 24:47). The remission of sins is in His Name: "Neither is there salvation in any other: for there is none other name under heaven given among men, whereby we must be saved" (Acts 4:12).

Our decadent society searches frantically but in futility for solutions to societal problems. At the same time it blatantly and willfully denies the sin problem. Sociologists blame environs for wrong humans; the Bible blames humans for wrong environs. Liberal theologians blame sinful institutions for man's sad plight; the Bible blames sinful man for our institution's sad plight. Honest students of history understand the relationship between righteousness and a healthy society. The transformation of English society by the preaching of the Wesleys and George Whitefield proves that effective evangelism is the antidote and the only antidote for decadence.

---

1. Gaines S. Dobbins, *Evangelism According to Christ* (New York: Harper & Brothers, 1949) 22.

2. Ibid., 37.

3. Ibid., 43.

4. G. Cambell Morgan, *The Great Physician* (New York: Fleming H. Revell Company, 1924) 67.

5. Dobbins, 57.

6. Ibid., 100.

# 10

# The Primacy
# of Evangelism
# in the Book of Acts

The Book of the Acts of the Apostles, an inspired history of the New Testament Church, traces the spread of the gospel from Jerusalem, to Judaea, then to Samaria, and finally out to the ends of the earth. How impoverished we would be without this great document and its record of epochal events that changed the course of history by changing the hearts of men. The whole book throbs with evangelistic outreach as it chronicles the early church's commitment to obey Christ's commands to be His witnesses to all the world.

Those of us who admire the Apostles are prone to idealize them and to idolize the Apostolic Church. But they had their defects too. Let me point out a defect often overlooked. The Apostles and the Jerusalem Church did an amazing feat of evangelizing Jerusalem. On the day of Pentecost 3,000 were added to the Lord and to the church (Acts 2:41). People were saved daily (Acts 2:47), and in a few months the number of men disciples was about 5,000 (Acts 4:4).

The success of their evangelism incurred the wrath of the Jewish leaders. The Apostles were arrested and put in the common prison (Acts 5:18), released by the Angel of the Lord, and later rearrested by the authorities. The High Priest said to Peter and the other apostles, "Did not we straitly command you that ye should not teach in this name? and, behold, ye have filled Jerusalem with your doctrine, and intend to bring this man's blood upon us" (Acts 5:28). This speaks well of the evangelistic efforts of the Jerusalem Church.

But at the same time they were filling Jerusalem with the teaching of Christ, they were ignoring and forgetting Judaea, Samaria, and the rest of the world. God does not tolerate disobedience. He did not tolerate it in the Jerusalem Church; He will not tolerate it in this day in our churches. Disobedience brings pressure. This pressure manifested itself in the form of persecution. "And at that time there was a great persecution against the church which was at Jerusalem; and they were all scattered abroad throughout the regions of Judaea and Samaria" (Acts 8:1).

As a result of persecution, the Jerusalem Church was scattered and the ones scattered continued to evangelize. The evangelization of Judaea and Samaria represents the involuntary phase of obeying the Great Commission. In Acts 13, we see a different picture. The leaders of the Church at Antioch fast and pray. The results of their prayers intimate the nature and purpose of their gathering. Their prayer meeting was interrupted by the Holy Spirit, the Lord of the Harvest, commanding the Church to set aside Paul and Barnabas for the work of reaching out to the ends of the earth. Here we see the voluntary phase of obeying the Great Commission.

The Book of Acts selectively records those events that the Holy Spirit wants us to know. The book is well-ordered and follows the outline found in Acts 1:8: "But ye shall receive power, after that the Holy Ghost is come upon you: and ye shall be witnesses unto me both in Jerusalem, and in all Judaea, and in Samaria, and unto the uttermost part of the earth." The first seven chapters tell of the exploits of the Jerusalem Church; Acts 8 records the spread of the gospel to Samaria by the person of Philip; Acts 9 to the end deals mainly with Paul and his missionary journeys, but also includes Peter's opening the doors of faith to the Gentiles.

## EVANGELISM IN
## THE JERUSALEM CHURCH

Acts 1:8 assures the primacy of evangelism. Last words are important words. No one takes lightly last words. The early church took seriously the last words of their risen Lord. First, He told them to tarry and wait for the promise of the Father, which was the Holy Spirit. They waited and on the day of Pentecost the Holy Spirit came and endued them with power to witness. Second, they became bold witnesses, testifying of the resurrected Christ. It is true their receiving the Holy Spirit was more dramatic than we experience today. Yet the same Holy Spirit that endued them and gave them the ability, the courage, the will to witness, that same Holy Spirit indwells our hearts and will enable us to be true witnesses for our Lord.

In Acts 2, the Holy Spirit records for us New Testament evangelism in action. Important lessons relating to evangelism will certainly present themselves. First, God used men and women as His witnesses. God has so arranged His program to use people to reach people. Peter was the main spokesman, but all the disciples were busily engaged in communicating the gospel. "And they were all amazed and marvelled, saying one to another, Behold, are not all these which speak Galilaeans" (Acts 2:7)?

Second, God uses men and women who are obedient. They had waited, they had been filled, and now they were evangelizing, and their labors were honored of the Lord. Third, God uses men and women who speak forth the message of the gospel. Peter preached the death, the burial, the resurrection, and the ascension of Jesus, who is both Lord and Christ (Acts 2:23-36). He called for repentance, and he got it (Acts 2:38).

Also in this chapter we see how evangelism affected those being reached. The message of Peter convicted the hearers who were guilty of crucifying the Lord of glory. Conviction, fear, and remorse characterized the effect of Peter's message on those who heard. They cried out for help: "what shall we do"

(Acts 2:37)? Then those that were convicted, gladly, willingly, received the word, were baptized, and continued in the Apostles' fellowship and teaching (Acts 2:41). This is New Testament evangelism. Defective evangelism is better than no evangelism at all. But, oh, how our hearts hunger to see conviction of sin, to see people fear for their souls, to hear them cry out in desperation "what must I do to be saved?", to repent of their sin of ignoring and rejecting God, to humbly, thankfully, believingly receive the Lord Jesus Christ as Savior, to gratefully and eagerly enter the waters of baptism, and to join a Bible believing church and serve with a body of believers. This is the pattern, and when our practices veer from it, then we are leaving New Testament evangelism.

## GREAT ROLE MODELS

What marvelous servants Peter, James, John and the others were! Several of their attributes need mentioning so that we might be more like them. First was their fearlessness. In spite of threats, intimidations, whippings, and the real possibility of execution, they continued their witness. Several times the apostles were arrested and brought before the authorities. In the face of these powerful men, who humanly speaking, controlled their destiny, an unbelievable boldness filled the hearts and minds of the apostles. On one occasion Peter answered his accusers this way: "Be it known unto you all . . . that by the name of Jesus Christ of Nazareth, whom ye crucified, whom God raised from the dead, even by him doth this man [the crippled man] stand here before you whole" (Acts 4:10). Is it any wonder after seeing this boldness "they marvelled; and they took knowledge of them, that they had been with Jesus" (Acts 4:13).

How did they get this fearlessness and boldness? They asked for it. Note their prayerfulness. Following their run-in with and arrest by the authorities and their release, they all gathered together for a prayer meeting. It is interesting to note what they did not pray for. They did not pray that God would destroy their enemies. Neither did they pray that God would save them from further harassment. Listen to their prayer in Acts 4:29: "And now, Lord, behold their threatenings: and grant unto thy servants, that with all boldness they may speak thy word."

To them was given unusual spiritual power. "And with great power gave the apostles witness of the resurrection of the Lord Jesus: and great grace was upon them all" (Acts 4:33). This power manifested itself not only toward those who were without, but also toward those who were within. Theirs was a spirit of generosity. "Neither was there any among them that lacked: for as many as were possessors of lands or houses sold them, and brought the prices of the things that were sold, And laid them down at the apostles' feet and distribution was made unto every man according as he had need" (Acts 4:34-35). Who would not want to be a part of a fellowship like that!

Let me give one final example of their loyalty and love to their risen Lord. The miraculous deliverance from the common prison and the apostles' continued successful witness caused the enemies to question as to how far this movement would grow (Acts 5:24). God used Gamaliel to save the apostles from execution by warning the chief priests that if this movement was not of God, it would fizzle. If it were of God, there was no way they could stop it (Acts 5:34-39). So they spared their lives and gave them a beating—a hard one at that—and a warning to speak no more in this name. "And they departed from the presence of the council, rejoicing that they were counted worthy to suffer shame for his name. And daily in the temple, and in every house, they ceased not to teach and preach Jesus Christ" (Acts 5:41-42). Indeed, evangelism was a primacy with the Jerusalem Church.

## WILLING SERVANTS

In Acts, the Holy Spirit favors us with the conversion experiences of five individuals. In our study of evangelism, it will be extremely edifying to note these conversions. In all five of them, we find a willing servant, a wanting sinner, and a wooing

Spirit.

The first willing servant we see is Philip. There are many admirable traits in this man. Philip was adaptable. As a result of the persecution that arose surrounding Stephen's death, Philip finds himself in Samaria. Philip broke out of the mold (Jewish evangelism) and preached the gospel to the Samaritans. Philip was a pioneer in that great task of cross cultural evangelism. He took a risk, he went out on a limb, he broke new ground, he evangelized Samaria (evangelistic target number three), and as a result his work appears in the pages of the Book of the Acts. "Then Philip went down to the city of Samaria, and preached Christ unto them" (Acts 8:5). How beautiful, how sublime!

Not only was Philip adaptable, but he was accountable. When news of Philip's success in evangelizing Samaria reached Jerusalem (headquarters), the apostles sent Peter and John to see what was going on (Acts 8:14). The point to see is that Philip welcomed Peter and John and in doing so his ministry gained a new dimension. Before Peter and John came, even though many had believed and had been baptized, the Holy Spirit had not been given. By the laying on of Peter and John's hands, the believers received the Holy Spirit (Acts 8:17). Everyone in Christian service is accountable to someone besides to God.

Philip was also attentive to the leading of the Holy Spirit. His sensitivity to the Holy Spirit manifests itself several times. First, Philip was having a fruitful harvest of souls in the city of Samaria. Just when things were going so well, Philip receives instructions to move out and go down to Gaza (Acts 8:26). Evangelists are in the people business. There are no people in Gaza, which is desert. But Philip went and was amply blessed of the Lord.

The second leading of the Holy Spirit comes as Philip meets a caravan in the desert. "Go near, and join thyself to this chariot" (Acts 8:29). By being in the right place, at the right time, with the right message, and with the right attitude Philip received from God the joy and privilege to introduce an influential man to the Lord Jesus Christ (Acts 8:35).

Note Philip's attentiveness to the command of Christ in obeying the ordinances. The command was not just to preach the gospel; not just to see people receive Christ as Lord and Savior. Baptism was included in the command. The new believer, seeing a pond of water, asked, "What doth hinder me to be baptized" (Acts 8:36)? His desire for Christian baptism indicates that Philip had instructed this new convert of this duty. Philip discipled the man well, as tradition tells us that the Ethiopian officer went home, won people to Christ, and founded the church of Christ in Ethiopia!

Philip also gave attention to his family. He later settled in Caesarea and raised a family. Paul and his companions had a brief stay with Philip and his family. "And we entered into the house of Philip the evangelist, which was one of the seven [deacons]; and abode with him. And the same man had four daughters, virgins, which did prophesy" (Acts 21:8-9).

## GOD'S ALL INCLUSIVE LOVE

A close study of Acts reveals that God is much concerned about world evangelism. In Acts 8:27 we see an Ethiopian officer, servant of Queen Candace. Ethiopia is in Africa and was populated by the sons of Ham, the son of Noah. In Acts 9:1, we read of Saul of Tarsus who was a citizen of a country in the Middle East, which is in Asia. Paul, being a Jew was from the line of Seth, the son of Noah. In Acts 10:1, we find Cornelius, a centurion of the Italian band. Italy is in Europe and is peopled by the sons of Japheth, the son of Noah. In these three men we have representatives of peoples from Africa, Asia, and Europe which takes in the whole world.

None of these men seemed a likely candidate for salvation. The Ethiopian was a man of great authority. Under his control were all the resources of the famous Queen Candace. In this man we see money power. Rich people are often neglected because of a mistaken notion the rich are not interested in spiritual things. However, this rich man was very hungry for God.

Next, see Saul, the persecutor of Christians. It is unlikely he will ever be saved. He was man of great intellect, having what we would call a double Ph. D. degree. In him we see mental power. Intelligent people believe the gospel, and intelligent people disbelieve the gospel. People choose to believe or to disbelieve, not according to their intellect but according to their wills.

Finally, Cornelius, a Roman army officer, would not be interested in spiritual things, would he? Indeed he was. In him we see military power. How often we steer away from men of position and prominence, thinking they will not be approachable.

Financial success, educational attainments, and official position do not alter the fact that all are sons of Adam and as such are sinners. People in all walks of life have a heart-ache of sin, a heart-hunger for God, and they need a heart hope in Christ.

In the conversion of these men, there is a common denominator: human help. Philip, as we have seen, left a fruitful harvest in the city to be used of God in bringing this man of prominence to Jesus Christ. Saul of Tarsus also needed human help. The Lord got his attention and instructed him to go into the city, and it would be told him what to do (Acts 9:6). The Lord called on a faithful nobody, Ananias, to be the human instrument in becoming the spiritual father and discipler of Paul the Apostle (Acts 9:10-16). Ananias took a big risk in going to Saul of Tarsus who was the known enemy of the Christians. His questioning yet faithful obedience shows us his expendability.

Peter was prepared by a vision from the Lord to minister the gospel to Cornelius and his household and thus open the doors of the church to the Gentiles (Acts 10:3-8). It was unheard of for a Jew to associate with Gentiles. Peter's ministry to Cornelius and his household speaks of Peter's availability to do God's will. Those of us who would be used of God in the great work of reconciliation must likewise be adaptable, expendable, and available.

In these three conversions, God is sovereignly working out His will. In all three men, the sovereign power of God is evident. Who put that hunger for God in the breast of that well-heeled Ethiopian? Who stopped Saul of Tarsus in his fanatical persecution of Christians? Who caused this Roman officer to be a man of prayer even before he came to know Christ? "For it is God which worketh in you both to will and to do of his good pleasure" (Philippians 2:13). God's sovereignty is not to make us lazy in seeking to reach men for Christ; rather it is to make us confident. How beautiful is His sovereign working! Money power, mental power, and military power are no match for the mighty sovereign power of God. Even though God works sovereignly He works through means: the Word of God and the people of God.

## FOUR COMMANDS

The command to preach the gospel keeps surfacing in the Book of the Acts. The Angel of the Lord opened the prison doors and sent His imprisoned apostles back to the Temple with this message: "Go, stand and speak in the temple to the people all the words of this life" (Acts 5:20). Go is an integral part of the gospel. If you take "go" out of the gospel, all you have left is a "spel." A church can go and not grow, but it can never grow without going. The early church was a going church and thus it was a growing church.

There is a grave danger of good people retreating from a bad world. It is bad for the world to be in the church, but it good for the church to be in the world. To fulfill this command, churches must go with the gospel. They need to go to the houses closest to them and then systematically work out from the church. It is a matter of obedience.

Along with the command to go comes the command to stand. The gospel has moral and social ramifications; hence, there is a moral imperative to stand for everything that is good, wholesome, clean, beneficial, uplifting, and godly. At the same time, those that preach the gospel are under divine obligation to stand against everything that is wrong, dirty, harmful, debasing, and ungodly. In an ungodly society, gospel preachers who stand for decency, for righteousness, for truth, for the family, for morality and for the Bible will not win popularity contests. Those who will dare to stand against false teaching and false teachers who have ingratiated themselves with many Christians will be severely criticized in some quarters.

Next comes the command to speak. The devil's people are walking and talking. They are beating the bushes to add to their ranks. All the while, God's people, for the most part, are keeping quiet. Oh, how we need to speak out for God, for the Bible, for the salvation of the lost! There are several reasons why we need to speak out for God. First, speaking for God is important service. "So then faith cometh by hearing, and hearing by the word of God" (Romans 10:17). According to this verse, speaking for God generates faith in the one hearing. "It pleased God by the foolishness of preaching to save them that believe" (I Corinthians 1:21). One of the God ordained means of saving the lost is through preaching or speaking.

Speaking for God is costly service. Abel, the first man to speak for God and suffer for it, was murdered by his unbelieving brother. According to tradition, wicked King Manasseh executed Isaiah the prophet by having him cut in two after putting him in a hollow log. John the Baptist lost his head. Peter was crucified upside down. Both Paul and James got it in the neck for speaking for God. Right up to this present hour people are still paying the price for speaking for God.

I have seen people pay the price for speaking for God in Bangladesh. I saw missionary Victor Barnard hike miles to tribal villages to preach while suffering excruciating pain of arthritis. Later the Barnards buried their beautiful 14 year old daughter, Mary, in the black dirt of Bangladesh. Paul Miller, faithful missionary to China, Tibet, and Bangladesh died of bulbar polio, leaving his wife, Helen and four small children. Harry Goehring, strong, intelligent, dedicated missionary to the tribals, died of chemical poisoning. Who, why, and how he was poisoned remains a mystery. If the Lord does not come soon, it is going to become more costly for gospel preachers in the United States of America.

But let me hasten to say that speaking for God is rewarding service. To be the human instrument God uses to bring people out of darkness into His marvelous light brings great joy. "They that sow in tears shall reap in joy. He that goeth forth and weepeth, bearing precious seed, shall doubtless come again with rejoicing, bringing his sheaves with him." (Psalm 126:5-6). Only those who have experienced the soul-winner's joy know the ecstasy it brings to the human heart.

The fourth command our Lord gave to His freed apostles was about living service. We are to speak the words of this life. Serving God, preaching the gospel is not a vocation, not a job, not a profession. It is a life. To live this life of service, necessitates a warm, close, and loving fellowship with the Lord of life. The Chinese proverb is so apropos: "no walkee walkee, no talkee talkee!" The Angel of the Lord reminded His messengers that they preach with both their mouths and their lives.

As a result of the persecution of Stephen, the believers were scattered as far as Antioch of Syria (Acts 11:19). Their presence and their preaching in Antioch resulted in a solid gospel preaching church. At first, they preached only to the Jews, but some of them began to minister to the Grecians. These believers broke out of their ghettos, they gossiped the gospel of Christ, and the hand of the Lord was with them, and a great number turned to the Lord. Again we see New Testament evangelism in action. No longer is the church an extension of Judaism, but now it is a growing body incorporating in its fellowship all who will believe, whether Jew or Gentile.

## MODEL CHURCH

Following the persecution of Stephen, the curtain comes down on the church at Jerusalem. In its place God raises up the great church at Antioch. New Testament evangelism centers in the local church. The church at Antioch stands as a model, a pattern for local church evangelism. The strength and success of this church's ministry and outreach lay in its relationships. First, these folks enjoyed a relationship with God. Their presence in Antioch resulted from persecution and disruption. Did not Paul say in II Timothy 3:12, "All that will live godly in Christ Jesus shall suffer persecution." The depth of their relationship with God manifests itself in that they did not buckle under pressure, but were strong in their witness. In Acts 11:21, we see the reality of their relationship with God: "the hand of the Lord was with them." This expression refers to God working in and through them in such a way it was evident that what was being done was the work of God and not of man.

It may be well to point out that in this church there is no mention of miracles, healings, or signs. The hand of the Lord working with them manifested itself in causing many to turn to the Lord. Their fruitfulness evidences the validity of their relationship with God. Without a deep, real, and valid relationship with God, no local church will impact its community with the message of the gospel.

Then in Acts 11:23, Barnabas confirms the proof of their relationship with God. "Who, when he came, and had seen the grace of God, was glad." How was Barnabas able to see the "grace of God?" He saw it in the lives of these believers. Ephesians 2:8-10 alerts us as to how to see the grace of God: "For by grace are ye saved through faith; and that not of yourselves: it is the gift of God: not of works, lest any man should boast, for we are his workmanship, created in Christ Jesus unto good works, which God hath before ordained that we should walk in them." Barnabas saw a group of people who had been saved by the grace of God, who were filled with good works, and who were praising the Lord for the new life and liberty that was theirs in Christ.

A proper relationship with God will ensure a right relationship with man. Though no specific mention of their relationship with one another appears in the account, we are led to believe that theirs was a harmonious and caring fellowship. Why do I assume this? Because the hand of the Lord was working and the grace of God was present. The writer of the book of Hebrews tells us the results of an absence of grace: "Looking diligently lest any man fail of the grace of God; lest any root of bitterness springing up trouble you, and thereby many be defiled" (Hebrews 12:15). The magnet that drew multitudes to Christ in the early church was the love the Christians had for one another. Evangelism cannot flourish in a local church racked with bitterness and strife.

The visit of some prophets from the church of Jerusalem provided an opportunity for the church of Antioch to demonstrate their relationship with their sister churches. It came to the attention of the church that the saints in the Jerusalem church were in real need. Notice their generous response: "Then the disciples, every man according to his ability, determined to send relief unto the brethren which dwelt in Judaea: which also they did" (Acts 11:29-30). God is showing us the type of church He uses in evangelism.

The church at Antioch certainly had a great relationship with God, with one another, and with their sister churches in Judaea. But how did they relate to the Jewish and heathen community of which they were a part? The Word speaks plainly to this point. First, they preached the word to their community. Some preached only to the Jews; others branched out to reach the Grecians. Whether preaching to Jew or Greek, they had one message: the Lord Jesus Christ.

Instead of isolating themselves they penetrated the neighborhoods and preached to their neighbors. A careful study of Acts 11:19 and 20 reveals two methods of evangelism. In verse 19, the word for "preach" has the idea of informally telling the message, i.e., gossiping the gospel. The word for "preach" in verse 20 means to proclaim publicly. Privately and publicly the church at Antioch communicated the message orally, and they backed up the message with their lives. As a result of their labors two things happened: a great number turned to the Lord, and the disciples were first called "Christians" at Antioch.

In Acts 13:1-3, the Holy Spirit draws back the curtain and gives us a peep at the Antioch church leaders' prayer meeting. From this glimpse we learn who is present (verse 1), and we learn what they were doing (verse 2). The outcome of this meeting had far reaching effects. By a direct command of the Holy Spirit, Saul and Barnabas were to be separated for missionary work. In verse 3, the church concurs with the Holy Spirit, identifies with Paul and Barnabas by the laying on of hands, and sends them on their way to begin the great task of world evangelism.

From this we see that the Antioch church had a relationship with the world. This relationship cost them dearly as two of their leaders were sent forth to evangelize the world. It seems that the church of Jerusalem never caught the vision of world evangelism and now the church at Antioch eclipses the church at Jerusalem by becoming the first missionary church that began a movement that continues to this very day.

## IRREDUCIBLE MINIMUM
## OF MISSIONS

Each chapter of the Book of Acts concerns itself with evangelism. Yet the primacy of evangelism is highlighted more in some chapters than others. In Chapters 8, 9, and 10 the conversions of the Ethiopian officer, Cornelius, and Saul received attention. The Holy Spirit zeroes in on the conversions of Lydia and the Philippian jailer in Chapter 16. Three irreducible minimums of evangelism confront us in chapter sixteen: loyal servants, lost sinners, and Lord Spirit (Holy Spirit).

Without loyal servants there would be a **cessation** of evangelism. In the New Testament, Paul traveled with companions, such as Barnabas, Silas, Timothy, and Luke, to name just a few. Let us note three things that characterize loyal servants. First, we note their sensitivity to the guidance of the Holy Spirit. Paul wanted to preach in Asia, but the Holy Spirit forbad him (Acts 16:6). Then he endeavoured to go to Mysia, but the Holy Spirit permitted him not (Acts 16:7). In a vision, Paul saw the man of Macedonia who asked him to come over and help (Acts 16:9). Luke, the writer of the Book of Acts, gives the result of the vision on Paul and the others: ". . . immediately we endeavoured to go into Macedonia, assuredly gathering that the Lord had called us"

(Acts 16:10). For the first time, the gospel of Jesus Christ entered the continent of Europe.

Second, loyal servants depend on the Word of God to do the work of God. It seems in Philippi there was no synagogue so services were conducted by the river. On this particular occasion a group of women gathered on the Sabbath. Paul and his gospel band met with them. We are told that one lady, Lydia, attended (listened) unto the things spoken by Paul (Acts 16:14). In this account, the message of Paul is not revealed. Previously, the Holy Spirit shared with us a typical sermon preached by Paul in the synagogue of Antioch of Pisidia. The gist of the message was this: "Be it known unto you therefore, men and brethren, that through this man is preached unto you the forgiveness of sins: And by him all that believe are justified from all things, from which ye could not be justified by the law of Moses" (Acts 13:38-39). Paul preached the Word and in preaching the Word he preached Christ's death, burial, and resurrection.

Third, loyal servants are noted for their obedience in following the commands of Christ. Paul's obedience manifested itself in three ways: he faithfully preached the gospel, he baptized those that believed, and subsequently he organized a local church in the home of Lydia. This humble, seemingly insignificant work of preaching the gospel to a small group of women eventuated in the great church of Philippi. One of the secrets of New Testament evangelism is the thoroughness of their obedience to all of the Lord's commands.

Next, lost sinners are a necessary part of evangelism. Without sinners there would be no **cause** for evangelism. The Bible teaches that all are sinners. In evangelism, it is needful to classify sinners. Some are saved sinners and others are unsaved sinners. Unsaved sinners can be classified as either receptive or resistant.

Paul and his band found themselves by the guidance of the Holy Spirit in the great city of Philippi, a Roman colony. In that city were heathen temples filled with sinful men and women. The whole system was corrupt. Priest and follower both walked in darkness and shame. These people were resistant to the message of righteousness and purity preached by Paul. The gospel band did not make a frontal assault on the heathen temple, but rather they made their way to find and to minister to a group of women who had gathered to worship God. Being receptive, they would listen to the Word of God. Sound evangelistic strategy teaches us to look for receptive people while not ignoring the resistant.

## MODEL CONVERSIONS

The interesting account of Lydia's conversion serves a definite purpose: it typifies true conversion and gives us an example to follow. Notice five things about her conversion. First, Lydia had a seeking spirit. She is identified as one who worshipped God. The expression "worshipped God" tells us that she was a Gentile proselyte. She had turned from her idols to worship the God of Israel. Second, she had a listening ear. She gave attention to the Word of God being spoken by God's loyal servant, Paul. "Faith cometh by hearing, and hearing by the word of God" (Romans 10:17). Then right between her seeking spirit and listening ear was an open heart. Paul did not open her heart; he opened the Word of God and his mouth. Lydia did not open her own heart; she opened her ears and listened to the Word of God. The Lord opened her heart, "whose heart the Lord opened" (Acts 16:14). The loyal servant's task is to introduce receptive sinners to the Great Soul-Winner and Heart-Opener, the Lord Jesus Christ.

Now that she has received the Lord Jesus as Savior and Lord we find in her an obedient spirit. She and those of her household who believed followed the Lord in believer's baptism, the first step in the Christian life. Without the first step there will be no other steps. Finally, Lydia had a generous spirit. She begged Paul and his friends to abide in her house and partake of her hospitality. The opening of her home to God's servants resulted in the beginning of the church at Philippi.

The Lord Spirit (Holy Spirit) is a vital ingredient in evangelism. Without the Holy Spirit there would be no **compulsion** for evangelism. Each of the conversions described are similar in that there is a wanting sinner, a willing servant, and a wooing Spirit. In salvation the trinity is at work. The Father planned salvation—He thought it; the Son purchased salvation—He bought it; the Holy Spirit provided salvation—He brought it. Our Lord Jesus Christ presently busies Himself with three important works, two in heaven and one on earth: He is preparing a mansion for those who love Him (John 14:2), He is interceding for us as our High Priest (R< mans 8:34), and He is building His church (Matthew 16:18).

In that great 16th chapter of Acts, another striking conversion experience is found. As a result of casting out the demon of soothsaying from a young girl, Paul and Barnabas incurred the wrath of those who profited from her fortune telling. They were severely beaten and thrown into jail. At midnight these faithful servants of Christ sang and prayed (Acts16:25). God applauded their faithfulness by sending an earthquake. Miraculously, the chains fell off the prisoners and the prison doors opened. The jailer, witnessing these things, despaired and sought to end his life. Paul stopped him by crying, "Do thyself no harm: for we are all here" (Acts 16:28). Then came that question of all questions: "Sirs, what must I do to be saved?" (Acts 16:30). The answer is so simple, yet so profound. "Believe on the Lord Jesus Christ, and thou shalt be saved, and thy house" (Acts 16:31). The Church of Christ [Campellites] would answer, "Believe on the Lord Jesus Christ and be baptized and thou shalt be saved." Some charismatics would say, "Believe on the Lord Jesus Christ and speak in tongues and thou shalt be saved." Others would say, "Believe on the Lord Jesus Christ and hold out unto the end and thou shalt be saved." Salvation is by grace though faith plus or minus nothing.

Acts 16:32 is often overlooked. "And they spake unto him the word of the Lord, and to all that were in his house." The gospel is not a magic formula; it is a divine system of truth. Would it not have been great if we could have recorded for our hearing and instruction the words Paul and Barnabas spoke to this man and his family? This instruction would have included the sinfulness of man, the holiness of God, the love of God in sending His Son to die on the cross, the necessity of faith, and the result of believing on Christ, i.e., a new creature with a new nature. New Testament evangelism inevitably resulted in changed lives. Note some changes in the newly converted jailer. He listened to the Word of God; he ministered to Paul and Barnabas by washing their stripes; he submitted to the ordinance of believer's baptism; he provided food and lodging for his teachers; and he rejoiced greatly in his new found faith in Christ (Acts 16:33-34). The next Lord's Day he and his household worshiped in the church which was in formation at Lydia's house.

## MODEL PREACHING

Passing from Paul who is preaching to a group of worshiping women, we now see him addressing a group of philosophers on Mars Hill in Athens (Acts 17:22-34). His approach to these philosophers will be much different than his approach to people schooled in Judaism. It will be helpful if we learn how to approach people who are strangers to the Word of God.

First, Paul found a point of common interest. The men of Athens were incurably religious. Fearing that they might neglect some god who could hurt them, they erected an altar TO THE UNKNOWN GOD. Paul uses this UNKNOWN GOD to gain and hold their attention. Ingeniously, Paul inoffensively introduces these pagans to the true God who is their Creator. In doing so he quotes from their poets to further gain their attention. Next, Paul brought them face to face with a common need. "And the times of this ignorance God winked at; but now commandeth all men every where to repent" (Acts 17:30). He reminded these learned men that God had appointed a day in which He will judge the world in righteousness. Paul raises their wrath by preaching Jesus Christ and His death and resurrection. Since the resurrection of the body ran contrary to their inherent beliefs, many mocked him. Paul refused to compromise his message to tickle the ears of his listeners.

The reactions to Paul's message in Athens typifies the reaction the gospel will receive today. Some will abhor the message and hate the messenger; the majority will ignore it; and a few, comparatively speaking, will adore the message and love the messenger. In this unlikely place, God drew people to Himself. "Howbeit certain men clave unto him, and believed: among the which was Dionysius the Areopagite, and a woman named Damaris, and others with them" (Acts 17:34).

## EVANGELISTIC NECESSITIES

Studying the Apostle Paul and his evangelistic message and methods will challenge the heart of every earnest Christian. His faithfulness to His Lord and to the message stirs the heart. An example of his faithfulness appears in Acts 24:24-26. Felix, the governor and his wife, Drusilla, a Jewess, driven by curiosity wanted to hear about Paul's faith. If we had the opportunity to address the governor, his wife, and his court, what would our message be? Paul did not vary but stayed right on course. "And as he reasoned of righteousness, temperance, and judgment to come, Felix trembled" (Acts 24:25). Paul's message is a far cry from what is being preached today in the name of evangelism.

Paul's defense before King Agrippa recorded in Acts 26 brings into focus many truths related to evangelism. There are certain essentials for those who would engage in evangelism. There is no substitute for a vital, fresh conversion experience with the Lord in the heart and life of one who would turn men away from sin to Christ. In his witness for the Lord, Paul often used the testimony of his conversion. Some conversions are dramatic and some prosaic. Whatever the nature of our conversion we need to remember that a conversion is not a once-and-for-all experience, but a once and forever one. Conversion has two phases: turning from sin—repentance toward God and turning to Christ—faith in the Lord Jesus Christ. Both of these activities continue throughout our life.

## MODEL MINISTRY

Next, every Christian should recognize God's general call. We have been programmed to relegate the call to the missionary or to the minister, but every Christian should be aware of a twofold call: to be a servant and to be a witness (Acts 26:16). The high privilege of serving God and witnessing of the saving power of Jesus Christ belongs to every Christian. In verse 18 we see five important ministries mentioned. These ministries are open to those who are willing to serve and to witness.

First, we can have a ministry of revelation—"To open their eyes." "The entrance of thy words giveth light; it giveth understanding unto the simple" (Psalm 119:130).

Second, we can have a ministry of repentance—"to turn them from darkness to light." The ministry of revelation gets people to see right and believe right. The ministry of repentance encourages them to live right and walk right.

Third, a ministry of redemption—"to turn them from the power of Satan unto God" can be ours by preaching the blood of Christ. "Forasmuch as ye know that ye were not redeemed with corruptible things, as silver and gold, from your vain conversation . . . . But with the precious blood of Christ, as of a lamb without blemish and without spot" (I Peter 1:18-19).

Fourth, the ministry of remission—that they may receive remission of sin" is extended to the gospel preacher. No man can forgive sins, but we preach the words of Him who promises forgiveness to those who believe and repent. And finally we have a ministry of riches—"that they may receive an inheritance among them which are sanctified by faith that is in me." Jesus speaks of the true riches which indicates there are false riches. Those that preach the Word share the riches of His grace—the riches of salvation (Ephesians 1:7); the riches of His goodness—the riches of this present life (Romans 2:4); and the riches of His glory—the riches of eternity (Romans 9:23).

After rehearsing the various ministries Christ had entrusted to him, Paul shouts to King Agrippa, "I was not disobedient unto the heavenly vision" (Acts 26:19). This strong statement suggests two dire essentials in the life of faithful servants of God: conviction and consecration. Conviction is defined as a strong belief. The first conviction to grip the heart is "to obey God rather than men" (Acts 5:29). Heavenly vision could well be translated "heavenly revelation." Paul was informing Agrippa that he had no intention of disobeying God. Second, God's servant must have a conviction concerning the nature of the "heavenly revelation." He must believe strongly in the accuracy of the Word of God. "The words of the LORD are pure words: as silver tried in a furnace of earth, purified seven times" (Psalm 12:6). The Word of God is not on trial; it has already been tested and found true.

Likewise, he must be assured of its authority. "Thou hast magnified thy word above all thy Name" (Psalm 138:2). Those who preach the Word must trust its ability. "For the word of God is quick, and powerful, and sharper than any two-edged sword, piercing even to the dividing asunder of soul and spirit, and of the joints and marrow, and is a discerner of the thoughts and intents of the heart" (Hebrews 4:12). Praise God, we do not go to battle with a broken or dull sword.

A strong conviction concerning man, his nature, and his need, is vital also. First, we must be convinced that man's greatest need is spiritual. The sad plight of homeless men and women, the pitiful sight of those whose bodies have been ravished by alcohol, drugs, and sexually transmitted diseases tear at our heartstrings. The answer to man's problems cannot be found in the science laboratory and cannot be solved with government spending programs. Man has a sin problem, and until the sin problem is solved, the effects of sin will remain. Sin is the root; suffering is the fruit.

Second, the fact that people without Christ are lost must dominate our thinking. "Ye were without Christ, being aliens from the commonwealth of Israel, and strangers from the covenants of promise, having no hope, and without God in the world" (Ephesians 2:12). Nice people, gentle people, cultured people, and yes, helpful people without Christ are lost. Of equal intensity must be the conviction that people are savable. "This is a faithful saying, and worthy of all acceptation, that Christ Jesus came into the world to save sinners; of whom I am chief" (I Timothy 1:15). Paul reinforces the savability of sinners in the next chapter: "Who will have all men to be saved, and to come unto the knowledge of the truth" (I Timothy 2:4). Last, we must be convinced that preaching the gospel to all men is a God-given responsibility. O Lord, help us to be obedient to the heavenly vision.

The last essential I will mention involves consecration. Paul kept on track. He was able to say at the end of his ministry, "I have fought a good fight, I have finished my course, I have kept the faith," (II Timothy 4:7). Two traits are found in consecrated people: a heavenly vision and human obedience. Heavenly vision is not man-made but God-given. Let us ask God for a heavenly vision. Substitutes abound. However, there is no substitute for obedience. General Douglas MacArthur, that great soldier and diplomat said, "In war there is no substitute for victory."[1] In our life and labors for God, there is no substitute for obedience. What is the heavenly vision that Paul would not disobey? "Go ye therefore, and teach all nations, baptizing them in the name of the Father, and of the Son, and of the Holy Ghost: teaching them to observe all things whatsoever I have commanded you" (Matthew 28:19-20).

---

1. Bergen Evans, *Dictionary of Quotations* (New York: Delacorte Press, 1968) 225.

# 11

# The Primacy
# of Evangelism
# in the Book of Romans

Before dealing with specifics we need to see how the Book of Romans relates generally to the subject of evangelism. The theme of Romans is "the Gospel of God" and with divine precision the Apostle defends the doctrine of grace. The whole world stands guilty before God (Romans 3:19) and a redemptive plan capable of saving a guilty world unfolds (Romans 3:22). This redemption comes not by human works but by divine grace responding to faith (Romans 4:5). Saving faith justifies the sinner (Romans 5:1) and at the same time sets in motion the process of sanctification (Romans 5:2-5). The law of sin and death has been superseded by a higher law of the Spirit of life in Christ Jesus (Romans 8:2). By identification with Christ the believer can be dead to sin and alive to righteousness (Romans 6:11). Chapters twelve through fifteen urge believers to live dedicated lives which is a reasonable spiritual expression of people who belong to the family of God (Romans 12:1-2).

It does not take Paul long to get to the subject of evangelism. His purpose for going to Rome was to gain fruit, to reap a harvest for the glory of God (Romans 1:13). In verses 14 to 16 we see the "three I am's" of Paul. "**I am debtor**" (Romans 1:14). Salvation is free, but along with the gift comes responsibility, a moral and spiritual obligation to share the gift.

Paul was a "world" Christian, i.e., he felt obligated to Greeks, barbarians, as well as to the educated and uneducated. His burden to communicate Jesus Christ knew no bounds, and none were beyond his concern.

Next, he says "**I am ready**" (Romans 1:15). Paul's delay in getting to Rome was not of his choosing. He would have been there before but he had been hindered (Romans 1:13). With eagerness of soul and intense desire, Paul longed for the opportunity of preaching the gospel at Rome. His statement "as much as in me is" (Romans 1:15) speaks of his willingness to give of himself in this great venture. By preaching, winning, and perfecting people in Rome, he knew his influence would emanate to all points of the Roman empire. Danger never deterred Paul. When warned of the danger of going to Jerusalem Paul responded: "I am ready not to be bound only, but also to die at Jerusalem for the name of the Lord Jesus" (Acts 21:13).

## GLORY OF THE GOSPEL

"**I am not ashamed**" (Romans 1:16). Paul's statement could be restated: I am proud of the gospel. Perhaps some had succumbed to worldly ridicule to become ashamed of the gospel. The message of Christ crucified and risen, evoked scorn and ridicule from Jew and Gentile (I Corinthians 1:23). However, those who had experienced the power of the gospel were able defenders of the gospel. Gospel preachers have a dual responsibility relative to the gospel: to defend it and to declare it. Paul, in Romans 1:16, tells us several reasons why he is proud of the gospel.

First, the gospel "is the power of God." Paul was proud of the **potential** of the gospel. As one who had been saved and served by the gospel, Paul was "exhibit A." A Christ-hating, Christian-killing fanatic whose whole purpose in life was to bring the gospel to naught, but by that gospel was caught. He was transformed from a hater of Christ to a herald of Christ by that gospel. Paul had the assurance that what the gospel did for him it was capable of doing for others.

Then Paul exulted in the **universality** of the gospel—"to everyone that believeth." The relevance of the gospel in all ages, in all climes, in all classes, in all nations, in all circumstances impresses the mind. People of humble means can benefit as well as the learned and noble. Also Paul boasted in the gospel because of its **simplicity**—"to everyone that believeth." The gospel challenges the greatest minds while at the same time it comforts the mind of the child that receives and believes.

Finally, Paul rejoiced in the **equality** of the gospel—"to the Jew first, and also to the Greek." All are included; none are excluded.

## BELIEVING AND CONFESSING

Next we come to Romans chapter ten which is one of the richest portions of the Word of God. This great chapter begins with Paul sharing his awe-inspiring evangelistic burden for his own people, the Jews. "Brethren, my heart's desire and prayer to God for Israel is, that they might be saved" (Romans 10:1). They had zeal; they had ritual; they had rules; but they failed to submit themselves to the righteousness of God (Romans 10:2-3). Righteousness comes not by keeping the law, but by faith in Christ (Romans 10:4).

Romans 10:8 tells us three things that are necessary for those of us who would evangelize. "The word is nigh thee, even in thy mouth, and in thy heart: that is, the word of faith, which we preach." First, Our **mouths** must be filled with the Word of God. God has chosen to use His Word to save the lost. "It pleased God by the foolishness of preaching to save them that believe" (I Corinthians 1:21). Second, our **hearts** must be filled with faith. The Word of God fuels faith. "Faith cometh by hearing, and hearing by the word of God" (Romans 10:17). But the Word in our mouths and faith in our hearts must join to give a witness for Christ. Witnessing is not a popular pastime. Statisticians tell us that only five percent of Christians ever witness

for Christ. Why is this? Real witnessing results from an over-
flow of a Christ-filled life sharing the source of its blessings with
others. True witnessing comes from a **life** abiding in and com-
muning with Christ. "Abide in me, and I in you. As the branch
cannot bear fruit of itself, except it abide in the vine; no more
can ye, except ye abide in me" (John 15:4).

The verses found in Romans 10:9 and 10 speak plainly
as to how to be saved. "That if thou shalt confess with thy mouth
the Lord Jesus, and shalt believe in thine heart that God hath raised
him from the dead, thou shalt be saved. For with the heart man
believeth unto righteousness; and with the mouth confession is
made unto salvation." As we look at these two verses we see
two actions by two members of the body. The mouth confesses
Jesus as Lord; the heart (not the organ that pumps blood, but
the inner man) believes unto righteousness. The twofold emphasis
of heart and mouth in both verses nine and ten is important: the
mouth without the heart would be **hypocrisy**, while the heart
without the mouth would indicate **cowardice**. Since confessing
and believing are such inestimably important actions relating to
salvation it would be of immense value to understand these actions.

First, let us consider the word "confess." It means to express
or profess our agreement and our concord to a statement that
it is true. I like what Albert Barnes says:

> A profession of religion then denotes a public
> declaration of our agreement with what God has
> declared, and extends to all his declarations about
> our lost estate, our sin, and need of a Saviour;
> to his doctrines about his own nature, holiness,
> and law; about the Saviour and the Holy Spirit;
> about the necessity of a change of heart and
> holiness of life; and about the grave and the
> judgment; about heaven and hell.[1]

To be saved one must confess the Lord Jesus or confess
Jesus as Lord. In commenting on confessing the Lord Jesus,

Albert Barnes again writes:

> Shalt openly acknowledge attachment to Jesus
> Christ. The meaning of it may be expressed by
> regarding the phrase, 'the Lord,' as the *predicate;*
> or the thing to be confessed is, that *he is Lord.*
> Comp. Acts ii. 36. Phil. ii. 11, 'And that every
> tongue should confess that Jesus Christ is Lord.'
> Here it means to acknowledge him as Lord, i.e.,
> as having a right to rule over the soul.[2]

Then the statement "believe in thine heart" needs
consideration. Griffith Thomas in his commentary on Romans
writes sensibly as to what it means to believe:

> The term 'heart' in Scripture always means the
> centre [sic] of the moral being, and invariably
> includes the three elements of intellect, feeling,
> and will. We never find in the Bible that contrast
> between 'head' and 'heart,' between 'intellect'
> and 'emotion,' which is so characteristic of our
> usage today. Trust always includes the assent of
> the mind and the consent of the will; the cre-
> dence of the intellect and the confidence of the
> heart. Saving faith dominates the entire being,
> mind, feelings, and will, and as a consequence,
> this faith will express itself in confession.[3]

In Romans 10:10, the two actions of confessing and
believing are reiterated. By faith the believer is declared righteous,
i.e., justified. By confession salvation is attained. This time the
"believing" comes first and the "confessing" comes last. Faith
is an inward, God-ward, invisible, and intensely spiritual reality
(Hebrews 11:1). Conversely, confession is an outward, man-ward,
visible, and practical manifestation. Albert Barnes also gives words
of wisdom concerning our confession of Christ:

And we may here learn, (1.) that *a profession* of religion is, by Paul, made *as really* indispensable to salvation as *believing.* According to him it is connected with salvation as really as faith is with justification; and this accords with all the declarations of the Lord Jesus. Matt. x.32, xxv.34-46; Luke xii. 8. (2.) There can be no religion where there is not a willingness to confess the Lord Jesus. There is no true repentance where we are not willing to *confess* our faults. ... (3.). ... The *real* feelings of the heart will be expressed in the life. And they who profess by their lives that they have no regard for God and Christ, heaven and glory, must expect to be met in the last day as those who deny the Lord that bought them, and who bring upon themselves quick destruction, 2 Pet. ii.1.[4]

## FOUR IMPORTANT QUESTIONS

In Romans 10:13 the Apostle makes a dynamite of a promise: "For whosoever shall call upon the name of the Lord shall be saved." That statement raises four important questions: the how of **calling**, the how of **believing**, the how of **preaching**, and the how of **sending**. "How then shall they call on him in whom they have not believed? and how shall they believe in him of whom they have not heard? and how shall they hear without a preacher? And how shall they preach, except they be sent" (Romans 10:14-15)? In verses nine and ten we see the **message;** in verse fourteen we see the **masses;** and in verses fourteen and fifteen we see the **messengers**.

## SOVEREIGNTY AND RESPONSIBILITY

Sometimes the Bible emphasizes God's sovereignty in bringing men to faith. But human responsibility explodes in these verses. If the masses are to hear the message, then the messengers must tell them. The *Harper's Study Bible* has a good note on these verses:

> A basic truth is taught here that bears on the missionary task of the church. Salvation is possible only when certain indispensable conditions are met. One must have faith ([Romans] 10:11), but faith is not possible unless the gospel is communicated, and the gospel can be communicated only by the preaching of the Word of God. Therefore the ultimate source from which salvation springs is necessarily the Word of God. This may be given to men a variety of ways, such as by word of mouth or the printed page; but however it is conveyed the Word of God is indispensable to salvation.[5]

As we come toward the end of this Epistle, Paul once again puts the matter of world evangelism before his readers. In chapter fifteen, Paul brings before his Roman readers an overview of his ministry. He considered the Gentile believers who came to Christ by the Gospel of God to be an offering to God. He gloried in being a minister of Jesus Christ and praises God's grace and power that enabled him to do an effective work for God among the Gentiles. Paul had a noble ambition: not to make money, not to make a name, not to build an empire, but to preach the gospel where Christ had never been named. "Yea, so have I strived to preach the gospel, not where Christ was named, lest I should build upon another man's foundation" (Romans 15:20). May that noble ambition fill the hearts of God's servants in our day.

---

1. Barnes, 624.
2. Ibid.
3. W. H. Griffith Thomas, *St. Paul's Epistle to the*

*Romans* (Grand Rapids: Wm. B. Eerdmans Publishing Company, 1947) 278.

4. Barnes, 625.

5. Harold Lindsell, *Harper's Study Bible* (Grand Rapids: Zondervan Bible Publishers, 1985) 1435.

# 12

## The Primacy
of Evangelism
in the Corinthian
and Galatian Epistles

In I Corinthians Paul deals with thorny church problems. Immorality threatened the purity and testimony of the church. Pride and carnality weakened its harmony and fellowship. Abuse and misunderstanding of spiritual gifts prompted Paul to spend three chapters, 12 to 14 in order to put the gifts in proper perspective.

### SCANDAL IN THE CHURCH

One of the serious problems addressed, concerns evangelism. Not only was there moral scandal in the church, but spiritual scandal was lurking in the shadows. Paul rebukes this scandal in unmistakable terms: "Awake to righteousness, and sin not; for some have not the knowledge of God: I speak this to your **shame**" (I Corinthians 15:34).

Failure to share the gospel of Jesus Christ scandalized the Church of Corinth and that same scandal continues to the present day. Paul's sharply worded exhortation purposed to lift the Corinthians from their lethargy. "Awake to righteousness" —**wake up**! Nero fiddled while Rome burned. The church plays while our world gets farther and farther from God. Activities abound for teenagers and keenagers, but where are the dedicated harvesters who go out reaping and return with rejoicing bringing their sheaves with them?

"And sin not"—**shape up**! The sin Paul rebuked was not something they were doing; rather it was what they were not doing. It was the sin of omission, i.e., the church's failure to impact its community for Christ. The sin of omission hides behind a cloak of respectability. Is the church's failure to evangelize just an unpleasant fact? Has a successful outreach come to be seen as a pesky problem without a solution? Paul faces this question with the answer that failure to reach ones community, or at least to make a determined effort to do so is dereliction of duty.

"Some have not the knowledge of God"—**speak up**! The church at Thessalonica proved it was not an impossible task: "For from you sounded out the word of the Lord not only in Macedonia and Achaia, but also in every place your faith to Godward is spread abroad; so that we need not to speak any thing" (I Thessalonians 1:8). In a missionary conference, the participating missionaries joined with some members of the church in an afternoon of soul-winning visitation (visiting with the purpose of leading people to faith in Christ). The family next door to the church was visited, and the family had lived there for 20 years, and no one from the church had ever contacted them.

Paul sums up his evangelistic challenge with this stinging indictment: "I speak this to your shame"—**confess up**! If the Church at Corinth deserved such a rebuke, what about our churches? A sinful silence lies like a gloom over our nation and world. The church's neglect has created a spiritual vacuum that refuses to remain empty. Religious humanism, the New Age movement, Islam, cults, and Satanism rush to fill the void. These sinister spiritual forces continue to gain ground. According to experts, the traditional Protestant population of the United States will have shrunk from two-thirds to one-third between 1900 and 2000 A.D.[1] In 1900 there were 27 churches for every 10,000 people. Now there are only 12 churches for every 10,000.[2] There are an estimated 30,000,000 hard core pagans that are anti-

Christian. The unchurched number is at least at total of 169,000,000.[3]

The crisis is here! The gates of hell armed with government and media support relentlessly press the battle against our traditional Christian values and institutions. The temptation to close ranks, retreat inside the walls of our churches, and lock the doors beguile us. Nothing could be worse. The church got into trouble disobeying the Great Commission; the only way out is to obey the Great Commission. Will the church of Jesus Christ deal with its scandal? Will she wake up, shape up, speak up, and confess up? The future of America and our world depends upon it.

Moving on to II Corinthians we find several passages dealing with evangelism. This is the most personal of Paul's Epistles. In it he bears his heart as he defends his apostleship, his honesty, and his motives.

## BLINDED BY SATAN

We will deal first with II Corinthians 4:3-7. "But if our gospel be hid, it is hid to them that are lost" (II Corinthians 4:3). Anyone who does personal work will soon realize that the god of this world (Satan) has blinded the minds of men lest they understand the gospel and be saved (II Corinthians 4: 4). In the parable of the soils, the devil's main strategy is to keep the Word of God out of the minds and hearts of people.

In our evangelistic work, we use a neighborhood religious survey which helps us plant the Word of God in our neighbors' hearts. It includes this question: "If you were to die today and stand before God, and He should ask you why He should let you into heaven, what would you say?" People who have been to church all their lives cannot answer the question. One lady in Wisconsin said she had been going to church for 80 years, and she did not know what she would tell God. Thankfully, before we left her home she had heard a careful explanation of the gospel, confessed her sin, and received Christ as her Lord and Savior.

## SERVANT PREACHERS

After discoursing on the blindness of man and his inability to comprehend the gospel, Paul mentions the subject of preaching. "For we preach not ourselves, but Christ Jesus the Lord; and ourselves your servants for Jesus' sake" (II Corinthians 4:5). Already in our study, the importance of the Word of God and our preaching, teaching, explaining, and applying that Word has been pointed out. Two important aspects of an evangelistic ministry present themselves in this verse: our **message** and our **manner**.

The message is Christ Jesus the Lord. New Testament preaching presents Christ as Lord. The attempt to separate Jesus as Savior from Jesus as Lord flies in the face of biblical teaching. Those who do so emasculate the message and put at peril those they seek to reach for the Lord.

Then notice the humble manner of those who preach Christ Jesus the Lord. "Neither as being lords over God's heritage, but being ensamples to the flock" (I Peter 5:3). People not only hear the message, but they carefully observe the messenger. May we be delivered from modern day Diotrephes who usurp authority and set themselves up as lords. "But Diotrephes who loveth to have the preeminence among them, receiveth us not" (III John 9). For effective evangelistic work we need the right message and the right manner of communicating that message.

"But we have this treasure in earthen vessels, that the excellency of the power may be of God, and not of us" (II Corinthians 4:7). Ask the man on the street what he thinks of "evangelists." Unfortunately, the image of an evangelist is a huckster, a deceiver, a charlatan. The world pictures him as one who wears outlandish suits, adorns his fingers with rings, drives expensive cars, and lives in luxurious homes. Thanks and no thanks to televison! The Word of God pictures an evangelist as a common clay pot. The treasure, the power, and the excellency all belong to God, not to the evangelist. Spiritual disaster and eternal harm follows in the wake of those who promote themselves and take to themselves glory which belongs to God.

## RECONCILED TO BE RECONCILERS

The great doctrine of reconciliation appears in II Corinthians 5:18-21. "All things are of God, who hath reconciled us to himself by Jesus Christ, and hath given to us the ministry of reconciliation" (verse 18). We have a hard time believing that God really wants to save people. It is time we realize that judgment is God's strange work, and salvation is His glorious work. "Salvation is of the LORD" (Jonah 2:9).

Adam and Eve offended God and in the reconciliation process, since the offender usually makes the first move, we would have expected them to make things right with God. However, in the Garden of Eden, God came seeking Adam, not Adam seeking God (Genesis 2:8-9). "God was in Christ, reconciling the world unto himself" (II Corinthians 5:19) thereby taking the initiative to bring alienated mankind back to Himself.

Amazingly, God not only reconciles us to Himself, but He includes us in reconciling others to Himself. In II Corinthians 5:18, God gives us the **ministry of reconciliation;** in II Corinthians 5:19 the **word of reconciliation;** in II Corinthians 5:20 the **responsibility of reconciliation;** and in II Corinthians 5:21 **the message of reconciliation.**

Paul declares that we are ambassadors for Christ. In this world, ambassadors play impressive roles in world politics. The analogy of an ambassador with that of a witness for Christ shows the position and authority God gives us. An ambassador represents the head of a nation. A Christian witness represents the head of the Church. An ambassador has **no program** of his own, but initiates the program of his country. We have no program of our own, but seek first the kingdom of God. An ambassador has **no power** or authority of his own, but his is a delegated authority. Likewise, ours is the power and authority of the Holy Spirit. An ambassador acts in the stead of, or in the place of the one he represents. "Now then we are ambassadors for Christ, as though

God did beseech you by us: we pray you in Christ's stead, be ye reconciled to God" (II Corinthians 5:20).

God certainly wants people to be saved for He says in His word "Who [God] will have all men to be saved, and to come unto the knowledge of the truth" (I Timothy 2:4). The responsibility of beseeching sinners to be reconciled to God rests squarely upon the shoulders of the redeemed.

Before real reconciliation takes place, the grievances that caused the alienation must be removed. Both parties must knowingly and willingly enter into the reconciliation process. God was infinitely offended by man's sin. At the same time sin produced spiritual death and alienation in the life of the sinner. The scene at the cross highlights reconciliation. Jesus Christ, the sinless Son of God, takes upon Himself the sins of the whole world (I John 2:2). "He [God] hath made him to be sin for us" (II Corinthians 5:21). On that cross, Jesus was our sin bearer and as such suffered for our sins. By this act of identifying with sinners and receiving in His own body our punishment, He is able to bring us to God or reconcile us (I Peter 3:18).

On the either side of Jesus were two thieves. One of them by faith recognized Jesus Christ for Who He was. The believing thief repented—had a definite change of mind—as he confessed his own guilt and confessed the innocence of Christ (Luke 23:39). He then asked to be remembered which was the same as asking to be saved or forgiven (Luke 23:42). Reconciliation was complete when Jesus said, "Verily I say unto thee, To day shalt thou be with me in paradise" (Luke 23:43). The soiled rags of sin were taken away and a robe of righteousness clothed the dying thief. The enmity was gone; reconciliation was complete. "That we might be made the righteousness of God in him" (II Corinthians 5:21).

## PRIMACY OF EVANGELISM
## IN GALATIANS

Solomon said in Ecclesiastes "There is no new thing under

the sun" (Ecclesiastes 1:9). Those concerned about evangelism are cognizant that debates about the gospel which began in Paul's day continue to this very hour. Various charges that are followed by counter charges are hurled. Books, articles, and sermons appear which seek to set forth the true gospel. Bible-preaching men are accusing each other of preaching "another gospel." The charges of preaching "another gospel" are basically two-fold: on the one hand some are accused of preaching "cheap grace," and on the other hand, others are accused of preaching salvation by works or Lordship salvation.

The debate raging concerning the true gospel is no light matter. Paul puts an eternal curse on anyone who preaches a false gospel "But though we, or an angel from heaven, preach any other gospel unto you than that which we preached unto you, let him be accursed" (Galatians 1:8). It behooves everyone who preaches the gospel to carefully give attention to the message as Paul warns young gospel preacher Timothy: "Take heed unto thyself, and unto the doctrine; continue in them: for in doing this thou shalt both save thyself, and them that hear thee" (I Timothy 4:16).

My desire is to set forth biblical truth concerning evangelism and the nature of the gospel without involving personalities, naming names, and quoting various authors and their works. Let the Bible speak.

In Galatians, Paul meets head on with the Judaizers that were preaching "another gospel" contrary to the grace of Christ (Galatians 1:6). The error of the Judaizers was twofold: obedience to the law mingled with faith is the basis of justification, and the justified sinner must keep the law to remain saved. Paul took care of the first error by taking his readers back to the Abrahamic covenant, and he summed it up in this way: "But that no man is justified by the law in the sight of God, it is evident: for, The just shall live by faith" (Galatians 3:11). The second error is answered by Paul's question: "Are ye so foolish? having begun in the Spirit, are ye now made perfect by the flesh?" (Galatians 3:3). The believer is saved by grace and kept by grace.

In his beautiful salutation in Galatians 1:1-5 Paul speaks

of both the resurrection in verse 1 and the sufferings of Christ in verse 4: "Who gave himself for our sins, that he might deliver us from this present evil world, according to the will of God and our Father." Consistently, the Bible presents salvation as accomplishing two great works on behalf of the believer: a **present** deliverance and a **future** deliverance. Here we see the present deliverance. Christ saves us from this present evil world system by giving a new nature enabling us to escape the corruption that is in the world through lust (II Peter 1:4). "Therefore if any man be in Christ, he is a new creature: old things are passed away; behold, all things are become new" (II Corinthians 5:17). A salvation experience that does not result in new desires and a different lifestyle is suspect.

## FREE GRACE IS NOT CHEAP GRACE

Salvation is by grace and not of works. The teaching of free grace (not cheap grace) comes under fire by those who would mix grace and works The question was asked in New Testament times, and it is asked today: "shall we continue in sin, that grace may abound?" (Romans 6:1). Paul deals with this issue in Galatians. After teaching salvation by faith apart from the law (Galatians 2:16), he asks this pertinent question: "But if, while we seek to be justified by Christ, we ourselves also are found sinners [living a sinful lifestyle], is therefore Christ the minister of sin? God forbid" (Galatians 2:17). Paul gives the two keys of the Christian life in two similar verses. In Galatians 5:6, "For in Jesus Christ neither circumcision [law] availeth any thing, nor uncircumcision [lawlessness]; but faith which worketh by love." Here we see a living, working, loving faith. Then in Galatians 6:15 we have a similar verse: "For in Christ Jesus neither circumcision availeth any thing, nor uncircumcision, but a new creature."

---

1. *Focus on Missions,* Vol. 17. No. 1, America–The Mission Field (The Win Arn Growth Report, No. 13, February,

1986) 5.

    2. Ibid.

    3. Donald A. McGavran, *Today's Task, Opportunity, and Imperative in The World Christian Movement,* Ralph D. Winter and Steven C. Hawthorne, eds. (Pasadena: William Carey Library, 1981) 770.

# 13

# The Primacy
# of Evangelism
# in the Prison
# and Pastoral Epistles

While in a Roman prison, Paul wrote the following letters: Ephesians, Philippians, Colossians, and Philemon. The reason there are few exhortations to evangelize in these epistles lies in the fact that these churches were busily reaching out with the gospel. Acts 19:10 confirms this fact. "And this [teaching] continued by the space of two years; so that all they which dwelt in Asia heard the word of the Lord Jesus, both Jews and Greeks." Paul began a Bible school in Ephesus. His students not only studied the Word, but they preached the Word. From Paul and his disciples the whole area came to hear of the Lord Jesus.

At the very end of the Ephesian Epistle, Paul beseeches the Ephesian saints to pray for him. First, he requested that they pray for all saints (Ephesians 6:18), but then he said, "And for me, that utterance may be given unto me, that I may open my mouth boldly, to make known the mystery of the gospel, For which I am an ambassador in bonds: that therein I may speak boldly, as I ought to speak" (Ephesians 6:19-20). Boldness is a missing ingredient in many gospel presentations. The enemies of Christ seek to intimidate those who preach the gospel. We need to pray for one another that with all boldness we may preach the Word of God.

## EVANGELISTIC CHURCH

The church at Philippi must have been a great joy to the heart of Paul. This church more than any other supported him in his missionary endeavors (Philippians 4:15). He also speaks of fellowship in the gospel with this church. The Philippians participated with Paul "in the defence and confirmation of the gospel" (Philippians 1:7). Paul encouraged them to let their conversation or manner of life be such as becomes the gospel (Philippians1:27). The enemies were seeking to terrify these believers which caused Paul to exhort them to be of one mind and to stand "together for the faith of the gospel" (Philippians 1:27).

It seems that some of the folks in Philippi experienced difficulty in their relationships with one another. In his exhortation for them to be of one mind, we learn something about these people. They labored with Paul in the gospel. One is called a "yokefellow" and others are referred to as "fellowlabourers" who labored with Paul in the gospel. (Philippians 4:2-3). From all this, we surmise that the church of Philippi was an evangelistic church, determinedly reaching their area with the gospel.

The Colossian Epistle deals mainly with the errors of legalism and false mysticism. However, the rapid spread of the gospel is evidenced by Paul's statement in his apostolic greeting: "which [the gospel] is come unto you, as it is in all the world; and bringeth forth fruit, as it doth also in you, since the day ye heard of it, and knew the grace of God in truth" (Colossians 1:6). By this statement, I take it not to mean that all the world had been evangelized, but simply that the gospel was rapidly spreading over the known world.

Colossians 2:6, "As ye have therefore received Christ Jesus the Lord" indicates that the apostles encouraged people to receive Jesus Christ as Lord, not just as Savior. The new believer is to walk in fellowship with the Lord, to be grounded and edified, and to abound in thanksgiving (Colossians 2:7). Evangelism which incorporates, indoctrinates, and integrates new believers into the fellowship of the church blesses a church. The superficial evangelism that rejoices in professions of faith, but which fails to follow through will lead to disappointment.

In the fourth chapter of Colossians, Paul's burden for evangelism surfaces. He once again asks for prayer but the request differs from the request in Ephesians. In his request, Paul asks for two things: "that God would open unto us a door of utterance, to speak the mystery of Christ" and "that I may make it manifest [clear or understandable]" (Colossians 4:3-4). Some people just do not want to hear the gospel. Others desire to hear it. As we go out to evangelize we must pray for God to open doors, to lead us to receptive people.

In our ministry of dealing with literally thousands of people, we find that few, even who profess to be saved, understand the gospel. People who have been to church all their lives cannot verbalize the gospel. Therefore, we need to pray that we may make the gospel plain. Colossians 4:5 and 6 follow the same thought as they encourage right living and right talking toward them that are without faith. We need to live so people will ask us concerning the hope we have in Christ. Then we need to prepare our hearts and minds to be able to give the right answer.

## PRIMACY OF EVANGELISM
## IN THE PASTORAL EPISTLES

Bible teachers call the church of Thessalonica the model church. Paul was very thankful for them and mentions why he was thankful. "Remembering without ceasing your **work of faith**, and **labour of love**, and **patience of hope** in our Lord Jesus Christ, in the sight of God and our Father" (I Thessalonians 1:3). The gospel worked mightily in this place. Notice that Paul mentions how the gospel came unto them. "For our gospel came not unto you in word only, but also in **power**, and in the **Holy**

**Ghost**, and in **much assurance**" (I Thessalonians1:5). The gospel brought them two contrasting conditions: "much affliction" and the "joy of the Holy Ghost" (I Thessalonians 1:6). Thessalonica was a church on fire. This church became an example to believers in other places such as Corinth (I Thessalonians 1:7). The gospel radiated out from Thessalonica, and the faith, love, and hope of these believers became common knowledge. Their testimony was loud and clear as people could see that they had turned to God away from idols, that they were now serving the true and living God, and that they were waiting expectantly for His Son from heaven (I Thessalonians 1:9-10).

## MODEL EVANGELIST

In Chapter 2, we have Paul, the model evangelist. Just before coming to Thessalonica, Paul and Silas had been whipped, humiliated, and chased out of Philippi. This persecution never fazed them as he says "we were bold in our God to speak unto you the gospel of God with much contention" (I Thessalonians 2:2). The word for "contention" is *agon* from which our word agony derives. It speaks of striving with great exertion. Is it any wonder their coming unto the Thessalonians was not in vain? (I Thessalonians 2:1).

In the next verses Paul describes his ministry among them. There was no guile, deceit, or uncleanness in his methods. He did not resort to flattery; neither did he covet their possessions. Instead of being burdensome, he paid his own way. Rather than lording it over the new believers, he cherished them as a nurse cherishes her little ones. His ministry of love not only caused him to give them the gospel, but if necessary, he would have given his very soul also (I Thessalonians 2:8). Living above reproach, he was an example to them that believed.

Paul established the church in Thessalonica in a few short weeks. He sums up his ministry in Thessalonica with these words: "When ye received the word of God which ye heard of us, ye received it not as the word of men, but as it is in truth, the word of God, which effectually worketh also in you that believe" (I Thessalonians 2:13).

II Thessalonians speaks of a falling away, an apostasy, a turning away from truth. Certainly those days are upon us. Men who have been faithful to the Bible are turning from the doctrine of eternal retribution. Paul was not in that number, as under the inspiration of the Holy Spirit he taught specifically about that subject. "In flaming fire taking vengeance on them that know not God, and that obey not the gospel of our Lord Jesus Christ: Who shall be punished with everlasting destruction from the presence of the Lord, and from the glory of his power" (II Thessalonians 1:8). The language Paul uses does not match the popular, watered-down, wimpy presentations that we hear today.

## PRAYER IN EVANGELISM

Paul gives another prayer request that shows his interest in evangelism. "Finally, brethren, pray for us, that the word of the Lord may have free course, and be glorified, even as it is with you: And that we may be delivered from unreasonable and wicked men: for all men have not faith" (II Thessalonians 3:1-2). In these verses three requests are made: that the Word may be unhindered, that the Word may be effective, and that God would protect His servants from ungodly men. In Thessalonica, the Word had free course and accomplished great things. In Athens, the Word was bound by prejudice and philosophy, and the results were scanty. When the Word is believed and obeyed, God receives glory. When the Word is rejected, men rob themselves of the blessings that could be theirs.

In Bogota, Colombia, Harold Davis, missionary with Association of Baptists for World Evangelism, was coming home by bus after church visitation. Evil men took him to a vacant lot, shot him through the head, and robbed him. Three missionaries with New Tribes Mission are being held hostage in Columbia. More recently guerillas entered a mission school in Colombia and kidnapped two missionaries and shot them to death. These incidences should be a call to prayer that God's servants may be protected from wicked men.

It is interesting to note how prayer and evangelism relate in the Epistles. Paul's burden for the unreached manifests itself in his prayer requests. In I Timothy we find another prayer request: "I exhort therefore, that, first of all, supplications, prayers, intercessions, and giving of thanks, be made for all men" (I Timothy 2:1). We are instructed to pray for those in authority that peace and godliness may be enjoyed (I Timothy 2:2). A violent society is a godless society; a peace-loving society forwards the work of God. In referring to a peaceful society, Paul says, "This is good and acceptable in the sight of God our Saviour; Who will have all men to be saved, and to come unto the knowledge of the truth" (I Timothy 2:3-4). Dr. E. Y. Mullins, Southern Baptist theologian, makes some wise remarks concerning these verses:

> There are two choices necessary in a man's salvation: God's choice of the man and man's choice of God. . . . Salvation never comes otherwise than through God's choice of man and man's choice of God. . . . Free-will in man is as fundamental a truth as any other in the Gospel and must never be canceled in our doctrinal statements. Man would not be man without it and God never robs us of our true moral man-hood in saving us. . . . The decree of salvation must be looked at as a whole to understand it. Some have looked at God's choice alone and ignored the means and the necessary choice on man's part. . . . Election is sometimes said to indicate arbitrariness and partiality in God. But this is an error. God wills that all men should be saved and come to a knowledge of the truth (I Timothy 2:4), as Paul assured us. Certainly Jesus died for the whole world (John 3:16).[1]

Dr. William Pettingill gave wise counsel concerning this controversy of election and free will:

> The relation between God's sovereignty and elective purpose on the one hand and free grace and human responsibility on the other has perplexed the commentators throughout the ages. The best course is to believe all that God says and wait for Him to make it plain. God insists upon His sovereignty and also upon man's responsibility. Believe both and preach both, leaving the task of 'harmonizing' with Him.[2]

"For there is one God, and one mediator between God and men, the man Christ Jesus; Who gave himself a ransom for all, to be testified in due time" (I Timothy 2:5-6). In our pluralistic society, preaching One God and One Mediator runs contrary to public policy, is not politically correct, and raises the ire of free thinkers. The same was true in Paul's day. Timothy needed encouragement, and Paul gives it in II Timothy 1:7 and 8: "For God hath not given us the spirit of fear; but of power, and of love, and of a sound mind. Be not thou therefore ashamed of the testimony of our Lord, nor of me his prisoner: but be thou partaker of the afflictions of the gospel."

During my several years of conducting Jerusalem Outreach conferences in 54 churches, I have seen a desperate need for a spirit of faith, of power, and of right thinking in the hearts and minds of those who go into out their neighborhoods with the gospel. Right thinking should always cause us to be unashamed of the testimony of our Lord Jesus Christ and of those who serve Him. Paul did not tell Timothy there would be no trouble, but rather he urged him to be a partaker of the afflictions of the gospel. In Paul's life there was much suffering, but he was not ashamed of that suffering because he knew the Lord was faithful and would amply reward him at that day (II Timothy 1:12).

# PRIMACY OF EVANGELISM
# IN II TIMOTHY

The devil hates God and God's people so it is no surprise that he puts that same enmity in the hearts of his servants. Paul was accused of being a troublemaker. "Wherein I suffer trouble, as an evildoer" (II Timothy 2:9). Today, the media, educationalists, sociologists, New-Agers, and humanists combine to blame godly Christians, those who stand for purity, decency, and righteousness, for the troubles of society.

In this context, Paul makes a most interesting statement: "I endure all things for the elect's sakes, that they may also obtain the salvation which is in Christ Jesus with eternal glory" (II Timothy 2:10). For the elect to be saved, it was necessary for Paul to preach the gospel and thus incur the wrath of men. Election in no way removes human responsibility. God uses the preached gospel to bring the elect to salvation and glory. No preaching, no salvation.

From the beginning of II Timothy to the end, Paul continues to warn Timothy to be prepared for hardships. "But watch thou in all things, endure afflictions [hardships], do the work of an evangelist, make full proof of thy ministry" (II Timothy 4:5). This is the third and last time the word "evangelist" appears in the New Testament. Every servant of God should strive to have an evangelistic ministry–a ministry that brings Jesus Christ to people and people to Jesus Christ.

## THREE GRAVE DANGERS

In looking back over his life and ministry, Paul compared his work to a **boxing match**, to a **race**, and to a **trust**. "I have fought a good fight, I have finished my course, and I have kept the faith" (II Timothy 4:7). If we hope to be able to echo these words of victory, then there are some things to avoid. Paul not only fought a good fight, but he fought the right fight. In our Christian service we must avoid **distractions**. Many good things keep us from doing the best thing. How sad to see people giving themselves for the wrong causes.

It is not enough to start well, but we must also end well. To do so we must be watchful of **discouragement**. God does not use discouraged people. Faith is the victory, and those that win will keep the faith.

Due to the pressures and disappointments of life, some fall prey to **disbelief,** and as a result fail in the battle of life. "Keep thy heart with all diligence; for out of it are the issues of life" (Proverbs 4:23). Faith is the issue.

## GRACE THE GREAT TEACHER

The short letter of Titus relates to evangelism in several ways. The phrase "good works" appears four times. Paul emphasizes right living and denounces professed Christians that fail to prove the reality of their faith. "They profess that they know God; but in works they deny him, being abominable, and disobedient, and unto every **good work** reprobate [worthless]" (Titus 1:16). Evangelism that majors on profession of faith, but ignores repentance, a changed life, and a new nature can hardly be called New Testament evangelism. It is a facade and a counterfeit, not the real article.

In Titus 2:11-14, Paul gives basic teaching on grace, salvation, the Christian life, and the Second Coming of Christ. As preachers of the gospel we must rightly divide the Word of truth (II Timothy 2:15), and we must compare Scripture with Scripture. Preaching grace without works needs qualifying. No doubt we are "saved by grace through faith; and that not of yourselves: it is the gift of God: Not of works, lest any man should boast" (Ephesians 2:8-9). "But to him that worketh not, but believeth on him that justifieth the ungodly, his faith is counted for righteousness" (Romans 4:5). Faith is absolutely essential. And if that is all the Bible said about the subject of works, we could believe that grace, faith, righteousness, and justification stand alone and are completely unrelated to works.

Without denying salvation by grace through faith and justification by faith and not by works, we must look at Titus 2:11-15 and correlate the two passages.

> For the grace of God that bringeth salvation hath appeared to all men, Teaching us that, denying ungodliness and worldly lusts, we should live soberly, righteously, and godly, in this present world; Looking for that blessed hope, and the glorious appearing of the great God and our Saviour Jesus Christ; who gave himself for us, that he might redeem us from all iniquity, and purify unto himself a peculiar people, zealous of **good works**. These things speak, and exhort, and rebuke with all authority.

The same grace that saves (justifies) also sanctifies. Grace not only delivers from the penalty of sin, but it also delivers from the power of sin. Grace is not only a saving force; it is also a teaching force. The grace of God is the teacher. The teaching that we are saved by grace and then later a second work of grace sanctifies receives no support from the Scripture. If a person is saved by grace and his life is unaffected by that grace, the whole purpose of redemption is thwarted. Christ died to redeem (free) us from all iniquity, to make us pure, a people with a godly lifestyle, delighting in being good. This is not to be interpreted that a new-born Christian immediately changes all his bad habits and instantaneously achieves Christian maturity. What it does mean is at the time of salvation, the process begins just as in physical birth the processes are set in motion that will eventuate in a full-grown person.

---

1. E. Y. Mullins, *Baptist Beliefs* (Louisville: Baptist World Publishing Company, 1913) 26-27.

2. William Pettingill, *Bible Questions Answered* (Finlay, Ohio, Fundamental Truth Publishers, n.d.) 209.

# 14

# The Primacy
# of Evangelism
# in the Epistles of James
# and I and II Peter

Faith is the key that opens to us all the blessings of God. "But without faith it is impossible to please him" (Hebrews 11:6). "Believe on the Lord Jesus Christ, and thou shalt be saved" (Acts 16:31). Since faith plays such an important function in both salvation and the Christian life, our study of evangelism would not be complete if we did not take a careful look at this subject. An understanding of faith is crucial since so much is riding on our faith.

Where are we to learn about faith? The controversy over the nature of faith continues unabated. I will not quote Bible teachers and give their views since the Holy Spirit speaks eloquently on the subject in James. So again let the Bible speak. Critics accuse the Bible of contradicting itself because of seemingly contradictory statements by Paul and James on the subject of faith and works. Paul says, "Therefore we conclude that a man is justified by faith without the deeds of the law [works]" (Romans 3:28). James, on the other hand says, "Ye see then how that by works a man is justified, and not by faith only" (James 2:24). The seeming contradiction vanishes when it is understood that Paul is looking at justification from the divine viewpoint and James from the human viewpoint. Faith alone justifies a man before God; a faith that proves itself by good works justifies a man before men. Faith alone saves, but the faith that saves is never alone. The faith that saves is a living faith, and according to verse 18 it is a working faith.

In our study of other portions, we have seen various kinds of faith mentioned: **temporary** faith (Luke 8:13), a **false** faith (John 2:23-25), and a **spurious** faith (Acts 8:20-21). Here in James we see a **dead** faith: "For as the body without the spirit is dead, so faith without works is dead also" (James 2:26).

The Bible speaks plainly on the matter of saving faith. It links faith and repentance together which implies undoubtedly at the time of salvation certain changes occur. I am a great advocate of following up and encouraging new Christians. But every Christian worker experiences resistance and disinterest on the part of many who profess to be saved. Can we believe people are genuinely converted that after professing to receive Christ as Lord and Savior, have no appetite for the things of the Spirit? "As newborn babes, desire the sincere milk of the word, that ye may grow thereby: If so be ye have tasted that the Lord is gracious" (I Peter 2:2-3). One of the strongest signs of new life is a hunger for the Word of God. Without this desire for the study of the Word, Christian fellowship, service, and obedience to the commands of Christ, we are justified in doubting the genuineness of that profession of faith.

## PRIMACY OF EVANGELISM
## IN I PETER

In looking at I Peter, we will deal with two portions that speak directly to evangelism. I Peter 3:1 assures wives that they can win their husbands to faith in Christ. "Likewise, ye wives, be in subjection to your own husbands; that, if any obey not the word, they also may without the word be won by the conversation [lifestyle] of the wives." We could call this **silent** evangelism, **loving** evangelism, and **living** evangelism. The wife need not preach, nag, or coerce her husband in the things of Christ, but rather demonstrate to him the reality of her faith and her submission to God by a virtuous life. For a wife to be submissive to an unsaved husband and her Lord at the same time requires divine wisdom. Over involvement in Christian activities resulting in neglect of husband and home is not the way for a wife to win her husband to Christ.

The first example of evangelism in I Peter was silent evangelism, but our second example encourages speaking out for the Lord. In this verse, Peter gives sound instructions for those involved in biblical evangelism. "But **sanctify the Lord** God in your hearts: and be ready always to give an answer to every man that asketh you a reason of the hope that is in you with meekness and fear" (I Peter 3:15). By sanctifying the Lord in our hearts, we are recognizing Him as holy, we are honoring Him, and we are declaring our dependence upon Him. Peter's knowledge and use of Scripture is evident as he refers to Isaiah 8:13: "Sanctify the LORD of hosts himself; and let him be your fear, and let him be your dread."

## THREE ESSENTIALS
## FOR WITNESSING

Witnessing for Christ, involving ourselves in the spiritual and private lives of others, evokes fear in normal people. Fear deters many earnest Christians from witnessing for Christ. "The fear of man bringeth a snare: but whoso putteth his trust in the LORD shall be safe" (Proverbs 29:25). By sanctifying the Lord in our hearts we choose to fear God more than we fear man. By obeying this injunction, we will witness because we fear God, love Him, and want to please Him.

An important factor in witnessing is our relationship with the Lord. Once this matter is settled, another hindrance to witnessing must be removed. Lack of preparation prevents many Christians from being a bold witness. "Be ready always to give an answer to every man" (I Peter 3:15). Readiness in any endeavor requires preparation. First, there must be that **spiritual preparation** of heart mentioned above. Then **mental preparation** is necessary. A thorough knowledge of Scripture coupled with an ability to answer common complaints against God, the Bible, Christianity, etc., enables the witness to give an intelligent answer. I just read *I'm Glad You Asked—In-Depth Answers to Difficult Questions About Christianity* published by Victor Books and written by Kenneth Boa and Larry Moody. I found it very helpful. Sorry to say, some books written on the subject of evangelism overemphasize methods, techniques, presentations and neglect the spiritual aspects such as the message, prayers, right relationship with God, and the convicting power of the Holy Spirit.

The third essential, besides spiritual and mental preparation is an **assured hope.** "Be ready always to give an answer to every man that asketh you a reason for the hope that is in you" (I Peter 3:15). It is a fact of life that we cannot give what we do not have, and we cannot teach what we do not know. The "hope" mentioned in this verse suggests assurance, not doubt. "Which hope we have as an anchor of the soul, both sure and steadfast" (Hebrews 6:19). Relativism, the absence—yes, the very denial of truth—robs men of hope. What a blessing to meet despairing people who have lost all hope and assure them that our hope in Christ holds and sustains us in the conflicts of life.

Peter's last instruction closely connects with our bearing witness of hope and assurance in Christ. "And **be ready** always to give an answer to every man that asketh you a reason of the hope that is in you with meekness and fear" (I Peter 3:15). I am a fundamentalist and unashamed of my faith and assurance in Christ. Also I am proud of most of my fellow laborers. But there are some who are proud, arrogant, uncouth, rude and by their actions bring disgrace on the name of Christ. They seem to enjoy offending people. Our message will certainly offend, and we are willing to bear the offense of the cross. But our manners, our attitudes, our disposition, and our demeanor should be characterized by humility and a great fear of offending either God or man. "A brother offended is harder to be won than a strong city: and their contentions are like the bars of a castle" (Proverbs 18:19).

## PRIMACY OF EVANGELISM
## IN II PETER

A great encouragement to evangelism and to Christian life and service appears in II Peter 1:3: "According as his divine power hath given unto us **all things** that pertain unto life and godliness, through the knowledge of him that hath called us to glory and virtue." Evangelism certainly comes within the scope of life and godliness. God has promised to give us all we need to live for Him and to serve Him. What do we need? Do we need wisdom? Do we need boldness? Do we need facility of speech? Do we need zeal? Name what you need, and God's promise is like a blank check ready to be filled out and cashed.

## NECESSITY OF REPENTANCE

In I Timothy we learned of God's willingness to save all who will come to the truth (I Timothy 2:4). Peter gives the same teaching as Paul on the subject of God's willingness to save the lost. "The Lord is not slack concerning his promise, as some men count slackness; but is longsuffering to us-ward, not willing that any should perish, but that all should come to repentance" (II Peter 3:9). Peter's use of "repentance" in this verse needs comment. Those Bible teachers who equate repentance with works are hard put to explain Peter's–or rather–the Holy Spirit's choice of words. These Bible teachers who deny repentance are well-intentioned as they are purporting to protect the doctrine of grace. But to protect one great doctrine of Scripture by denying another is not the way to go.

An old Southern Baptist Declaration of Faith has this to say on the subject of repentance:

> We believe that Repentance and Faith are sacred
> duties, and also inseparable graces, wrought in

our souls by the regenerating Spirit of God; whereby being deeply convinced of our guilt, danger, and helplessness, and of the way of salvation by Christ, we turn to God with un-feigned contrition, confession and supplication for mercy; at the same time heartily receiving the Lord Jesus Christ as our Prophet, Priest, and King, and relying on him alone as the only and all-sufficient Saviour.[1]

Contrast this sound teaching with a statement that sums up the new idea about repentance:

Any teaching that demands a change of conduct toward either God or man for salvation is to add works or human effort to faith, and this contra-dicts all Scripture and is an accursed message.[2]

In fundamental circles today there is much confusion about repentance. Ernest Reisinger in his book, *Today's Evangelism: Its Message and Methods* capsulizes the biblical teaching on repentance. Note what he says:

To set forth more explicitly what Christian Re-pentance is, it may be stated that it includes:

1. An intellectual and spiritual perception of the opposition between holiness in God and sin in man. It does not look at sin as the cause of punishment, but, abhors it, because it is vile in the sight of God and involves in heinous guilt all who are sinners.

2. It consequently includes sorrow and self-loathing, and earnest desire to escape the evil of sin. The penitent soul does not so much feel the

greatness of its danger as the greatness of it [sic] sinfulness.

3. It also includes an earnest turning to God for help and deliverance from sin, seeking pardon for guilt and aid to escape its presence.

4. It is also accompanied by deep regret because of the sins committed in the past, and by determination with God's help to avoid sin and live in holiness hereafter. The heart that was for sin and against God is now for God and against sin.[3]

The term "inseparable graces" ascribed to faith and repentance by the framers of the New Hampshire Confession of 1833 argues that one cannot exist without the other.[4] It is like one coin with two sides. One side is faith; the other side is repentance. Many lost church members have never repented, but only signed a card, giving mental assent to the truths of the gospel, and as a result fall victim to defective evangelism.

———————————

1. W.J. McGlothlin, *Baptist Confessions of Faith* (Philadelphia: American Baptist Publication Society, 1911) 304.

2. Ernest C. Reisinger, *Today's Evangelism: Its Message and Methods*, Quote is by Dr. A. Ray Stanford, from his *Handbook of Personal Evangelism*, not available to the author. (Phillipsburg, New Jersey: Craig Press, 1982) 31.

3. Ibid., 33-34.

4. Wallace, O. C. S. *What Baptists Believe: The New Hampshire Confession: An Exposition* (Nashville, Tennessee: Sunday School Board Southern Baptist Convention, 1919) 83.

# 15

# The Primacy
# of Evangelism
# in the Epistles of John
# and The Revelation

The Epistle of I John follows the Gospel of John in declaring its intended purpose: "These things have I written unto you that believe on the name of the Son of God; that ye may **know** that ye have eternal life, and that ye may believe on the name of the Son of God" (I John 5:13). The theme of the Epistle is assurance of salvation. Many professed Christians think it impossible to know for sure if one is saved. If salvation depended on us, then we would be fearful and insecure. Since it depends upon the promises of God, we can be absolutely certain.

To be effective in evangelism, the evangelist and anyone else who seeks to win people to Christ must enjoy the assurance of salvation. This assurance should engender a spirit of **humility**, **gratefulness**, and **joy** because "it is God which worketh in you both to will and to do of his good pleasure" (Philippians 2:13). But how can one be sure? Is there not a danger of presumption? Could we be deceived into a false assurance? Yes, and for the very purpose of giving divine guidelines for assurance the Epistle of I John was penned.

The devil counterfeits the works of God. He gives a counterfeit faith for real saving faith, a worldly sorrow mimicking real repentance, and he also gives a false assurance of salvation for scriptural assurance. False assurance leads to pride, self-indulgence, and self-satisfaction. True assurance has just the opposite effect of producing humility, holiness, and self-examination.

## GROUNDS FOR ASSURANCE

John, under the inspiration of the Holy Spirit, gives three grounds upon which to base our assurance: the witness of the **Word**, the witness of the **Holy Spirit**, and the witness of a **changed life**. First, let us discuss the witness of the Word. "And this is the promise that he hath promised us, even eternal life" (I John 2:25). In I John 5:11-12, the promise is clear: "And this is the record, that God hath given to us eternal life, and this life is in his Son. He that hath the Son hath life; and he that hath not the Son of God hath not life." When saving faith is exercised in believing and receiving Christ, the Holy Spirit gives the assurance as I John 5:10 says, "He that believeth on the Son of God hath the witness in himself." The personal worker gives the Word, but only the Holy Spirit can give assurance. Jesus said, "The words I speak unto you, they are spirit, and they are life" (John 6:63).

Second, the Holy Spirit testifies with our spirit that we are the children of God (Romans 8:16). I John 5:10 says, "He that believeth on the Son of God hath the witness in himself." The assurance of salvation comes to us by the indwelling Spirit. The Word gives **light**; the Holy Spirit gives **sight**. "Hereby know we that we dwell in him, and he in us, because he hath given us of his Spirit" (I John 4:13). This witness of the Spirit is hard to describe. It is intuitive; somewhat mystical but very real. If you have that witness, you will know it. It also seems reasonable to expect the fruit of the Holy Spirit in the life of one indwelt by the Spirit.

The third grounds of assurance is a changed life. Defective evangelism fails to change lives so those who dare make a changed life a basis for assurance are accused of preaching salvation by works. Legalism is the belief that a "changed life" can result in salvation. The "changed life" presented in I John is the result of salvation, not the cause of salvation. Notice some changes in the life that will give assurance. First, there is a change of **belief**. "Whosoever believeth that Jesus is the Christ is born of God: and every one that loveth him that begat loveth him also that is begotten of him" (I John 5:1). This belief results in the introduction of a new life principle, a new birth into the family of God. Second, there is a change of **allegiance**. "And hereby we do know that we know him, if we keep his commandments" (I John 2:3). This obedience comes not from outward pressure, but from an inner desire to please Him, our new Lord. A Christian does not work to be saved, but he works because he is saved. Third, there is a change of **affection**. "We love him, because he first loved us" (I John 4:19). Not only do we love our new found Lord, but we also love His children. "We know that we have passed from death unto life, because we love the brethren. He that loveth not his brother abideth in death" (I John 3:14).

Counterfeits fear examination; the genuine welcomes inspection. Both Paul and Peter exhorted Christians to examine themselves as to the genuineness of faith. "Examine yourselves, whether ye be in the faith; prove your own selves. Know ye not your own selves, how that Jesus Christ is in you, except ye be reprobates [worthless counterfeits]" (II Corinthians 13:5)? Peter said the same thing this way: "Wherefore the rather, brethren, give diligence to make your calling and election sure: for if ye do these things, ye shall never fall" (II Peter 1:10). Christians are not perfect, but they are different. In I John 3:10, the litmus test of being a true Christian is this: "In this the children of God are manifest, and the children of the devil: whosoever doeth not righteousness is not of God, neither he that loveth not his brother." Let us not be satisfied with an evangelism that produces converts that fail the litmus test of true faith.

## ASSISTING EVANGELISTS

In III John there is a passage that speaks to the local church as to its responsibilities to traveling evangelists. "Beloved, thou doest faithfully whatsoever thou doest to the brethren, and to strangers" (III John 5). In the early church, small groups itinerated from place to place preaching the gospel. For the most part, these preachers were dependent upon the local churches and believers for their sustenance and support. The assembly of which Gaius was the elder had been good to these itinerant preachers and John is commending him and the church. "Which [the traveling preachers] have borne witness of thy charity before the church" (III John 6). John the Apostle had heard from these men of the kindness of Gaius and the church of which he was elder and he is using this as an occasion to praise and to exhort. "Whom if thou bring forward on their journey after a godly sort, thou shalt do well" (III John 6).

Local churches and individual believers can be a great blessing to evangelists and missionaries by helping them in practical ways. III John 7 explains why the church has this responsibility. "Because that for his name's sake [the Lord Jesus Christ] they went forth [to preach the gospel], taking nothing of the Gentiles." These men had cast themselves upon God and upon His people and were not depending upon the unsaved to support them. John closes this passage by reminding God's people to receive preachers of the gospel and in receiving them and caring for their present and future needs they would be fellow helpers in spreading the truth. (III John 8). Dr. Charles Kempf has authored a book, *Let's Have An Evangelist,* published by Unusual Publications, which instructs churches on how to take care of evangelists that minister in churches.[1]

## PRIMACY OF EVANGELISM
## IN THE BOOK OF REVELATION

A look at a few references to evangelism in the Book of

the Revelation will conclude our study of evangelism in the New Testament. Our Lord was a faithful shepherd and a great teacher. Revelation 1:5 calls Jesus Christ the **faithful witness**. A faithful shepherd will not send his sheep where he himself is unwilling to go. A good teacher will not command his pupils to do what he himself is not willing to do. Our Lord, being a faithful witness, gave us a great example to follow. Every Christian, not just pastors and Christian workers, are to be witnesses.

## IMPORTANCE OF WITNESSING

In Acts 1:8 we see the **command** to witness. "Ye shall receive power, after that the Holy Ghost is come upon you: and ye shall be witnesses unto me." Witnessing is an integral part of evangelism. Where there is no witness, there will be no evangelism; where there is a witness, evangelism will be present. Neglecting our witnessing responsibilities is sin. We need to confess and forsake the sin of failing to be a witness for our Lord.

The **impact** of witnessing must be recognized. The early church impacted the Roman Empire by joyful, fearless, and consistent witnessing of their newly found faith and newly found Lord. Let me give an example from my ministry in Bangladesh. Two Tipperah tribesmen who had come to know and love the Lord stopped in a heathen village to spend the night. As they sat around the fire talking with the headman and his friends, one of them mentioned that he was no longer afraid to die. And besides that he was no longer afraid of the dark. Death and darkness terrified these heathen villagers, and they were eager to know how this could be so. The Tipperah Christian joyfully spoke of his newly found Savior who promised a home in heaven to those who truly believe. He also told them about the Holy Spirit that lived in him who was greater than the evil spirits that lived in the darkness. That witness resulted in Oncherai Tipperah, a faithful evangelist and me being invited to visit this village. We did visit and the majority of the village trusted Christ and built a "Jesus House" (church) that continues to this day to worship and serve the Lord Jesus Christ.

As I look back over my life, I can remember the people who witnessed to me. Even though I resisted their witness and laughed it off, an impression was made. These people who witnessed to me contributed to my being saved. Your witness to someone may be the only witness they will ever have. The people who receive your witness will never forget the fact that you were willing to share with them. Never minimize the power and potential of a witness for Christ. We can witness and not win anyone, but we can never win anyone without witnessing. The first step in bringing a person from no faith to mature faith in Christ is a witness.

Two of the fastest growing cults in the world, Jehovah's Witnesses and Mormons, teach us the impact of witnessing. Each of these cults have odious doctrines that defy the imagination. But in spite of persecution, harassment, and contempt, they continue to grow. Their faithful witness, their willingness to share, and their conviction that what they teach is true, wins people over. I do not like their doctrines and their methods, but I am impressed with their leaders' ability to instill in their members the desire and the skill to witness.

## LAST COMMAND

The Church at Ephesus speaks to me about evangelism or shall I say the lack of evangelism. The Lord of the Church commended the Ephesians for the good works they were doing. But He levels a charge against them: "Nevertheless I have somewhat against thee, because thou hast left thy first love" (Revelation 2:4). True evangelism flows out of a fervent love for the Lord. In the next verse, He orders them to remember and to repent. They were to remember from whence they were fallen and to repent and to do the first works. The first works were His last command: "ye shall be witnesses unto me." Failure to do the first works (witnessing) resulted in the removal of the church's candlestick, i.e., the love, the power, and the glory of the Lord in their midst. Churches that neglect evangelism will suffer the loss of their candlestick.

The Church of Philadelphia received no rebuke from the Lord. "I know thy works: behold, I have set before thee an open door, and no man can shut it: for thou hast a little strength, and hast kept my word, and hast not denied my name" (Revelation 3:8). The statement "hast kept my word" says volumes about this Church. This was an obedient church that marched through open doors with the Word of God. They were a missionary, evangelistic church. Though not strong in the eyes of the world, they were faithful to the command of Christ to evangelize. The promise of Christ given to them because of their faithfulness should encourage all in our day who are seeking to emulate this Church of Philadelphia. "Because thou hast kept the word of my patience, I also will keep thee from the hour of temptation [testing], which shall come upon all the world, to try them that dwell upon the earth" (Revelation 3:10). I take the "hour of temptation" to be the Great Tribulation which means we will be delivered from that terrible event.

The primacy of evangelism, the Word of God, and the Second Coming of Christ, three important subjects, receive attention just before the Bible closes. Concerning the Second Coming, we see a promise and a prayer. The Lord affirms His coming: "Surely I come quickly" (Revelation 22:20). John welcomes His coming: "Even so, come, Lord Jesus" (Revelation 22:20). A terrible curse rests upon any man, church, or organization that dares to add to or subtract from God's Word: "If any man shall add unto these things, God shall add unto him the plagues that are written in this book: And if any man shall take away from the words of the book of this prophecy, God shall take away his part of out the book of life, and out of the holy city, and from the things which are written in this book" (Revelation 22:18-19).

We can learn from this last invitation in the Bible. First, both the Holy Spirit and the bride (church) extend the invitation to come. "And the Spirit and the bride say, Come" (Revelation

22:17). We see divine-human cooperation. The Spirit joins with the church members in gladly issuing that sweet word to unworthy sinners—come. Then individual believers who have heard (obeyed) the invitation are urged to join the task of inviting sinners to come. "And let him that heareth say, Come" (Revelation 22:17). The very last statement in the Bible concerning this great subject of evangelism emphasizes human responsibility. "And whosoever will, let him take the water of life freely" (Revelation 22:17).

---

1. Charles A. Kempf, *Let's Have an Evangelist! Preparing Your Church for Revival* (Greenville, South Carolina: Unusual Publications, 1987) 1-4.

# A
# Practical
# Perspective
# of
# Evangelism

"And [they] so spake, that a great multitude both of Jews and also of the Greeks believed"(Acts 14:1).

# 16

## Persons
## Involved
## in Evangelism

Evangelism is extremely personal. People are born into this world one at a time. Likewise, people are born into the kingdom of God one at a time. Every child has a father and a mother. Paul reminded the Corinthian believers that he was their spiritual father: "For though ye have ten thousand instructors in Christ, yet have ye not many fathers: for in Christ Jesus I have begotten you through the gospel" (I Corinthians 4:15). Everyone reading this sentence who is saved can point to someone that led him or her to Christ, either directly or indirectly. I am so thankful for Mr. Johnny Harper, a machinist by trade, but a man who loved his Bible and His Lord. When I was desperate to have my sins forgiven, Johnny Harper was there. My soul still thrills as I remember how he opened his large Bible and explained to me salvation by grace through faith (Ephesians 2:8-9). He was the human instrument the Holy Spirit used to bring me to faith in Christ.

Evangelists and all that join with them in this great endeavor of spreading the gospel are in the people business. In every instance of evangelism, three persons are present: the person of the Holy Spirit, the person of the soul-winner, and the person of the sinner. In this chapter we want to look at these three important persons in evangelism.

The Holy Spirit is not our Savior in any sense of the word, but without His divine operations the atoning virtues of the death of Christ, the justifying, and the sanctifying power of a risen Christ would not be ours. Effectiveness in evangelism depends upon the presence and power of the Holy Spirit. Therefore, we need to know how the Holy Spirit works in the heart of the sinner, in the heart of the new believer, and in the heart of the soul-winner.

The initial work of the Holy Spirit in the heart of the sinner is **conviction** of sin, i.e., causing the sinner to see his need of salvation. In John 16:7-9, our Lord promised the coming of the Holy Spirit and described His work in evangelism. "But if I depart, I will send him unto you, And when he is come [into you], he will reprove [convict] the world of sin, and of righteousness, and of judgment." In convicting men of sin, the Holy Spirit uses the man and woman of God who gives the sinner the Word of God. Our responsibility is to give the message of the gospel; the Holy Spirit alone can do the convicting of sin. Without the convicting work of the Holy Spirit, the sinner feels no need for Christ; hence he rejects the message and often the messenger. Ah, but when the Holy Spirit convicts of sin and shows the sinner his great need of salvation, then the guilty sinner turns imploringly to Christ to be saved.

Along with convicting men of their sin, the Holy Spirit also bears testimony to the truth of Christ. "But when the Comforter [Holy Spirit] is come, whom I will send unto you from the Father, even the Spirit of truth . . . he shall testify of me: And ye also shall bear witness" (John 15:26-27). Once again we see the Holy Spirit and the soul-winner working together in reaching men for Christ. All that we can do is preach to the ears of people. The message will not be fruitful unless the Spirit at the same time preaches to their hearts. Man can and does preach to the ears of people, but he cannot preach to their hearts. The Spirit does not preach to the ears of people, but He can and does preach to their hearts. In other words there is a co-dependency in witnessing: the Holy Spirit depends upon us to preach to the ears and we depend upon Him to preach to the hearts. So we desperately need the Holy Spirit, and the Holy Spirit has chosen to need us. Jesus said, "For without me ye can do nothing" (John 15:5). Soul-winning is a joint venture: a divine-human endeavor of bringing men into a right relationship with God.

The third work of the Holy Spirit in the life of a sinner is regeneration. Man has nothing to do with this divine work. Two agencies regenerate the sinner: the water and the Spirit. "Except a man be born of water [Word of God] and of the Spirit, he cannot enter into the kingdom of God" (John 3:5). The means whereby the sinner is regenerated or born of God is faith in Christ. "Whosoever believeth that Jesus is the Christ is born of God" (I John 5:1). This new birth results in a new creation "Therefore if any man be in Christ, he is a new creature" (II Corinthians 5:17) and the impartation of the divine nature (II Peter 1:4). A belief in Christ that fails to impart a new life and a new nature (desires) is not saving faith.

Not only does the Holy Spirit convict, but He also bears His sacred and powerful testimony in the heart and conscience. Responding to faith, which is also the gift of God "Not of works, lest any man should boast" (Ephesians 2:9), the Holy Spirit regenerates the believing sinner, giving a new life and a new nature. But that is not all. The Holy Spirit **indwells** the new believer. "Now if any man have not the Spirit of Christ, he is none of his" (Romans 8:9). We learned in our definition of evangelism that the work does not stop at conversion but continues on through life. Likewise, the Holy Spirit continues His work in the life of the believer.

The believer in Christ has the assurance that the Holy Spirit will give guidance (Romans 8:14), victory (I John 5:4), and power in service (Acts 1:8). For evangelism to be successful, the one evangelized must become an evangelist, the soul won must become a soul-winner, and the disciple must become a discipler. Since the person and work of the Holy Spirit is so vital in the work of evangelism, only the haughty, the ignorant, or the careless would dare to engage in this divine work without

His presence and power.

## THE SOUL-WINNER

I hesitate to use the term "soul-winner" because it gives the impression that man is doing the winning. Nothing could be further from the truth. This does not mean that human instrumentality is inconsequential. It is absolutely essential. However, God does not place upon us the responsibility of saving people, but He does place upon us the duty of witnessing and doing our human best to influence people for God. When man believes he can "win souls," there is no end to the tricks, the pressure, the persuasion, the inducements offered to people to "decide for Christ." Eugene Myers Harrison, in his excellent book, *How to Win Souls,* makes a good statement:

> To 'make disciples of all nations,' or even to win one soul to Christ, is a supernatural assignment which demands supernatural equipment. Without it, the work is impossible. 'Apart from Me ye can do nothing,' said our Lord. It is possible to get people to 'make decisions' and 'join the church' by the use of salesmanship techniques or other carnal methods, but the person who, by any such method, endeavors to lead a lost soul into the holy experience of redemption is doomed to failure. Methods of approach and of dealing with different types of individuals may be of tremendous help but they are worse than useless unless the soul winner himself is spiritually prepared and supernaturally equipped. . . . What the soul winner *is* in his spiritual life and relationship to God, is much more significant than anything he may say or any method he may use.[1]

For men to function in various fields of service, they must meet certain qualifications. If you were to go a surgeon for a serious operation, you would want to know before hand that the man is experienced and qualified. Let us look at some of the qualifications needed in the lives of those who would point others to the Savior. First, he must have experienced new life in Christ. Evangelism is spiritual reproduction. To reproduce physically requires life and a measure of health. Spurgeon said, "God will not use dead tools for working living miracles."[2] Those who would minister life to others must first receive that life themselves.

The life of the soul-winner must be characterized by cleanness and wholesomeness. People are watching and will gleefully point out any defect they find in the life of Christ's servant. Worldliness, indiscreet actions, an uncontrolled tongue, and secret sins clog the power-ducts from God. Indulgence in worldly pleasures, wrong attitudes, and questionable behavior short circuits our effectiveness. "Be ye clean, that bear the vessels of the LORD" (Isaiah 52:11). Jesus was aware of the importance of a good testimony when He said: "Let your light so shine before men, that they may see your good works, and glorify your Father which is in heaven" (Matthew 5:16).

Pointing lost souls to Jesus Christ is the highest and holiest business known to man. To succeed in this holy business requires spiritual preparation. George Jaffray, Jr. speaks of superficial preparation in his book, *Explosive Evangelism:*

> Lack of proper training is no small reason for the failure of personal evangelism. Almost everyone has at one time or another come across a Christian leader who has advocated the trial and error approach. The argument for this goes as follows: All Christians are witnesses. They cannot help but be witnesses if they are walking in fellowship with the Lord. A person cannot be a Christian himself without knowing the Gospel message.

Therefore, all Christians are capable of giving the message to someone else. . . . Most Christians will have an unsuppressible fear to try to lead someone to Christ unprepared; it is holy ground that they stand on, and they fear to dishonor Christ by what they say and that they may harm the one to whom they speak . . . . Christians are witnesses, it is true, but that does not make them qualified in personal evangelism.[3]

## PRINCIPLES OF PERSONAL EVANGELISM

The first principle of personal evangelism to be considered concerns the fitness of the worker. Jesus said in Matthew 10:16, "Behold, I send you forth as sheep in the midst of wolves: be ye therefore wise as serpents, and harmless as doves." There is a bad world out there and people who go with the gospel must be wise and brave. Those in places of leadership must first go into the harvest themselves and then work to prepare others to go into the harvest fields who are spiritually prepared. John Mark went before he was ready and turned back (Acts 13:13). Under the tutelage of Peter, Mark developed and became profitable in the work of the Lord (II Timothy 4:11). Severe spiritual harm to both the sinner and would be soul-winner can result from lack of spiritual preparation.

Three traits will be found in the life of a soul-winner: conviction, compassion, and courage.

The realization that, apart from Christ, men are hopelessly and eternally lost was a powerful motivation in the lives of all the great soul winners of history. More than once the students in the geography class saw tears rolling down the cheeks of their cobbler-teacher, William Carey, as he pointed to the map he made of left-over pieces of leather and exclaimed, 'Many millions of immortal souls live here, and there, and they are *lost*, knowing nothing of our Saviour.'[4]

L. R. Scarborough writes challenging words about compassion:

A compassionless Christianity drifts into ceremonialism and formalism and dries up the fountains of life and causes the world to commit spiritual suicide. A compassionate leadership in the Christian movements of the world is now our greatest need. Every niche of this lost world needs the ministry of a fired soul, burning and shining, blood-hot with the zeal and conviction of a conquering Gospel. Spiritual dry rot is worse than the plagues of Egypt, the simoons of a thousand Saharas, to the churches of Jesus Christ throughout the world. Many a minister is in a treadmill, marking time, drying up, living a *professional life,* without power, not earning his salt because he has no passion for God or souls and no power for effective service. May our God kindle holy fires of evangelism in all churches and pulpits where such is needed.[5]

Courage is not the absence of fear. Brave men fear but they refuse to let fear stop them. The soul-winner's courage is in the Lord. Evil spiritual forces are at work in our land (Psalm 55:8). Those who go out to preach the gospel can expect to be challenged by evil forces. We are no match for the weakest demon. But if we go prayerfully, depending upon the Holy Spirit, claiming the blood of Christ, and for the purpose of preaching the gospel to win souls, and to glorify God, the devil himself cannot stop us. If you believe that say, Amen.

The presence of courage does not mean the lack of tact. All the common sense, kindness, and good judgment one has should be brought into play in personal and public evangelism. God forbid that our lack of social graces and decorum should turn people away from the gospel. We need to learn all we can about the mindset of the unsaved and unchurched to help us gain a hearing. I read with profit *Inside the Mind of Unchurched Harry and Mary*[6], a book by Lee Strobel. Yet a sincere love for Christ and the unsaved will be the best safeguards against tactlessness. Honest mistakes are over-looked if there is unmistakable love and concern. The matter of tact can be summed up by I Corinthians 13:5, Charity "doth not behave itself unseemly."

The last two qualifications I will mention are determination and dedication to soul-winning. I like what Dr. Roland Leavell said about soul-winning:

> Personal soul-winners do not happen automatically. Christians do not become personal evangelists by birth, by accident, or by assuming a church position. Soul-winners are inspired by the Holy Spirit. They are trained in the church. They gain experience by self-discipline within their own wills, directing them in personal efforts to win souls. Christ paid the price of taking a personal interest in the needs of human beings. Christians must pay the price of purpose, consecration, and self-discipline in order to win souls. One must engage in rigid self-discipline to become a soul-winner.[7]

As I travel among the churches, now and then, men and women are found that are dedicated to the task of reaching out with the gospel. In one church, I met a retired couple who have dedicated one day a week to personal evangelism. They go from door to door giving the gospel to all who will receive their witness. We often dedicate ourselves to good things such as prayer, Bible study, church attendance and other wholesome activities and at the same time fail to dedicate ourselves to the main thing, evangelism.

## THE SINNER

In a previous chapter the subject of the sinner's standing before God has been dealt with. In our study of evangelism in the New Testament, we saw Christ dealing with different types of sinners such as Nicodemus, the woman of Samaria, and Zacchaeus. In The Acts of the Apostles, the five conversion experiences recorded happened to people of diverse backgrounds. As we consider the person of the sinner, we will look at people with various needs in our present society.

Eugene Myers Harrison has some wise words about the different types of unsaved people:

> All sinners are lost but all sinners do not have the same basic attitude or problem, hence all cannot be dealt with in the same manner. A variety of spiritual states calls for a variety of methods. That this is true is indicated by a study of the soul-winning incidents in the life of our Lord and confirmed by the experience of all those who deal with souls today. The technique used in fishing for perch would never catch trout and a still different technique must be used in catching whales. Similarly, your methods as a soul winner must be determined by the type of human fish you are trying to land.[8]

Dr. Harrison goes on to list eight different categories of sinners:

1. The concerned, seeking sinner.

2. The self-righteous person.
3. The indifferent person.
4. The religious person.
5. The person with intellectual difficulties.
6. The willful, antagonistic sinner.
7. Roman Catholics.
8. Cult followers.[9]

His book was published in 1952, over forty years ago, so there are new categories of sinners today that were unknown in his day.

Great changes have revolutionized religious thinking in America and in Europe. The process of secularization has done its worst. All around us the foundations have been destroyed (Psalm 11:3). Fundamental Christians that venture out to share their faith will find five belief systems competing for the souls of men.

First there is monism. Many people in our churches have never heard the word nor have any idea what it might be though it is everywhere about them. It is the philosophical position underlying both Hinduism and Buddhism. It is sweeping America and Canada in the form of the New Age Movement. In their reaction against crass materialism, many people, especially the wealthy and famous, find excitement and liberation in its precepts. What makes it exciting and liberating? Several things. It categorically rejects the materialistic philosophy and celebrates personhood and spirituality. Monism views all as one and rejoices in unity. According to this philosophy, good and evil, truth and falsehood, divine and human are all one. This illogical reasoning transcends truth and nullifies the law of non-contradiction. Monists gain much comfort by believing all are right and no one is wrong. However, only those who believe in Jesus Christ as Lord and Savior are set free by the truth (John 8:32).

Religious humanism has become the religion of the sophisticated, the liberated, and the well-educated. It is, to all intents and purposes, the worship of mankind by man. A humanist does not believe in God, heaven, or hell. This life is all there is. All mankind's problems have been caused by man and can be solved by man. In spite of much evidence contrary to the fact they continue to have great faith in man and are highly optimistic that things will get better. Evolution and atheism are the basic tenets of humanism.

The "me" generation worships at the shrine of narcissism, the preoccupation with self. The name comes from Narcissus, a character in Greek mythology who fell in love with himself and as a result could not love anyone else. He saw his reflection in the water, and trying to embrace himself, he fell in and drowned. So many in our day are consumed with themselves, their pleasure, their comfort that they find it impossible to love anyone else. People under this sinful influence are preoccupied with their private world of self-reliance, self-love, self-fulfillment. Other people are not to be served but manipulated. It hates authentic Christianity which calls for renunciation of self and living for others. As poetic justice would have it, Narcissism starts with optimism and ends in despair. Christianity, on the other hand, begins with loss and ends with great gain.

## HONEST CONFESSION

Worldly wise people, young and old, claim agnosticism as their creed. This is the belief that it is impossible to know God. Humanistic philosophers use the ploy that the Infinite cannot be known by the finite. However, they willfully overlook the fact that the Infinite revealed Himself in the person of His Son Jesus Christ. The willfulness of their ignorance and sin reveals itself in the writing of Aldous Huxley's *Ends & Means* where he writes:

I had motives for not wanting the world to have
a meaning; consequently assumed that it had
none, and was able without any difficulty to find

satisfying reasons for this assumption. . . . The philosopher who finds no meaning in the world is not concerned exclusively with a problem in pure metaphysics. He is also concerned to prove that there is no valid reason why he personally should not do as he wants to do, or why his friends should not seize political power and govern in the way that they find most advantageous to themselves. . . . For myself as, no doubt, for most of my contemporaries, the philosophy of meaninglessness was essentially an instrument of liberation . . . . Sexual (and). . . . Political . . . .[10]

Huxley told the truth one time in his life. A whole generation of young people have been under the spell of these deceivers. Let us pray that God will raise up servants of His that will be able to minister to those who have been blinded by agnosticism.

The last sinful thought system we will discuss is pragmatism. The idea behind this system is that actions are more important than words. Success is more important than truth. It judges truth, instead of letting truth judge it. "For truth is fallen in the street, and equity cannot enter" (Isaiah 59:14). Their question is not so much "Is it true?" but "Does it work?" Relevance takes priority over truth and success exceeds faithfulness in importance. This philosophy has invaded our churches. Doctrinal teaching which exalts Christ is being replaced by self-fulfillment teaching.

Those are the five faces of modern unbelief. Of course, most of these have not reached the common man as yet. But as the media, the schools, and the universities spew out these false doctrines, more and more people will come under their evil influence. There are many more sinful lifestyles and godless pathways luring people away from God and the Bible. Unless we want to keep preaching just to the choir, it is incumbent that we prepare ourselves to do battle with these powerfi l forces of unbelief. The one blessing that none of these "isms" can give is a personal relationship with the Creator of this universe through Jesus Christ His Son.

## POWER OF THE GOSPEL

But we need to put things in the proper perspective. Men's hearts are failing for fear. Many are fed up and disappointed with hedonism, the belief that life's greatest blessing is pleasure and comfort. Those with eyes willing to see will see through the deception of these man made philosophies. When we look out over this world of lost sinners, it is encouraging to hear Christ's true assessment of the situation: "The harvest truly is plenteous, but the laborers are few" (Matthew 9:37). In another place he said the fields are white unto harvest (John 4:35). The harvest speaks of sinners who need to be saved and the whitened harvest indicates sinners are ready to be saved. Today nothing is wrong with the harvest. The trouble lies with the harvesters.

With God there are no hard cases. "He is able also to save them to the uttermost that come unto God by Him" (Hebrews 7:25). To encourage our hearts in reaching out to sinners who seem most unlikely to respond, let me tell of God bringing Bob to Himself. In the course of my duties as a missionary in Bangladesh, I met a handsome, single American engineer named Bob. His dad was a rancher out West and Bob had seldom attended church. I manifested an interest in Bob by inviting him to our home for meals and to our English services. We developed a good relationship, and since Bob was an avid reader, I began lending him books on Christian apologetics. From time to time, I and other missionaries would urge Bob to trust Christ and be saved. Bob kept saying he was not ready. He faithfully attended the English worship services and became interested in our ministry of spreading the gospel and planting a church. After about six months, Bob knelt by his bed and received Christ as his Lord and Savior.

With great enthusiasm Bob set out to live the Christian life. Out went the "Playboy" magazines, etc., and he sought every opportunity to serve and help us. Bob was a new creature in Christ (II Corinthians 5:17). I had developed a series of lessons to prepare new believers for baptism and church membership. Bob had his secretary type these notes and bound them in a book entitled, *What Every Christian Should Know and Do.* On completion of our study with Bob, he was baptized. Several hundred people gathered to witness Bob's baptism. Many of these people had never before seen a baptism. Bob gave a glowing testimony of new life in Christ and I carefully explained to the crowd the meaning of baptism.

Next, another missionary and I had regular studies with Bob teaching him Old and New Testament survey. Bob was independently wealthy so he decided to take a leave and attend Piedmont Bible College for a year. On arriving home, Bob led his mother and sister to the Lord. His mom was baptized and joined an independent Baptist church near her home. The church honored Bob's baptism and received him into their membership. Bob serves today as an engineer in Pakistan and to the best of our knowledge still loves the Lord.

The gospel works. For the gospel to work there must be the interplay of the Holy Spirit, the soul-winner, and the sinner. Not everyone we seek to win will respond like Bob. I could tell you of others in whom I invested much time and effort that did not come to know and love the Lord. In the instance above, several practical lessons should be noted. First, the matter of friendship is vital. Bob became our friend before he became God's friend. Second, our testimony will attract or repel. Bob saw in our family and the other missionary families a dimension he had never before seen. Third, people must hear the message. Information precedes faith. "So then faith cometh by hearing, and hearing by the word of God" (Romans 10:17). Bob was urged to act on the truths he was learning. This is exhortation. Babies need teaching, and babes in Christ need instruction. To see our spiritual children receiving the teaching of the Word brings great joy to the heart of the soul-winner. "I have no greater joy than to hear that my children walk in truth" (III John 4).

1. Eugene Myers Harrison, *How to Win Souls: A Manual of Personal Evangelism* (Wheaton: Van Kampen Press, 1952) 10.

2. Ibid., 11.

3. George R. Jaffray, Jr., *Explosive Evangelism* (MacDill Air Force Base, Florida: Tyndale Bible Society, 1972) 29-30.

4. Harrison, 13.

5. L. R. Scarborough, *With Christ After the Lost: A Search for Souls* (Nashville: Sunday School Board, Southern Baptist Convention, 1919) 40.

6. Lee Strobel, *Inside the Mind of Unchurched Harry & Mary: How to Reach Friends and Family Who Avoid God and the Church* (Grand Rapids: Zondervan Publishing House).

7. Leavell, 184.

8. Harrison, 54.

9. Ibid.

10. Aldous Huxley, *Ends & Means: An Inquiry into the Nature of Ideals and into the Methods Employed for Their Realization* (New York: Harper & Brothers Publishers, 1937) 312, 315-316.

# 17

# The Local Church
# and Evangelism

Evangelism cannot be separated from the local church. The Church of Jerusalem failed to obey the command to evangelize the world, and as a result, the torch of world evangelism passed to the Church of Antioch. On that momentous day when the leaders of the Church of Antioch gathered to pray, the Holy Spirit initiated a new thrust in world evangelism (Acts 13:1-3).

## LOCAL CHURCH
## MISSIONARY HEADQUARTERS

Therefore, I believe we can say that world evangelism was conceived in the local church. The local church is missionary headquarters. Mission boards certainly have their place when they serve the local church in facilitating the work of world evangelism. I would not be so narrow as to disregard the fine work many parachurch organizations have accomplished. But we must keep in mind that local churches are headquarters for evangelism both at home and abroad.

The local church as headquarters is a place of vision, action, and administration working to accomplish a predetermined goal: world evangelism. Since the local church has been divinely appointed (Matthew 16:18) by Jesus Christ as headquarters, the failure or success of evangelizing this planet rests with the local church. Only local churches can supply the three essential ingredients necessary for world evangelism. Parachurch organizations contribute, but these man-made organizations are here today and gone tomorrow. They flourish for a few years and then vanish or lose their intended purpose. The local church has been around since the day of Pentecost and will be alive and well until the Rapture.

The first ingredients supplied by the local church are men (and women). Without **personnel** the work of world evangelism would grind to a halt. Where do the workers for the harvest come from? They come from local churches. Many of these men and women go to Bible colleges, and they pass through these institutions, yet they come from local churches.

Second, local churches supply money for world evangelism. Without *materiel* (French word meaning all that is necessary to fight a war) the progress to evangelize the world is hindered. And where is this money to come from? It comes from the pockets of men and women in the churches that love God, love souls, and love evangelists and missionaries.

Third, the church supplies the motivation to keep moving ahead with the gospel. Without spiritual **morale**, men and women will not go forth, funds will not be available, and the dry rot of discouragement will settle over the church like a dark cloud. Where is this spiritual impetus to be found? Local churches is the answer.

Not only was world evangelism conceived in the local church, but we find that it was commanded by the Holy Spirit: "Separate me Barnabas and Saul for the work whereunto I have called them" (Acts 13:2). To discover what the "work" to which they were called is, it is necessary to study their ministry. Church planting evangelism was that work. Everywhere Paul went he left a functioning local church. We see his procedure of church planting evangelism in Acts 14:21-23. Local churches are points of light destined to shine the light of the gospel in their immediate area and through their missionaries spread that light afar.

This new thrust of reaching around the world with the gospel was conceived in the local church, was commanded by the Holy Spirit, and commenced as Paul and Barnabas and the

Church of Antioch obeyed. Some would try to tell us that the day of the missionary evangelist is over. No, no. Many things do change. Fashions change, methods change, emphases change, strategies change, but the command has not changed, the need of the world has not changed, the problem of man has not changed, and the only solution to solve man's problem has not changed.

## COMMANDER IN CHIEF
## OF MISSIONS

Throughout the history of the Church, the Holy Spirit has been calling men and women to do exploits for their God and conquer new territory for their King. God the Holy Spirit, commander in chief of missionary operations, has not changed or rescinded His program. He is still calling men and women to serve Him as ambassadors of Christ, as servants of God, and as stewards of the mystery of the gospel. Some would try to tell us that the missionary evangelist is replaceable. By what? Radio, television, videos, cassettes, tracts, books, bill-boards, gospel recordings, etc., is their reply. All these things are useful tools and good and proper in their place and order. But there is no substitute for God-called, gospel preaching, church planting, soul-winning, disciple-building missionaries. When a substitute is found for women to have babies, maybe a substitute will be found for missionary church planters to plant churches.

The emphasis the New Testament places upon prayer should teach us the importance of this duty and privilege. We are seeing that the modern missionary movement, which began in the Church of Antioch, was conceived in a local church, was commanded by the Holy Spirit, and was commenced as Paul and Barnabas sailed away to Cyprus. Note also that this divine initiative was covered by prayer. The leaders were fasting and praying when the summons of the Holy Spirit came to Paul and Barnabas. Again, the Church is fasting and praying as it lays hands on the first two missionaries and sends them forth to preach the gospel, to persuade sinners, and to plant churches. For fruitful missionary work, the entire mission must be covered and bathed in prayer. A prayerless endeavor is a powerless endeavor doomed to failure and disappointment. Lord, teach us to pray.

## CASE FOR THE LOCAL CHURCH

In our society, a vocal and powerful minority of religious humanists resent the Church of Jesus Christ and, if they had their way, would close every church, confiscate every Bible, and incarcerate every preacher. As in Bosnia an "ethnic cleansing" is under way, so in America a "religious cleansing" exists that puts our religious and moral values at risk. The media, the courts, and the entertainment industry take great delight in harassing and vilifying those who live godly in Christ Jesus (II Timothy 3:12).

In Matthew 16:18, our Lord Jesus Christ served notice on these enemies of the gospel that seek to destroy His church: "I will build my church; and the gates of hell shall not prevail against it." In this brief statement our Lord made a proclamation as to the foundation of the Church: "Upon this rock I will build my church." The rock is not Peter; the rock is not the Pope; the rock is not any man; the rock is Jesus Christ. Jesus used a play on words, and a mere cursory reading may lead some to conclude that Peter is the rock. Jesus said, "You are Peter [*petros*, which means a little rock], and upon this rock [*petra*, which means a massive rock] I will build my church." No, the Church is not built upon Peter, but upon Jesus Christ, the Son of God. "Other foundation can no man lay than that is laid, which is Jesus Christ" (I Corinthians 3:11). The Church's foundation is sure because it is none other than Jesus Christ Himself.

Next, Christ gives a promise as to the formation of the Church: "I will build my church." Praise the Lord that the formation of the Church does not depend upon frail men and women like us. Rather it depends upon Him who said, "Fear not;

I am the first and the last: I am he that liveth, and was dead; and, behold, I am alive for evermore, Amen; and have the keys of hell and of death" (Revelation 1:17-18). To be sure, men and women are co-laborers, and we cannot deny the human element, but He will build His Church. The responsibility is on Him. Since He promised it, the formation of the Church is sure.

We have every reason to be optimistic. Did not He give a prophecy concerning the **future** of His Church: "The gates of hell shall not prevail against it." Many have a mental picture of the devil and the forces of evil breaking down the doors of the Church. They see the Church as a fort to be protected. No, that is not the picture at all. Jesus is saying that the gates of hell, the headquarters of evil, will not be able to withstand the power of the Church. The "gates of hell" will not prevail but will fail. Emperors and dictators, philosophers and educators, and theologians and preachers have done their worst to destroy the Church, but the Church prevails, and it will prevail.

Have you ever thought what a grand society the Church is? How lonely and impoverished our lives would be without it! The local church is a nursery for new born babes (I Peter 2:1-2), a primary school for young believers (II Peter 3:18), a spiritual hospital for sin sick sinners and weak saints (Galatians 6:1), a social center for brothers and sisters in Christ (Acts 2:42), a hallowed shrine for adoring saints who worship God in spirit and in truth (John 4:24), a training center for Christian soldiers (Ephesians 4:11-13), and a headquarters for evangelizing and discipling at home and abroad (Matthew 28:19-20).

## FUNCTION OF THE CHURCH

What is the function of the Church? Titus 2:14 gives a broad hint as to the purpose: "Who gave himself for us [the church], that he might redeem us from all iniquity, and purify unto himself a peculiar people, zealous of good works." From this we learn that the Church will be zealous of good works. The Church will be a force for good and not for evil. In describing the function of the Church, I will use the pastoral metaphor: Jesus, the chief shepherd; the pastor, the undershepherd; the sheep, the saved church members; and the foal, representing the local church.

In discussing the function of the Church let us see first the **general** function. The general function of the Church is to develop human potential for the glory of God and for the good of mankind. Secular historians deny it or at least seek to minimize it, yet the Church has had great influence in world affairs. That is not surprising because Jesus said, "Ye are the salt of the earth....Ye are the light of the world" (Matthew 5:13-14). The Church has been a powerful influence for good both in England in the nineteenth century and America in the twentieth century. Listen to what a noted historian, H. W. V. Temperley said in the *The Cambridge Modern History*:

> The earlier half of the eighteenth century in England was an age of materialism, a period of dim ideals and *expiring hopes:* before the middle of the century its character was transformed; there appeared a movement headed by a mighty leader, who brought forth water from the rocks to make a barren land live again.[1]

When the night was cold and dark, the Wesleys and Whitefield built fires of evangelism. The power of the gospel saved England. Across the English Channel, the lack of the gospel catapulted France into the bloody, godless French Revolution.

What has made America the great nation she is? Ride through the countryside and see old deserted churches. At one time those churches were aflame with revival. The men and women who worshiped in these churches made America great. They taught their children to work, to respect authority, to love their country, and to serve their God.

Alexander deToqueville, a French philosopher, came looking for the secret of America's greatness in the early 1900's.

After a thorough investigation of its farms, factories, and universities, he visited its churches. His conclusion:

> I sought for the greatness and genius of America in her commodious harbours and her ample rivers —and it was not there . . . in her fertile fields and boundless forests—and it was not there . . . in her rich mines and her vast commerce—and it was not there . . . and in her democratic Congress and her matchless Constitution—and it was not there. Not until I went into the churches of America and heard her pulpits flame with righteousness did I understand the secret of her genius and power. America is great because she is good, and if America ever ceases to be good, America will cease to be great.[2]

But what about the **particular** function of the Church? Using the pastoral metaphor, we notice that the first function of the Church is to find sinful sheep. In the Bible, people are equated with sheep which we earlier referred to as very stupid animals that tend to self destruct: "All we like sheep have gone astray; we have turned every one to his own way" (Isaiah 53:6). People are lost, and Jesus in simple terms explained the purpose of His coming: "to save that which was lost" (Luke 19:10).

The Church functions as found sheep looking for lost sheep–saved sheep seeking to reach unsaved sheep. The Church in America is in trouble. We like to blame the Church's weakness on various scapegoats such as Rock music, television, sports, materialism, humanism, etc., etc., etc. But the trouble with the Church is not outside it is inside. The Church, for the most part, has forgotten its function. The light is dim and the salt has lost its savor. We must dedicate ourselves to evangelize, to spread the gospel, to contact, and to seek to rescue lost sheep. The Church that fails to assume this responsibility risks losing the candlestick, i.e., the love, power, and glory of Jesus Christ in His Church.

The second function of the Church is to feed saved sheep. It is wonderful when people are saved and join the Church. But if these people fail to grow, and continue in sinful lifestyles, they bring reproach and dishonor upon the name of the Lord and His Church. The Church's function is to integrate the teaching of the Bible into the life of the believer. Mature Christians are to take new believers under their wings and guide them in matters of faith, family, and finances. The Church should have a program to provide a counselor for every new convert. Have you ever dreamed of being part of a Church where everyone not only believed the Bible, but obeyed it? The model church at Antioch was that kind of church.

The third function of the Church is to fold or protect serving sheep. The foal represents the local church. The foal is not a luxury for a sheep. The foal is a matter of life and death. Outside the fold, the sheep is open game for all kinds of predators. Likewise, the local church is not a luxury to a new believer. His spiritual life depends upon his association and relationship with the body, the Church. Once a person makes a profession of faith, it is of the utmost urgency and importance to get him in fellowship with a Bible believing church. The truth hurts but it must be said: Evangelism that gets people to profess salvation, but fails to connect them with a local church is defective evangelism because it fails to meet the biblical standard (Acts 2:42).

Why is the local church so important to a new believer? There are several reasons. First, the Church offers the new believer protection. Sheep that stay close to their shepherd are safe. As the sheep graze, the howl of the wolf or the roar of the bear sounds in the distance. The sheep looks up, sees his shepherd nearby, puts his head down and contentedly continues to graze. The sheep knows by experience as long he stays close to the shepherd there is nothing to fear. The new believer in Christ who seeks the shelter, the counsel, and the protection of a local church will, likewise, be protected from false teachers and false paths. There is safety in a fellowship of mature believers who really care for one another.

But the Church is not just a protection agency or a security blanket. It also provides *preparation* for living for God and serving Christ. Sorrowfully, our churches do not have a good track record in the matter of preparing our people in serving and giving. Statistics prove that ten percent of the church members do ninety percent of the work. Also twenty percent of the people give eighty percent of the money. Thirty percent give the other twenty percent and fifty percent of the members do not give anything! The average church contributor gives 2.5% of his income.[3]

The Church has also failed in the area of making disciples. A statement from the *The Christian Century*, June 15-22, 1994, illustrates how the church has failed in making disciples:

> Jesus' scriptural admonition to 'make disciples of all nations' ranks far down the list of important church functions, according to a major survey of religious beliefs conducted for the *Atlanta Journal-Constitution* . . . . But today only 32 percent of the nation's Christians outside the South—and 52 percent of Southerners —consider converting people to the faith a 'very important' activity for the church, according to the poll . . . . Ninety-one percent of those surveyed in the South ranked moral guidance for young people a very important activity for the church, followed by worship opportunities (87 percent), helping the needy (86 percent) and converting others (52 percent) . . . . The poll was conducted by the Institute for Research in Social Science at the University of North Carolina in Chapel Hill.[4]

With proper guidance and prayerful programs these statistics can be changed. Thank God, every church is not failing, but far too many churches are not perfecting the saints for the work of the ministry (Ephesians 4:12).

The true success of a church is measured not by the attendance record nor by the finance record, but by the service record of its members. A church's ministry can be gauged by the quality and the quantity of laborers it sends to the harvest fields of the world. The church that functions scripturally will engather sinners, enrich and instruct the saints, and extol the greatness of our Savior.

## FAILURE OF THE CHURCH

The Church of Jesus Christ cannot fail. But lest we become smug, remember that local churches can and do fail. One generation of church members who sit in their pews and fail to evangelize will see their church gray and gradually die. In the United States 3,500 churches close their doors for the last time each year.

On visitation I talked to a woman from a dying church. She was in her early fifties and she said she was the youngest person there. In their large facility on Sunday morning, only about 20 were in attendance. The last one out, please turn off the lights!

I heard the story of a church that had a neon sign across the front of the outside of the church building: WHERE THERE IS NO VISION THE PEOPLE PERISH. One day a group of boys threw rocks at the sign. The next Sunday night when the sign was turned on, the members got a message: HERE IS NO VISION THE PEOPLE PERISH. Unlike faithful Paul the Apostle, they were disobedient to the heavenly vision (Acts 26:19).

During a missionary conference in an old, famous church in a large metropolitan area, an old missionary and a young missionary were roommates. This church had its glory years with great Bible teachers, and well attended Bible and missionary conferences. The church was a shell of what it once was. The old missionary kept telling the young missionary how things used to be. Finally, the young missionary tired of hearing about the glory that used to be.

He asked the old missionary, "What happened?"

The old missionary replied, "Son, this church has been good to me for many years, and I am not going to bad mouth these good people."

"I don't want you to bad mouth them. Only tell me what happened," replied the young missionary.

"Well, if you really want to know, I will tell you. As you drive to the church tonight, be on the look out for the traffic signs. One of those signs will tell you what happened to this church," the old missionary said sadly.

On the way to the church that night the young missionary looked carefully at every traffic sign. As he rounded a curve close to the church, he got the message. CHILDREN AT PLAY.

---

1. J. Wesley Bready, *England: Before and After Wesley,* Bready quotes from H. W. V. Temperley in *The Cambridge Modern History,* 1934, Volume VI, p. 76 (London: Hodder and Stoughton Limited, 1939) 141.

2. Suzy Platt, ed., *Respectfully Quoted: A Dictionary of Quotations from the Library of Congress* (Washington, DC: Congressional Research Service, Congressional Quarterly, Inc., 1992) 160.

3. Joe Miller, *The Church Planter,* Vol. 18. No. 4. (Florida: Lake Worth, 1994) 6.

4. *The Christian Century,* Vol. 111. No. 18, James Wall, ed. (Chicago: June 15-22, 1994) 199.

# 18

# Prerequisites
# for Local
# Church Evangelism

Few churches are organized to effectively, systematically, and continuously reach their areas of responsibility with
the gospel. By effectively, I mean to present the gospel so as to
be free of the blood of the people in the area of the church.
Systematically means reaching all the homes and not haphazardly
visiting the neighborhoods. Continuous means that neighborhoods change and need to be revisited periodically. Needless to
say, this is no simple task. In fact, it is a battle. To join and win
this battle requires desire, dedication, and determination. There
must be proper planning, preparation, personnel, and programs.
If a church gets serious in desiring to fulfill the Great Commission, starting at their Jerusalem, then certain prerequisites must
be met.

## RIGHT PERSPECTIVE

First, the church must have the right **perspective**. Church
workers who go into the neighborhoods with the gospel must
be prepared to be misunderstood. Today, the Apostle Paul is
honored and revered, but it was not always so. He writes in I
Corinthians 4:13, "Being defamed, we intreat: we are made as
the filth of the world, and are the offscouring of all things unto

this day."

Without the right perspective, house to house visitation can be damaging to the ego. Many people will think that these workers are Jehovah's Witnesses or Mormons. Others will think that they are insensitive, ignorant, Bible-thumping, air- sucking fundamentalists. We confess to being fundamentalists, but God help us not to be the kind mentioned above. Some will consider these Christian workers a nuisance, disturbers of the peace, and wish they would fall in a sinkhole and disappear. But servants of Christ must not let these false perceptions cloud their perspective.

To have the right perspective, several great truths must fill the mind. First, the fact that we are being obedient to God gives courage and motivation. Did not Jesus Christ command His disciples to go into all the world and preach the gospel? As church workers going house to house they are simply obeying the Great Commission. Others may mistake their motivation, but they know they are simply doing what Jesus told His Church to do.

Second, the importance of the work must be realized. Soul-winning visitation is not busy work. Without sowing there can be no reaping; without witnessing there can be no winning; without going there can be no growing. Knocking on doors, meeting neighbors,and presenting them the gospel are important steps in the great endeavor of bringing people from no faith to mature faith in Christ.

Third, in the mind's eye must be kept the truth that going to neighbors with the gospel is an attempt to do something for God and for the church. It is better to try and fail than to fail to try. Knowing that the attempt is commanded and its importance will urge the workers on.

Fourth, laborers in the harvest must keep a right perspective concerning results. The success of outreach varies. Sometimes the results will be gratifying; other times they will be disappointing. The focus must be on obedience, on doing our human best, and to remember that results belong to God. We cannot control what others may think, but keeping the right perspective will give encouragement in the arduous task of reaching neighbors for Jesus Christ and the Church.

## RIGHT PROMISES

The second prerequisite for local church evangelism is the **right promises.** Christian workers that venture out into the harvest fields must garrison their minds and hearts with the promises of God. God has showered promises upon faithful laborers, but we will only point out three of them. First, the promise of power emboldens the witness. Seeking to encourage his young disciple, Timothy, who seemed to have been of fearful nature, Paul gave him a promise of power, love, and a sound mind. "For God hath not given us the spirit [attitude] of fear; but of power, and of love, and of a sound mind" (II Timothy 1:7). The opposite of fear is faith. Faith removes natural timidity replacing it with spiritual courage. No matter how long one may have engaged in house to house visitation, the fear of the unknown, the question of who will answer the door, the uncertainty of the reception and the response, and the possibility of a man-eating dog causes anxieties. I have made it a practice when this attitude of fear seeks to enter my mind, to quote II Timothy 1:7. It does wonders to restore confidence and courage.

The devil gives a spirit of fear, but God gives us a spirit of faith, and this faith manifests itself in love. God enables His servants to love the unlovely, and as the Apostle Paul said, "Being defamed, we intreat" (I Corinthians 4:13). In visitation evangelism, love goes a long way in removing prejudices, overcoming obstacles, and reaching people for Christ.

Some people think that those who would be fool enough to participate in house to house visitation could not possibly be in their right minds. God has given us a sound mind and right thinking that enables us to answer the critics and gainsayers.

The promise of His presence gives assurance to those who evangelize. The promise of His presence, "Lo, I am with you alway, even unto the end of the world" (Matthew 28:20) follows the Great Commission. In context, His divine presence is promised to those who preach, baptize, and teach. Of course, we believe the Lord is with all His people all the time. But in a very special sense He is with those who obediently, reverently, and expectantly go out to evangelize and make disciples. We need to practice His "Presence." Never forget that as workers for Him He is with us in a definite way as we seek to be obedient in our witness for Him.

The third promise is a promise of productivity. "They that sow in tears shall reap in joy. He that goeth forth and weepeth, bearing precious seed, shall doubtless come again with rejoicing, bringing his sheaves with him" (Psalm 126:5-6). These beautiful verses speak directly to soul-winning visitation. First, we see the attitude of the soul-winner. "They that sow in tears. . . . He that goeth forth and weepeth." Soul-winning is serious work. It is not for the frivolous and the careless. The promise of productivity is given to men and women burdened for sinners to the point of tears.

Next, we note the actions of the soul-winner: "Bearing precious seed." The seed, of course, is the Word of God and the bearer (sower) of that seed scatters it on the soil (hearer). The promise of productivity is given to those that proclaim the Word of God to all who will hear.

Then we note with pleasure the accomplishment of the soul-winner: "Shall doubtless come again with rejoicing, bringing his sheaves [souls] with him." Pessimism and negativism permeate the atmosphere. As workers for Christ we must put away all ideas of defeat and go forth sowing seed with a burdened heart expecting God to bless our efforts with fruit that will remain. The harvest is plenteous, the harvest is ripe so that workers have every right to expect results. Claim the promise of productivity.

## RIGHT POWER

Now that the workers have the right perspective and the

right promises, what else do they need? They desperately need the right power. Going to neighborhoods, overcoming prejudices, and meeting and ministering to all kinds of people requires divine help. Behind God's commandments stand God's enablements. God never commands His servants to do something that He will not give them the ability to accomplish. In order that His workers can obey Him, He gives them the power of the Holy Spirit. "But ye shall receive power, after that the Holy Ghost is come upon you: and ye shall be witnesses unto me" (Acts 1:8). The power of the Holy Spirit is His enabling. As we yield to Him, trust Him, and obey Him, He will give us the strength, the courage, the ability, and the wisdom to be His witnesses. Somebody said, "If more people had the Holy Ghost, more people would have a holy go." It is not a matter of not having the Holy Spirit; it is a matter of the Holy Spirit not having us. Spirit-filled witnesses are the need of the hour. Our churches, our neighborhoods, our cities, our nation, and our world hurt for the lack of them.

Another source of power is the Word of God. The power of truth is on our side. Workers that go forth with their minds and mouths filled with the Word of God and their hearts filled with faith are equipped with a powerful weapon. "For the word of God is quick [living], and powerful [able to produce change], and sharper than any two-edged sword [cuts coming and going], piercing even to the dividing asunder of soul and spirit, and of the joints and marrow, and is a discerner of the thoughts and intents of the heart" (Hebrews 4:12). When the gospel comes not in word only, but also in power, and in the Holy Ghost, and in much assurance (I Thessalonians 1:5), hearts are convicted, sins are forsaken, and souls are saved. The powerful instrument producing the new birth is the Word of God. "Of his own will begat he us with the word of truth, that we should be a kind of firstfruits of his creatures" (James 1:18). Harvest workers gain strength, hope and courage from God's assurance to them that His Word will not return void. "So shall my word be that goeth forth out of my mouth: it shall not return unto me void, but it shall accomplish that which I please, and it shall prosper in the thing whereto I sent it" (Isaiah 55:11).

In this study of evangelism, we have learned that the ministry of reconciliation is a shared responsibility. God has chosen to involve us in reconciling the world unto Himself (II Corinthians 5:18-21). From His side, God has provided the power of the Holy Spirit and the power of the Word of God. From our side a power is required: the power of a dedicated life.

Looking back through history, we see the power of dedicated men. Some were dedicated to good and some to evil. Hitler was a rogue and a monster, but he was not short of dedication. In my visitation work, I entered the house of an old infirmed Jehovah's Witness. In the course of our conversation, he told me about his aunt that was a worker for that cult. This old gentleman told me that for forty-nine years she missed only three days without witnessing for Jehovah! Like it or not, that is dedication. There is no substitute for dedication.

As this age of grace comes to an end, as evil men continue to deceive and be deceived, are there men and women in our churches that will dare to dedicate themselves to the task of evangelizing their neighborhoods? Pray the Lord of the harvest to send forth laborers, laborers with a dedication to fulfill the ministry God has for them (Colossians 4:17).

## RIGHT PROGRAM

The church that purposes to evangelize its own Jerusalem certainly needs workers who have the right perspective, the right promises, and the right power, but what kind of practical help do they require? The next prerequisite we will discuss is very practical: the right program.

I have been traveling and ministering in churches for the past twenty years. Most of that time, my main emphasis has been missions and mission finances. The absence of outreach startled me. When the pastor was amenable and cooperative, we missionaries would do door to door visitation during the missionary conference seeking to involve members of the church.

Finally, I set out to develop a visitation program that would enable the local church to reach out effectively, systematically, and continuously. **Operation Doorstep**[1] resulted from that burden. In another chapter, I will explain that program. But now I want to talk about a concept called **Jerusalem Outreach**. Mel Lacock, former missionary to Taiwan and Hong Kong, developed an evangelistic and discipleship Bible study entitled Won By One.[2] As people learned about this tool and used it, the demand for this Bible study spread and it is now being used in many countries of the world.

I had developed **Operation Doorstep**, and Mel had authored *Won By One*. After Mel moved to the Greenville, South Carolina area, we joined together in a ministry of encouraging local churches in evangelism and discipleship conducting Jerusalem Outreach Conferences. To date we have conducted 54 conferences in 12 states.

Have you ever tried to do a job, but were frustrated because you did not have the right tool? We realized that tools can facilitate the work of evangelism. Let me share the tools we use and say a word about them. **Operation Doorstep** is a program designed to help church members meet and minister to their neighbors. Three tools are used: (1) neighborhood religious survey, (2) visitation record sheet, and (3) a gospel booklet, *Life's Most Important Question*.[3] The Neighborhood Religious Survey helps in two ways: to meet your neighbor and to minister to your neighbor. It gives a reason to be at the door and facilitates entrance inside the home.

The Visitation Record Sheet helps keep accurate records of streets, addresses, houses visited, the neighbor's church affiliation and spiritual condition, and whether a prospect or not.

*Life's Most Important Question* is a very thorough gospel tract that enables the worker to give a biblical presentation of the way of salvation. The *Won By One* Bible study is used in one of two ways: with a person who receives Christ for salvation, or with one who does not but is interested to know more.

**Jerusalem Outreach** is only one of several programs

available. Our program has two things going for it: it's free and it's simple. The task to evangelize our neighborhoods is formidable. With the finest of programs and workers it is an uphill battle. Without planning, organization, tools, and training the task will not get done.

## RIGHT PEOPLE

Programs alone will not do the job. Along with the right perspective, the right promises, the right power, and the right program, the fifth prerequisite for local church evangelism is the right people. Finding the right people has always been a problem. I say it reverently, but even God finds it troublesome sometimes to find the right people. "And I sought for a man among them, that should make up the hedge, and stand in the gap before me for the land, that I should not destroy it: but I found none" (Ezekiel 22:30). That is the case of no volunteers. Another time God called "Whom shall I send, and who will for us?" (Isaiah 6:8) and He found one who would answer His call, Isaiah.

The right people who will take the gospel prayerfully and powerfully to their neighbors will be characterized by love. First, they will be people who love God. Nearly all of us profess that we love God. But Jesus said it this way: "If ye love me, keep my commandments" (John 14:15). The chief motivating force to get people active in obeying Christ's commandment to evangelize is the constraining love of Christ. "For the love of Christ constraineth us; because we thus judge, that if one died for all, then were all dead: And that he died for all, that they which live should not henceforth live unto themselves, but unto him which died for them, and rose again" (II Corinthians 5:14-15).

The right people will not only love God, but they will love their church. As we have seen, the Church is close to the heart of God and it will be close to the heart of those who love God. People who love their church will give themselves for the Church just as Christ loved the Church and gave Himself for it.

Without evangelism the church cannot live and prosper.

The church will wither and die. People that love their church, will, with the help and blessing of God, work in the harvest for the good and ongoing of their church. The Northern Kingdom of Israel was destroyed because God could not find a man. Churches die because the right people are not doing the right things.

If a person loves God, and loves his church, then he will also love his neighbor. Jesus said the two great laws are: to love the Lord thy God with heart, soul, strength, and mind and to love one's neighbor as oneself (Luke 10:27). Our neighbors are lost; they are hurting. They need our help and above all they need God's help.

And finally, the right people love to work. In the modern church, play has replaced work. People learn all kinds of fun things at church. We need the right people who will work at evangelizing their neighborhoods by showing a heartfelt interest in their neighbors' physical, social, and spiritual well-being.

In thinking about Christians working for the Lord, I came across this humorous but profound poem.

## 10 LITTLE CHRISTIANS

10 little Christians came to church all the time; one fell out with the preacher, then there were nine.

9 little Christians stayed up late; one overslept on Sunday, then there were eight.

8 little Christians on their way to heaven; one took the low road, then there were seven.

7 little Christians, chirping like chicks; one didn't like the singing, then there were six.

6 little Christians seemed very much alive; one took a vacation, then there were five.

5 little Christians pulling for heaven's shore; one stopped to rest awhile, then there were four.

4 little Christians each as busy as a bee; one got

his feelings hurt, then there were three.
3 little Christians couldn't decide what to do;
one couldn't have his way, then there were
two.
2 little Christians each won one more; now don't
you see, two and two make four.
4 little Christians worked early and late, each
brought one, now there were eight.
8 little Christians, if they double as before, in
just seven Sundays we'd have one thousand
twenty-four.
In this little jingle there is a lesson true—you
belong either to the building or to the wrecking
crew.[4]

## RIGHT PASTOR (S)

Is there anything else necessary for the church to evangelize its area? Yes, one of the most essential factors has not been
mentioned: the right pastor(s). I don't know who said it first but
Dr. Lee Roberson is given credit for the saying, "Everything rises
and falls on leadership." People seldom, if ever, rise above their
leaders. Usually a congregation is a true reflection of its pastor.
Since this is true, pastors shoulder a heavy responsibility.

James, the brother of our Lord, in his book warns pastors,
teachers, and Christian leaders with these sobering words: "My
brethren, be not many masters [teachers], knowing that we shall
receive the greater condemnation" (James 3:1). If a church fails,
all will be guilty before God, but the heaviest guilt rests upon
the leaders.

In this matter of evangelism, the pastor is to be the model,
the trainer, and the encourager. For this very purpose God gifted
men in the Church: "And he gave some, apostles; and some,
prophets; and some, evangelists; and some, pastors and teachers;
For the perfecting of the saints, for the work of the ministry"
(Ephesians 4:11-12). The challenge, the guidance, the training,

the oversight, the accountability for a church's evangelistic outreach must come from the top.

The pastor has several responsibilities that I will mention. First, he must choose a program and initiate his people as to the program's purposes and possibilities. Second, he must implement the program by providing materials and teaching his people how to use them. Third, the pastor must participate and lead out by being an example to the flock. Fourth, the pastor must perpetuate the program of outreach. It is relatively easy to get something going, but it is extremely difficult to keep up the momentum. Fifth, from time to time the pastor needs to evaluate the program and make any necessary changes. Let us pray for pastors, evangelists and others in the places of leadership that they may be encouraged to accept and fulfill their responsibilities in the matter of reaching out to the unsaved in their communities.

## RIGHT PURPOSE

The last prerequisite for local church evangelism ranks first in importance. The right purpose for evangelizing must be biblical. What is the right biblical purpose? Is church growth a legitimate purpose? No, numerical, spiritual, and financial growth are not legitimate purposes, but they are beneficial by-products of an effective, systematic, and continuing evangelistic outreach. The glory of God is the right purpose.

Sometimes churches work hard to reach people, but it is for the glory of the church. To be known as the fastest growing church in Possum Gorge urges them on.

Again, pastors will labor intensively to reach people for Christ and the church, but if the truth were known, the motive behind their efforts is to bolster their own egos.

When the purpose is right—to glorify God; when the program is right—to bring people to a saving knowledge of Jesus Christ and to incorporate them as functioning members of His Church; when the people are right—serving because they love God, love their church, love their neighbors, and love to work, then blessing comes to the church, blessing comes to the community, and all glory goes to God.

---

1. Gene Gurganus, *Operation Doorstep*, a brochure explaining the philosophy of a systematic visitation program.

2. Melvin T. Lacock, *Won By One Bible Study* (Des Moines, Iowa: Bible Press, Inc., 1978)

3. *Life's Most Important Question* (Winona Lake, Indiana: Brethren Missionary Herald Tracts, n.d.)

4. Neil T. Anderson, *Living Free in Christ: The Truth About Who You Are and How Christ Can Meet Your Deepest Needs*, Footnote that author and source of "10 Little Christians" are unknown. (Ventura, California: Regal Books, 1993) 196.

# 19

# A Program
# for
# Local Church Evangelism

There is no dearth of programs designed to help the local church in evangelism. The need of the hour is for churches to utilize these programs. Programs are only as effective as the people that use them. Dr. Roland Leavell in his book, *Romance of Evangelism,* quotes these shocking statistics about the people who populate our churches. Even though given over 55 years ago they are still true today:

> 5% do not exist,
> 10% cannot be found,
> 20% never pray,
> 25% never read the Bible,
> 30% never attend church services,
> 40% never give to any cause,
> 50% never go to Sunday School,
> 60% never go to church Sunday night,
> 70% never give to missions,
> 75% never engage in any church service,
> 80% never go to prayer meeting,
> 90% never have a family worship, and
> 95% percent never win a soul to Christ.[1]

Since soul-winning is a deeply spiritual work and can only be done successfully by spiritually-minded people, the root cause of the failure of evangelistic programs lies in the shortage of Spirit-filled Christians in our churches.

But God has never used the majority to do His work. He uses those who have experienced a life-changing, soul-saving experience with Jesus Christ. I have noted in our conferences that the people most excited and willing to participate are people who came to know the Lord because someone came to their home to tell them how to be saved. A program of soul-winning visitation will not appeal to many church members, but there will be a core of people who see the need and will avail themselves of the training and the tools the program offers. In these people rest the hope of the Church, the hope of the nation, the hope of the world.

## OPERATION DOORSTEP

As I mentioned in the previous chapter, I developed a simple, straightforward program for helping local churches to effectively, systematically, and continuously reach out to their communities with the gospel of Christ. The program is called *Operation Doorstep.*[2] Why call it that? In my travels to West Virginia, I would often pass a drug store that had a proverb over the front door: "If everyone would sweep his own front yard, the world would be a cleaner place in which to live." I like that because it brings responsibility back home where it belongs. As I meditated on that proverb, I realized that if every Christian family would witness to the people in its neighborhood, the community would soon be evangelized.

In the course of time, I developed the Neighborhood Religious Survey and went out in my neighborhood to meet and minister to my neighbors. During that time, Mel Lacock and I joined *Operation Doorstep* and *Won By One* into *Jerusalem Outreach*, which is a program for evangelism and follow-up. I will first describe *Operation Doorstep* and then show how it fits into an expanded program of *Jerusalem Outreach.*

*Operation Doorstep* is a program. It is a **serious program** because our neighborhoods are faced with serious problems. The family is the basic building block of society. When families fail to function (dysfunctional families), the whole superstructure of society will eventually collapse. The family problem is a sin problem, and the Bible says that Jesus Christ was manifested to take away sin (I John 3:5). So *Operation Doorstep* is a serious program because of the **great need** in our neighborhoods. It is a serious program because of the **great lack** in our churches. Very few churches have a working program designed to reach every home in their community with the gospel. Many churches have visitation programs, and I commend those that are making an attempt. *Operation Doorstep* is not a gimmick, not a short-cut, and not a sure-fire secret for church growth, but it offers a church a workable program to help it reach its community.

Not only is *Operation Doorstep* a serious program, but it is a **Scriptural program**. A fisherman goes where the fish are. If we are going to reach our neighbors, the best place to talk with them is in their own homes. Paul used this method as we read in Acts 20:20, "and have taught you publickly, and from house to house." Also in Acts 5:42 we learn the practice of the Jerusalem Church: "And daily in the temple, and in every house, they ceased not to teach and preach Jesus Christ."

In building a scriptural base for this program, I chose four key verses that show the method, the means, the urgency, and the scope of the work to be done. The **method** is taught in Matthew 28:19: "Go ye therefore, and teach all nations, baptizing them in the name of the Father, and of the Son, and of the Holy Ghost: teaching them to observe all things whatsoever I have commanded you." The method is to win the lost by preaching the gospel, baptizing them that believe, and teaching them to be obedient to the commands of Christ.

Mark 16:15, "Go ye into all the world, and preach the gospel to every creature," indicates that the **means** is the preaching of the gospel. The **urgency** of the task is revealed in Luke

14:23, "Go out into the highways and hedges, and compel them to come in, that my house may be filled." Ours is not an arm-twisting, high-pressured program, but we go with a sense of urgency persuading sinners to be saved.

The **scope** includes the whole world. Acts 1:8, "But ye shall receive power, after that the Holy Ghost is come upon you: and ye shall be witnesses unto me both in Jerusalem, and in all Judaea, and in Samaria, and unto the uttermost part of the earth." If a church does not reach its own Jerusalem, there is little possibility of its being a force that will send missionaries around the world.

*Operation Doorstep* is a **simple program**. There are a variety of programs for outreach, but if you examine them you will find most are complicated, requiring notebooks, seminars, training, time away from home, etc. As a result many expensive, good programs never get implemented. In *Operation Doorstep* we use four basic tools: A Neighborhood Religious Survey, Visitation Record Sheet, a gospel booklet entitled *Life's Most Important Question*, and a New Testament.

The **Neighborhood Religious Survey** gives you a bona fide reason to be at your neighbor's door.[3] If you simply go to his or her door without the survey, there is a good possibility the conversation will take place on the porch. If the neighbor is already a member of a church or not interested in spiritual things, he is likely to close the conversation as soon as possible. By using the survey, you will be able to enter your neighbor's home and hold an extended conversation with him.

One of the most difficult areas of soul-winning visitation is the initial contact. At the top of the Neighborhood Religious Survey form, we have printed instructions for the visitors to use. Knowing what to say when a person comes to the door reduces anxiety and gives the visitor confidence. This is our introduction:

Good morning, I am_____ and this
is_____. We are your neighbors from_____Church. We

are visiting in your neighborhood getting to kn )w the people here. And the best way to get to know you is to come and see you. So we came to see you. You don't mind, do you? In order to get to know you, we are conducting a Neighborhood Religious Survey. May we have a few minutes of your time to come in and ask you a few questions?

To help people remember the above, we break it down into parts.

> **Greetings**: Good morning or Good afternoon.
> **Identification**: I am_____ and this is_____. We are your neighbors from_____Church.
> **Purpose**: We are visiting in your neighborhood getting to know the people here.
> **Request**: In order to get to know you we are conducting a Neighborhood Religious Survey. May we have a few minutes of your time to come in and ask you a few questions?

By using this simple approach, we gain entrance into 54 percent of the doors we knock on. The Neighborhood Religious Survey is structured to lead inoffensively into a presentation of the gospel. After several questions concerning church affiliation, three questions are asked requiring the person to think. "What do you expect from your church?" To help him or her in case the person cannot verbalize an answer, several questions appear. "Do you expect guidance in living a wholesome life?" "Do you expect help in raising your family?" "Do you expect the church to teach you the Bible way to go to heaven?"

The next question that logically follows is number eight: "Has anyone ever shown you from the Bible what you must do to go to heaven?" If the person answers negatively, politely ask permission by saying: "If someone could show you from the Bible how you could know that you would go to heaven if you died today, would you do what the Bible says or at least be willing to listen?" This is question ten. If the person agrees, at that point, you can take out the gospel booklet and your New Testament and say: "I have a booklet I want to give you, but first I want to share it with you."

"This little booklet is filled with Bible verses taken from the New Testament that I have here. For convenience sake, let us look at the verses from the Bible in this booklet." Carefully explain the verses contained in the booklet using appropriate illustrations.

In the event the person answers the question by saying, "Yes, someone has shown me from the Bible how to be saved," what do you do then? You then ask them question number nine in the survey: "Do you know for sure if you died today you would go to heaven or would you have some doubt?"

If they say, "I have doubts," then go to question ten which asks permission to show them from the Bible how they can know how to be saved. But if they say, "Yes, I know for sure," then what do you do? You take out your gospel booklet and say, "I want to give you this booklet, *Life's Most Important Question.* Do you know life's most important question? If you were to die today, and were to meet God, and He should ask you why He should let you into His heaven, **what would you say?**"

Now the person who has said he knows for sure he is going to heaven must tell the reason why he thinks so. If the person is basing his or her salvation on anything other than faith in the shed blood of Jesus Christ, then very carefully lead him through the booklet. If he is trusting the Lord Jesus for his salvation, rejoice with him.

The second most crucial time in soul-winning evangelism is closing the interview. After giving the gospel and the person has manifested an interest in what has been taught, if there is evidence of genuine desire and conviction, it is time to lead this person to trust Christ.

On the last page of the booklet is a question: "Can you

think of any reason why you wouldn't like to invite Christ into your life right now?" I also add to that by asking if they are willing to trust Christ as their personal Lord and Savior.

If they say there is no reason for not trusting Christ, then you need to deal more thoroughly with them to make sure they understand the gospel and are sincere in their desire to trust Christ as Lord and Savior. We want to lead people to faith in Christ, but we do not want to give people a false hope by preaching a watered-down gospel and rushing people who are unprepared into a spiritual decision. This is dangerous because it inoculates them to the real saving truth of the gospel. How many times when dealing with people and presenting the gospel they say, "Oh, I have already done that." But what they did had no effect upon their lives and they did not receive salvation though they went through the motions.

After they make a decision to receive Christ as Lord and Savior, we take time to study with them I John 5:11-13. As mentioned before, the personal worker can and should give the Word of God as to what it says about assurance, but only the Holy Spirit can use the Word to give the new believer assurance.

We then ask them when we can meet for a *Won By One* Bible study. Take down their telephone number and make a firm date for the first lesson.

The last page of the booklet tells three things a new Christian should do.

> 1. Make a public confession of your faith before others (Matthew 10:32; Romans 10:9-10).
> 2. Be baptized in obedience to Christ and in testimony of your faith (Matthew 28:19-20; Acts 8:35-38; Acts 16:30-34).
> 3. Attend a Bible-believing church where you can fellowship with other Christians and learn the Word of God (Acts 2:41-42; Hebrews 10:24-25).[4]

Another ticklish matter concerns getting the new believer

to attend church. Most people are already associated with a church of some kind or another. You need to tactfully remind them that the church they are attending may not be meeting their spiritual needs. Invite them to come with you to church. Often it will be necessary to work with the person for a period of time before he will be willing to leave his old church to attend yours.

The next important tool in *Operation Doorstep* is the **Visitation Record Sheet**.[5] Without keeping records no one will know what is being done and there could be embarrassing overlap and whole areas could be neglected. Let me explain the use of the Visitation Record Sheet. At the top of the sheet appear:

STREET NAME_____

NAME OF VISITORS_____

Each street is to have a separate sheet. If a street has more than thirteen houses on it, use another sheet with the same street name, and make it number two. Some long streets will have multiple sheets and each should be given the next higher number. It is important for visitors to fill in their names so that on a later date it will be known who visited these homes. It is suggested to start with the streets surrounding the church and systematically work out, making every effort to contact every home.

On the form are places for the following data: date, house number, name, at home, not at home, busy, call back, church affiliation, survey conducted, already saved, profession of faith, rededication, prospect, and interested in *Won By One*. A file will be kept of all these visitation records so the visitors will be able to revisit people who were not at home and to follow up the prospects.

During visitation, a brochure of the church is left with the people visited and also at homes where no one is at home. We also leave gospel tracts.

In Kansas, during Friday visitation no one was at home so a tract was left in the door. The lady of the house came home and found the tract. She read the tract, got down by her bed, and accepted Christ as her Savior. The next day Mel and the pastor revisited her home and conducted an interview with the lady. During the interview, she mentioned the tract, her reading it and praying to be saved. While this was happening, her husband came in. Mel asked the wife to share with her husband what she did the previous night. She gave him her testimony, and then Mel continued the survey. The husband accepted the Lord also. The next morning they were both in church. Since then they have been baptized and have become faithful members of the church. So leaving gospel tracts is important.

## ADVANTAGES OF
## OPERATION DOORSTEP

Before explaining how we correlate *Operation Doorstep* in a Jerusalem Outreach conference, I want to mention some advantages of *Operation Doorstep*. In most church visitation programs much time is lost and gas consumed trying to find some prospect to visit. Once you find the address there is a good possibility the person is not at home or otherwise occupied with company. Everyone who has worked at visitation knows the feeling of frustration after having spent several hours earnestly trying, yet never being able to contact anyone. In *Operation Doorstep* you can walk out in your neighborhood at the most convenient time when you know your neighbor is home. The fact that you are his neighbor will give credibility to your witness. In the event your neighbor is not open to the gospel, the visit has opened the door to future contacts. If your neighbor responds to the gospel, you are in a good position to help him and encourage him in the things of the Lord. Your witness in the neighborhood will become known, and people with spiritual needs may come to you or refer others to you. By using this neighborhood religious survey, you can extend your neighborhood to cover hundreds of families. When you have evangelized your neighborhood, you may help another church member evangelize his neighborhood. To avoid embarrassing situations, it is better to go out by twos, a married couple, two men, or two women.

## POSSIBILITIES IN
## OPERATION DOORSTEP

*Operation Doorstep* is not only a program, but it is a **possibility**. In fact, several opportunities present themselves. First, you will have the opportunity to meet your neighbors. You don't have to be afraid of your neighbors. Most of them will be happy to at last meet one. "Neighbor" is still a valued word in our society, and so we use it to gain rapport. You can meet your neighbor and not witness to him, but you can never witness to him without first meeting him.

The second possibility is to minister to your neighbor **spiritually**. In our discussion of using the Neighborhood Religious Survey, I pointed out how we use it to get to know our neighbor's spiritual condition and then present the gospel of Christ.

This also presents the possibility of ministering to your neighbors **socially**. There is the possibility of inviting your neighbor to church socials and picnics, to Sunday School parties, or just inviting him over for a meal. In evangelism that bears lasting fruit, we must not only win people to the Lord, but to ourselves also.

Sometimes it will be necessary to minister to our neighbors **physically**. "But whoso hath this world's good, and seeth his brother have need, and shutteth up his bowels of compassion from him, how dwelleth the love of God in him?" (I John 4:17).

## PLEASURE OF
## OPERATION DOORSTEP

Most people will not believe this, but working in *Operation Doorstep*, meeting and ministering to your neighbors can be a **pleasure**. Like any other task there are ups and downs. Some days will be discouraging; others will be exhilarating. Soul-winning visitation gives us the opportunity of being used of God in the lives of our neighbors. No other pleasure is as satisfying, refreshing, and lasting as to be used of God as the human instrument to bring people out of the darkness of sin into His marvelous light. Whether we are successful or not, whether people respond or not, we have the pleasure of knowing we attempted something for God. To see people saved, baptized, joining the church, and growing in grace and service will be a source of genuine pleasure.

## POTENTIAL OF
## OPERATION DOORSTEP

*Operation Doorstep* has great **potential** for ministry. As teams form to go out to meet and minister to neighbors, it will open up ministry opportunities. In a team, there can be a talker and a prayer helper. Some people love the Lord but are not good with words. These people can team up with one who likes to do the talking. The silent one can take care of crying babies, assist in prayer, and in many ways be a great encouragement.

As teams go out on a regular basis, they are going to find prepared hearts and will have the joy of leading these prepared people to faith in Christ. Again, some who are not fitted for soul-winning visitation can do a great job of teaching a *Won By One* class and being an encourager of a new convert. Others who are up in years and physically impaired can have a ministry of praying definitely for teams as they go out to witness.

As the teams circulate, they can tell children about AWANA and other ministries of the church. An active *Operation Doorstep* will open many ministry opportunities for the church.

## JERUSALEM OUTREACH
## CONFERENCE

To initiate and implement *Operation Doorstep* we conduct Jerusalem Outreach Conferences.[6] The conference usually begins on Wednesday night, at which time I introduce the *Operation*

*Doorstep* program with an overhead presentation. Mel introduces the *Won By One* program.[7] On Thursday at 9:30 a.m. we meet at the church for visitation. We spend a half-hour explaining the forms, forming teams, assigning areas, and praying. We visit from 10 a.m. until 12 noon. We all meet back at the church to rehearse how God led and used us. After lunch and rest, another visitation session is conducted from 3 p.m. until 5 p.m. Visitation continues Friday and Saturday according to the same schedule.

On Thursday night Mel and I demonstrate the four situations we meet in the neighborhood: some are already saved, some are busy, some are hostile, and some are receptive and want to be saved. With Mel taking the part as the neighbor and me the part of the visitor, we demonstrate how to lead a person to faith in Christ. Friday and Saturday nights we continue motivating and instructing in soul-winning and discipleship. In Sunday School, we give a review of *Operation Doorstep* and *Won By One* for those who were not at the midweek service on Wednesday night. At the morning worship service, Mel gives statistics of the meeting: number of homes visited, number at home, number not at home, number of surveys conducted, number of professions of faith, number interested in *Won By One*, and number of visitors. He compares how the statistics of this conference compare with our previous conferences. Then I preach on *Seven Dynamics for a Successful Local Church Outreach*. At the closing service, Mel gives guidelines for teaching *Won by One* and I challenge the people to go into the harvest.

The conference closes with a commitment service. There are three ministry opportunities: to work in *Operation Doorstep* with a team member one hour a week; to teach a *Won By One* Bible class; or to pray for those working in these two programs. People are given a commitment card and encouraged to prayerfully fill it out. Those who wish to participate in Jerusalem Outreach are invited to bring their cards and stand at the front of the church. The pastor closes with a prayer of dedication.

As a result of the 54 Jerusalem Outreach Conferences we have conducted, several widely held suppositions have been shown to be in error. First, during the hours of 10 a.m. until 12 noon and 3 p.m. until 5 p.m. people are at home. As a result of visiting 6,773 homes, we found 3,542 people at home and 3,231 people not at home. Fifty-two percent were at home and forty-eight percent were not at home.

Second, people are fearful and will not let you in to talk with them. Of the 3,542 people at home, 2,016 of them participated in a neighborhood religious survey. Fifty-seven percent of people at home took part in the survey.

Third, people are not interested in the gospel. Of the 2,016 people surveyed, 224 made a profession of faith in Christ. After carefully presenting the gospel, eleven percent made professions of faith in Christ. The harvest is ripe; the harvest is plenteous; the workers are few. The gospel works but it requires dedicated men and women to work it.

Initiating and implementing a Jerusalem Outreach Conference is relatively easy. Time is set aside for meetings and visitation, and for a few days people excitedly learn how to meet and minister to their neighbors. But the difficult aspect of Jerusalem Outreach is keeping it going. For the program to be successful, much planning and prayer must be given to perpetuating it. To help the pastor plan and prepare for a continuing Jerusalem Outreach we have prepared a brochure.[8]

The pastor functions as CEO (Chief Executive Officer) of the church. Ideally, a layman or an assistant pastor will assume the role of Jerusalem Outreach Coordinator. This person will have the responsibility to administer the program under the oversight of the pastor.

The Coordinator's first duty is to meet with the volunteers who signed a commitment card. It will be his responsibility to work closely with these workers by guiding, training, and encouraging them in their commitment to reach out in the neighborhoods. The Coordinator will see that all needed materials such as forms, tracts, booklets, and *Won By One* books are available. He will also oversee the formation of teams and correlate the areas of visitation to protect against both neglect and duplication. He will arrange a teacher for those interested in *Won By One*. Also getting pertinent information to the prayer partners is vital.

"Watch God work" is a valid motto. In order to know what God is doing and to keep the church informed, the Coordinator shall keep accurate records and will periodically report to the church. Reporting to the church serves three vital functions: it encourages the workers, it encourages the prayer partners, and it encourages the church. Nothing inspires God's people more than to know that the Church is obediently seeking to fulfill the Great Commission. To enable the church to know what is being accomplished, a system of reporting must be in place and in use. Without a faithful, dedicated Coordinator the possibility of a successful, systematic, and continuous outreach in the community is remote.

In our conferences, we use a theme chorus that expresses holy optimism and encourages individual participation.

## WIN THEM ONE BY ONE

If to Christ our only King
Men redeemed we strive to bring,
Just one way may this be done–
We must win them one by one.

**Chorus**
So you bring the one next to you,
And I'll bring the one next to me;
In all kinds of weather we'll all work together,
And see what can be done.

If you bring the one next to you,
And I bring the one next to me;
In no time at all we will have them all,
So win them, win them one by one.[9]

1. Roland Q. Leavell, *Romance of Evangelism* (New York: Fleming H. Revell, 1942) 89.

2. See Appendix A.

3. See Appendix B.

4. *Life's Most Important Question* (Winona Lake, Indiana, Brethren Missionary Tracts, n.d.).

5. See Appendix C.

6. See Appendix D.

7. Melvin T. Lacock, *Won by One, Bible Study Course* (Des Moines, Iowa: Bible Press, Inc, 1978).

8. See Appendix E.

9. C. Austin Miles, words and hymn tune, *Christian Service Songs* (Chicago: Rodeheaver Hall - Mack Co., 1939) Hymn 100. See also Appendix F.

# A
# Prophetical
# Perspective
# of
# Evangelism

"Nevertheless when the son of man cometh, shall he find faith on the earth?" (Luke 18:8).

"They shall not hurt nor destroy in all my holy mountain: for the earth shall be full of the knowledge of the Lord, as the waters cover the sea" (Isaiah 11:9).

# 20

# Prognosis
# for Evangelism
# 2000 A.D. and Beyond

Amos did not claim to be a prophet nor the son of a prophet (Amos 7:14), and neither do I. Nobody knows what will be on the morrow. God could intervene by sending a mighty Holy Spirit, sin-killing, life-giving revival. Every Wednesday morning a group of men meet at Hampton Park Baptist Church in Greenville, South Carolina, to pray for revival. Undoubtedly, hundreds of other groups are doing the same thing. "Behold, the LORD'S hand is not shortened, that it cannot save; neither his ear heavy, that it cannot hear" (Isaiah 59:1).

The expectation of, the desire for, and zealous prayer for revival must never cease. Revivals are not man made but are God sent. As we look at our nation and our times it is comforting to know that God is sovereign and works "all things after the counsel of his own will" (Ephesians 1:11).

## UNDERSTANDING THE TIMES

The children of Issachar had an "understanding of the times, to know what Israel ought to do" (I Chronicles 12:32). As the twenty-first century approaches, it behooves us to pray for wisdom (James 1:5). I thought it would be interesting to learn what various fundamental Christian leaders are thinking about evangelism in the future. Dr. Bob Jones III, President of Bob Jones University, shared these insights on evangelism 2000 A.D. and beyond.

> If the rapture has not occurred before the twenty-first century, and if revival in America tarries, the face of evangelism in my estimation, will look like this:
>
> ●The evangelistic message will contain less of sin, less of man's personal responsibility, less of Hell, less of grace.
>
> ● The church will spend less time seeking souls and more time trying to reform society. A message of societal reformation, rather than souls' salvation, will predominate.
>
> ●Compromising evangelicalism will declare a truce which isolates Catholics from being won to Christ, having embraced the seductive lie that Catholicism is just another Christian denomination. Those engaged in biblical evangelism will be persecuted by churches practicing ecumenical evangelism.
>
> ●There will be an increase in government encroachment on evangelization through regulations severely limiting or prohibiting proselytizing.
>
> ●America's law will restrict the church's function to the four church walls. An evangelizing church will be painted out of society by these laws which will allow for discussion of religion in the concourse of society only when the subject is broached by the 'seeker.' The laws will shield

him from being 'sought.'

●Even without such laws, Christians who sit in churches where sin, judgment, Hell, and man's personal accountability to a creator God are not preached will be devoid of the burden for personal evangelism

The picture is not encouraging. Luke 18:8 records that Christ asked the question, When the Son of man cometh, shall he find [the] faith on the earth? These words of the Lord reveal that as we approach the end of the age, His mandate to proclaim the Gospel to every creature will have been so neglected—or so distorted—that His saving Gospel will scarcely be heard. That being so, it is all the more incumbent upon Christians now to work before the night comes, when no man can work.[1]

Dr. Fred Moritz, Director of Baptist World Mission, sees both obstacles and opportunities in evangelism in the future. Consider his remarks:

I see **obstacles** to evangelism as we face the Twenty-first Century. Billy Graham popularized ecumenical evangelism, and the issue will not go away with his passing. Others, Luis Palau, e.g., carry the torch. There are theological attacks on evangelism, especially in the realm of missions. As we read the literature coming out of Fuller Seminary, and other places, we realize that the theological minimization of the place of Scripture in theology, and of Scripture's authority, waters down the gospel message. That has far-reaching implications in other areas of ministry, and in evangelism. American Christians need to shake the lethargy brought on by materialism and the wickedness of our age. We need revival, and to thus reverse the trend of Christians absorbing the wicked elements from our culture. Christians need to return to living as salt and light (Mt. 5), and thus impact a wicked culture instead of absorbing it into their lives.

I also see great **opportunities** in evangelism. We have unprecedented opportunities to evangelize in countries where we would have never thought it possible just a few years ago. A wicked culture leaves a vacuum and hunger in the hearts of sinful men that cries out to be filled with the gospel.[2]

Dr. Bob Jones, Jr., Chancellor of Bob Jones University, offered the following thoughts on the subject of evangelism:

We need new emphasis on the subject. I am certainly not a prophet; however, I do not foresee any kind of mass evangelism in the 21st century. I think the further we go into the century, if the Lord tarries, the more we will find the emphasis on ecumenical gatherings, one-world church, etc. It seems to me that any true, biblical, Christianity is going to be driven more and more underground. It is difficult, therefore, to envision how evangelism can work; but it would certainly be through individual contacts in most countries; and as in early years of the church, I think it will be accompanied by considerable persecution and rejection. We are already seeing the beginning of the days when men will not endure sound doctrine, and I think this increases and will increase until the coming of the Lord.[3]

Evangelist David Kistler, a young evangelist who is being used of God among fundamental churches, makes the following observations as to problems we face in evangelism:

> As I see things, the church today has adopted one of two approaches toward evangelism. Either that of being absorbed into the mainstream of this world's system, or that of being totally isolated from the world, with periodic invasions into the community in an attempt to reach people. Of course, neither of these is the correct Biblical approach. In attempting to become like the world in order to reach them, the new evangelicals have gained some audience but have lost their message. On the other hand, the fundamentalists who have practiced isolation from the world, have created another problem. We have maintained our Biblical message, but we have had no audience to whom we can direct that message. What I believe that we must do as fundamentalists is to certainly maintain our message, but adjust our methodology in order to reach our present generation. To fall into either of these errors is to arrive at the same tragic result. The world is never confronted with the truth.
>
> What I am seeing across America is that churches are either totally caught up in this materialistic age and therefore cannot impact it for Christ, or they have become so isolated from the world that the result is identical—no impact is made on a lost world. What we must have is confrontational, yet loving penetration into this degenerate society with the gospel. There must be some creative, Spirit-directed methods that we can employ that may not be at all traditional, but as long as they

are not un-biblical, surely we can utilize them in a way to once again reach our world with the clear Biblical message of repentance and faith.

May God grant us a new generation of men who have One Person to please and nothing to prove who will be effective evangelists in the twenty-first century and beyond, until our Lord returns. If our goal is to glorify God and reach men, then we must forsake the 'win them and leave them', 'my way or no way' philosophy that has prevailed in fundamentalism for so long.[4]

Dr. Bob Shelton has been used of God as a missionary to Vietnam, as a pastor in Michigan, and as an evangelist and prophecy teacher in many places for many years. His insights on evangelism 2000 A.D. and beyond reflect his study of prophecy:

The woods are now full of prophecy prognosticators who shower us with dates for the coming of Christ for His Bride. In recent years, four books have come to my attention in which the authors suggested the following dates for the rapture of the church: September 11-13, 1988; August 31-September 2, 1989; October 28, 1992; and September 15-27, 1994. To the embarrassment of the authors these dates have come and gone and the Church is still on earth.

Unbelievers are now beginning to respond as God's Word declared they would. They are asking, 'Where is the promise of his coming? for . . . all things continue as they were . . . .' (II Peter 3:4).

There is a challenge in all of this for those who know Christ as Savior. That challenge is associated with verse 9 of II Peter chapter 3, 'The Lord is not slack concerning his promise, as some men count slackness; but is longsuffering to us-ward, not willing that any should perish, but that all should come to repentance.'

As we await the coming of our Lord for His Bride, we must be about His business - reaching people with the Gospel story.

As you have noted, the conclusion of this book is entitled 'Prognosis for evangelism 2000 A.D. and beyond.' May I suggest the church may not be here when the turn of the century arrives.

There are many indications that we are quickly coming to the end of this age and our Lord may soon come for His waiting Bride. (Yes, I am a pre-tribulation rapturist).

The question is, will scriptural evangelism continue here on earth after the rapture?

First, we must understand that every believer will be caught away when Christ calls His Bride unto Himself. All who remain on this planet will be lost. A marvelous announcement is made, however in Revelation chapter 7. From each of the 12 tribes listed in verses 4 through 8 will come 12,000 virtuous men who will place their faith in God's crucified, resurrected Son. Twelve tribes with 12,000 from each tribe equals 144,000 believers. These 'servants of God' (Rev. 7:3) are referred to as 'the first-fruits unto God and to the Lamb' (Rev. 14:4). Notice they are called first-fruits not 'only fruit.' The fact is, millions of other Jews as well as millions upon millions of Gentiles will come to Christ as Savior during tribulation days (Rev. 7:9-14).

This great program of world evangelism was prophesied by Christ when He said, 'And this gospel of the kingdom shall be preached in all the world for a witness unto all nations; and then shall the end come' (Matt. 24:14).

In other words, the program of evangelism will continue on after the rapture of the Church. A witness will be given to 'all nations and then shall the end come.' (That is the end of the Great Tribulation).

What is the prognosis for evangelism 2000 A.D. and beyond? The prognosis is very good. If the Church is still here by the year 2000 it will be our responsibility to get the Gospel story into all the world. The great commission has never changed. We must strive to preach the Gospel to every creature.

When the Church is raptured, God's program will continue on as he uses tribulation Saints to proclaim His message, for His desire remains the same: 'He is not willing that any should perish, but that all should come to repentance.'[5]

Rev. Paul Seger, General Director of Biblical Ministries Worldwide, shares what he considers hindrances to effective evangelism now and in the future:

It is my opinion that there are at least five major trends that can greatly reduce the intensity of evangelism in the average American church today.

1. **PROSPERITY**: Our churches have come of age. We have moved from the rescue mission motif to a yacht club mind-set. We are not the church of the catacombs but of the cathedral. Our buildings and programs are respectable. We have moved from store-fronts to 'sanctuaries'. We have struggled through the years establishing ourselves as a credible movement of churches. It is in the midst of prosperity that we are tempted to lean back and relax because the struggle for existence is diminished. Nothing breeds failure like success (Revelation 3:14-19).

2. **PROFESSIONALISM**: In our search for excellence we have compartmentalized the ministry. We have trained specialists for every facet of church work. We have slick parachurch ministries using a myriad of media. We are now in a position to let the professionals do it. Yet in spite of all the modern tools at our disposal, we seem to impact our culture less than before we had them. Programmed evangelism by a professional can never replace relational evangelism by the people. The 'professional' evangelist must return to the biblical job description of training the saints to do it (Ephesians 4:11-12).

3. **POLITICS**: Our strategy has shifted from chopping at the root to whacking off branches. Though we realize theologically that the base problem in society is man's depraved heart we

seem to focus our efforts on changing government law. The political involvement of Christians continues to drain enormous amounts of financial and people resources away from the main thing of evangelism. If all the laws of America are rewritten to our satisfaction we will still have the job of evangelism ahead of us. We have simply made it a kinder gentler place from which to depart to hell. While political action may accomplish some things, we must keep in mind that at best it is a temporary solution to some surface problems. The main thing is to keep focused on eternity (II Corinthians 4:17-18).

4. **PATRIOTISM**: Our emphasis on love of country has molded us to see it as undesirable to leave these shores to be a missionary in some 'inferior' culture. Our infatuation with 'the way it once was' is a hindrance to receiving with open arms the hosts of foreigners flooding our land. The world has moved to our neighborhood but our patriotism has led to some bigotry which has caused us to view them as a nuisance rather than an opportunity for evangelism (Acts 10:28, 34-35).

5. **PHILOSOPHY**: We have drunk at the well of secular philosophy. This has been drawn up in the bucket of 'Christian' psychology, 'movements' within Christianity and humanistic ministry methods. We are in danger of diluting scripture by adding our own flavoring. If Scripture is no longer viewed as an adequate solution to every need of man, the result will be a human answer to a spiritual need. Anything added to the absolute dependence on the grace of God will dull the

cutting edge of evangelism (Colossians 2:3, 8-10).[6]

## BIBLICAL SCENARIO
## OF THE LAST DAYS

The biblical description of the last days aptly fits the conditions of our world today. I Timothy 4:1 speaks of the **religious** situation during the latter times [before the coming of the Lord]. "Now the Spirit speaketh expressly, that in the latter times some shall depart from the faith, giving heed to seducing spirits, and doctrines of devils [demons]." The New Age Movement continues to capture the minds and hearts of multitudes. An avalanche of evil rushes in to fill the spiritual vacuum existing in our secularized society. Texe Marrs comments on the seducing spirits and doctrines of demons:

Demonic spirits who appear as invited guests of human contacts wage war against the Word of God. The Bible instructs Christians to test the spirits to determine whether they are of God or Satan (I John 4:1-3). We are also told that light and darkness cannot coexist (II Cor. 6:14).

Using these Biblical guidelines, we can know that the clever spirits who are now deceiving New Age believers are of Satan, because they continually spread false doctrines that go against the Scripture.

In examining the utterances of these demons of the New Age, we find that among their many lies they consistently teach *eight spiritual false-hoods.*

1) A personal God does not exist.

2) Jesus is not the only begotten Son of God and is not the only Christ.

3) Jesus did not die for our sins.

4) There are no such things as sin and evil.

5) There is no Trinity of Father-Son-Holy Spirit.

6) The Bible is filled with errors.

7) There is no heaven and no hell.

8) Every man is God, and one's godhood can be realized through the attainment of a higher consciousness.

Satan is using demons to promote the New Age gospel, to defame Jesus Christ, and to discredit the Bible. He intends to soften up humanity for the arrival of the Antichrist, whom millions will believe is Christ because of the propaganda now being spread by these lying spirits. Element; of the Plan of Satan to bring in a New Age One World Religion and a one world political and social order are carefully woven into virtually every utterance of these demons.[7]

Then in II Timothy 3:1-5 Paul describes the moral and spiritual situation of our day.

This know also, that in the last days perilous [critical] times shall come. For men shall be lovers of their own selves, covetous, boasters, proud, blasphemers, disobedient to parents, unthankful, unholy, Without natural affection, trucebreakers, false accusers, incontinent, fierce, despisers of those that are good, Traitors, heady, highminded, lovers of pleasures more than lovers of God; Having a form of godliness, but denying the power thereof.

Is it any wonder, then, that the social fabric of our nation is unraveling, that the traditional family has been replaced by the dysfunctional family, and that our neighborhoods have become battlegrounds? Behavior that would have shocked and polarized concerted opposition a generation ago has become tolerable. The perpetrators of dastardly crimes are exonerated while society in general is blamed.

Many biblical scholars view the seven churches in the Book of Revelation as portraying the Church over the course of history. The Bible gives us a description of the churches situation in the last days prior to the Lord's coming.

> And unto the angel of the church of the Laodiceans write; These things saith the Amen, the faithful and true witness, the beginning of the creation of God; I know thy works, that thou art neither cold nor hot: I would thou wert cold or hot. So then because thou are lukewarm, and neither cold nor hot, I will spue thee out of my mouth. Because thou sayeth, I am rich, and increased with goods, and have need of nothing; and knowest not that thou art wretched, and miserable, and poor, and blind, and naked (Revelation 3:14-17).

Without a doubt the modern church is the Laodicean church. Beautiful edifices, fully equipped gymnasiums, programs and support groups for all with a variety of activities for folks from kindergarten to senior citizens characterize modern churches. But where is the fire? In his factual but depressing book, *The Vanishing Ministry,* Woodrow Kroll quotes from the Yearbook of American and Canadian Churches which gives a sad report of the state of the church in America and Canada.

> According to the 1990 edition of the Yearbook of American and Canadian Churches, a total of

145,383,738 or 58.7 percent of the population belonged to a church, a synagogue, or some other religious organization in 1989. There are 343,000 churches in America claiming a membership of 130,000,000 people. That sounds impressive, but dissecting this statistic does not generate confidence in the healthy state of the evangelical church in America. Of these churches, 23,500 are Roman Catholic, 6,900 Mormon; 6,000 churches are Jehovah's Witnesses' Kingdom Halls; 5,000 are actually Jewish synagogues; and 1,600 are the Orthodox Church.

Of the 70,000,000 Protestants in the United States, over 42,000,000 belong to churches associated with the National Council of Churches and would not ordinarily be considered evangelical. For this reason, the number of churches in the USA which can be launching pads for the gospel is not as large as we may think.

Moreover, many of these churches are not healthy. It is estimated that 80-85 percent of American churches have plateaued or are declining. Only 20 percent of all American churches have an attendance of more than 200 people. Sunday school watcher Elmer Towns says that the average church has only 87 people in Sunday school attendance.[8]

## DEVIL'S AGENDA

If the devil has a virtue it has to be tenacity. Down through the centuries, Satan has battled unceasingly against God and God's plan to reclaim fallen man. Today the devil has his program in high gear. In his excellent book, *The Gnostic Em-*

*pire Strikes Back—an old heresy for the New Age,* Peter Jones puts things in perspective.

> Have you ever asked yourself any of the following questions?
>
> Why is homosexuality on the rise? Why is it endorsed by *Time Magazine,* promoted on publicly funded radio, and featured in children's comic strips—with great moral fervor and in the name of democracy? Why is feminism such a powerful force today? Why is this movement developing its own goddess spirituality? Why is witchcraft taught in certain California school districts? Why is feminist spirituality making enormous inroads into Christianity? Why is abortion a vitally important part of the feminist manifesto? Is ecology just a neutral concern about the survival of the planet, or does it too have a religious agenda? Why is American Indian nature religion being actively promoted? Why is the work ethic no longer working? Why are multiculturalism and political correctness so important on many college campuses? Are these seemingly disconnected issues related in any way to the so-called New Age Movement? Why are the numerous New Age spiritual techniques for healing, peace of mind, and self-knowledge being publicized so vigorously in the media, and more and more utilized in the business world and the armed forces?
>
> The real question is this: Are these apparently disconnected issues really part of a coherent pagan ideology poised to impose its religious belief system on the New World Order (the Age of Aquarius)

of the twenty-first century? The following comparison of New Age objectives with the pagan Gnosticism that dominated society in the first three centuries of the Christian church would answer yes to that most important question.[9]

How does this agenda affect evangelism? Political correctness judges the gospel to be sexist, racist, anti-Semitic, patriarchal, chauvinistic, and homophobic. Tal Brooke, a converted New Ager, believes that the time of religious tolerance is coming to an end. Listen to his comments:

> At such a time, any non-inclusive faith or belief claiming unique revelation would be a supreme offense to the 'unity in diversity' mandate for public peace. . . . Evangelists could be arrested for committing 'crimes against the people,' while Christians could be dismissed for 'hate crimes' if they shared their faith with anyone.[10]

The proposed "religious harassment law" which would make it a criminal offense to mention spiritual matters in the market place would drastically hinder evangelism. It is becoming more and more difficult to witness for Christ. The time has come for Christians to wake up. Tim Stafford reports the view of J. Stanly Oakes, Jr., Director of Faculty Ministries for Campus Crusade as follows:

> Students have reason to be pessimistic. There are problems like we have never seen before. Lots of Christian positions will become illegal because of multiculturalism . . . . I see a tremendous chilling effect on Christian free speech. Western civilization is being blamed for all the problems of the world. I see it as a willful, hostile, orchestrated attempt to eradicate not just Christianity

from the university, but anything based on Christianity.[11]

## ARE WE READY?

For the past 21 years I have been holding missionary and
evangelistic conferences. As a result of ministering in over 500
churches I know the state of the church. God knows I do not
want to be critical or pessimistic, but fundamental churches are
in trouble. Many pastors have given up on trying to enlist their
people in reaching out to the neighborhoods. In fact many pastors
have quietly given up the battle to win souls. If Christians do not
witness when there is no persecution, how are they going to
witness when doing so could cause them serious trouble?

Peter Jones looks at our situation and comes to the
following serious conclusions:

> ●Our world is entering a new period of spiritual,
> demonic delusion cavorting about in the fake
> clothes of spiritual renewal.
> ●In step with a general optimism about the New
> World Order of the third millennium, such
> spiritual delusion could quickly sweep the globe,
> dragging millions into spiritual death.
> ●A serious infiltration of error into the Christian
> church may threaten unsuspecting believers,
> including our own children, with theological
> confusion and spiritual defeat.
> ●Difficult days may lie ahead for Christians who
> refuse to compromise. Perhaps, rather than the
> great advances of the Christian faith by the year
> 2000 touted by many mission strategists and
> statesmen, Christians one day, maybe sooner than
> later, would be considered a bothersome and
> dangerous minority group threatening the peace
> of universal tolerance for all kinds of faiths and

lifestyles. Even New Age tolerance has its limits! I am not a prophet, and I dearly hope I am wrong. But the phenomenal growth of this movement and the explicit menacing threats of New Age leaders against traditional 'intractable' Christianity, form an equation whose stubborn logic is difficult to avoid. This equation leads me to believe that those who profess absolute truth, the specific Creator and Redeemer God of the Bible, and biblical ethical behavior will be silenced by any means, in accord with the expedient norms of new-look Aquarian ethics.

●Christians should understand what is taking place now, both to avoid these chilling consequences, if this is still possible, and to recognize the level of commitment and public testimony required should these grim days come upon us.

●Those Christians who stand firm will be driven back to a fresh understanding of 'the faith once delivered to the saints,' especially since that faith was articulated in a pagan world very much like the one that ours is rapidly becoming. A renewed and realistic awareness of 'the mystery of iniquity' would not bring defeatism. On the contrary, it would promote an even greater conviction of the truth, and thus of the final victory of Jesus Christ who looked directly into the eyes of evil and was victorious.[12]

## WHAT WENT WRONG?

In North America, our people have known the highest quality of life and the longest uninterrupted time of peace and prosperity during all of history. An old proverb says, "Adversity has slain its thousands; prosperity its ten thousands." Too many have the idea that, like the economy, everything will keep getting better. Instead of looking for a city "whose builder and maker is God" the average Christian is caught up in the American dream. Just as Samson lost his power and did not know it, so the Church has been robbed.

Jesus used two powerful metaphors to describe the witness of the Church: salt and light. Douglas McLachlan speaks powerfully to this point in the following excerpt from his book *Reclaiming Authentic Fundamentalism:*

> What are the impurities which have weakened us, causing the salt to lose pungency and the light to lose brilliance? It may be **conformity**—becoming too much like the world; it may be **idolatry**—worshipping the gods of this world; it may be **hypocrisy**—wearing the masks of this world; and it may be **apathy**—expressing too little care and concern for the world. Together these and other deformities have robbed us of the power which is ours in Christ to radically impact our personal slice of the secular society.[13] (Emphasis added.)

Dr. McLachlan lays the blame on both the right and the left. On the right, fundamentalists have prided themselves on right doctrine and great preaching. But by a biblical separation that has degenerated into **sinful isolation** the fundamentalist has a small audience. The result: the culture never benefitted from the message. On the left, the evangelicals motivated by a desire to be successful and relevant attracted the multitudes. But **cultural absorption** short circuited their testimony.

Dr. McLachlan sums it up with these searching words:

> Tragically, the effect for both is identical: the culture never gets confronted with the truth. What they need is a healthy dose of divine holiness manifested in Biblical separation. What we need

is a healthy dose of divine love manifested in evangelistic penetration. And none of this is a possibility until we arise out of the dead ashes of Christian apathy. Perhaps instead of denouncing the secular world we should start repenting of our own sacred sins. Then perhaps we could intersect and maybe even inhibit the slide toward decadence in our culture, as we rediscover and reinstitute urgent and authentic Biblical evangelism in contemporary Fundamentalism.[14]

## EVIL FRUIT OF COMPROMISE

The publication of *Evangelicals & Catholics Together: The Christian Mission in the Third Millennium* exploded like a bombshell in the Fall of 1994. The statement is the product of a consultation beginning in 1992, between Evangelical Protestants and Roman Catholics. Outstanding leaders, both Catholic and Evangelical, are calling for a halt in proselytizing Catholics by Protestants and Protestants by Catholics. The signers of this document assume that baptized Catholics are born again and that baptismal grace is reawakened at the time of conversion.

These differing beliefs about the relationship between baptism, new birth, and membership in the church should be honestly presented to the Christian [?] who has undergone conversion. But again, his decision regarding communal allegiance and participation must be assiduously respected.[15] (Question mark is the author's.)

For the sake of a specious unity, the Evangelical signers of this document would discourage the evangelization of the lost. Who could have believed that Mr. Charles Colson, Prison Fellowship; Dr. Richard Land, Christian Life Commission of the Southern Baptist Convention; Dr. Larry Lewis, Home Mission

Board of the Southern Baptist Convention; Dr. Jesse Miranda, Assemblies of God; and Dr. John White, Geneva College and the National Association of Evangelicals; all professed Evangelical Bible teachers, would help draft and sign such a document? Who could have believed that men such as Mr. William Bentley Ball, Christian Lawyer; Dr. Bill Bright, Campus Crusade for Christ; Dr. Os Guinness, Trinity Forum; Dr. J. I. Packer, Regent College (British Columbia); Dr. Richard Mouw, Fuller Theological Seminary; and the Rev. Pat Robertson, Regent University;[16] would endorse such a travesty of biblical teaching and discourage the work of soul-winning among the host of baptized people, both Catholic and Protestant, that know nothing of God's saving grace through faith in the blood of Christ?

Thankfully, many voices of protest were heard. But the presence of such a document bodes ill for those who determine to be true to the task of preaching the gospel.

## IS ALL LOST?

Thus far in our prognosis of evangelism 2000 A.D. and beyond, I and those I have quoted have painted a dark picture. By this time, some of you readers may be in the pits. However, all is not lost. If the cause of Christ and the evangelization of the world depended on the likes of us, we would all have reason to despair. Never forget the words of our Lord: "I will build my church; and the gates of hell shall not prevail against it" (Matthew 16:18).

The enemies of the gospel are gloating because paganism is on a roll and seems to be capturing our culture. These neognostics, the New Agers, have imbibed a deep-seated hatred of God and the Bible. Peter Jones in the following statement has distilled from the gnostic teaching their thoughts about the God of the Bible:

The physical universe was never meant to be. Its existence, its creation if you will, resulted from a cosmic 'goof' committed by the foolish Creator God (the Demiurge) of the Bible. The ancient Gnostics understood very well that if their system was going to work, they would have to get rid of the God of the Bible. This explains the extremist anticreation and anti-Old Testament sentiment found in certain Gnostic texts. Yaldaboath (an obvious parody of Jahweh), the Chief Archon (Ruler-Creator) is vilified and mocked with a disdain bordering on hate . . . God the Creator is represented as blind, ignorant, arrogant, the source of envy and the Father of Death . . . .The Creator God is an impostor, masquerading as the true unknowable God.[17]

Not only do these New Agers vilify the God of heaven, but they also believe that God is evil, capricious, and of all beings most base. Madame Blavatsky, the demon-inspired founder of the Theosophical Society, died in 1891. Her writings *Isis Unveiled* and *The Secret Doctrine* are held in high esteem in the New Age Movement. Note how she blasphemes the God of the Bible:

Ialdabaoth, whom several sects regarded as the God of Moses, was not a pure spirit; he was ambitious and proud, and rejecting the spiritual light of the middle space offered him by his mother, Sophia-Akhamoth, he set himself to create a world of his own . . . he fabricated man, but this one proved a failure. It was a monster; soulless, ignorant, and crawling on all fours on the ground like a material beast. . . . Following the impulse of the divine light, man soared higher and higher in his aspirations. . . .Then the Demiurge was filled with rage and envy; and fixing his jealous eye on the abyss . . . . He is the union of all that is most base in Matter, with

the hate, envy, and craft, of a spiritual intel ·
ligence.[18]

Our God sees and hears and in due time He will deal with
these deceivers and blasphemers. Paul comforts the Thessalonian
believers with these reassuring words:

> And to you who are troubled rest with us, when
> the Lord Jesus shall be revealed from heaven with
> his mighty angels, In flaming fire taking ven-
> geance on them that know not God, and that obey
> not the gospel of our Lord Jesus Christ: Who
> shall be punished with everlasting destruction
> from the presence of the Lord, and from the glory
> of his power; When he shall come to be glorified
> in his saints, and to be admired in all them that
> believe (because our testimony among you was
> believed) in that day (II Thessalonians 1:7-10).

Martin Luther's great hymn, *A Mighty Fortress Is Our
God,* encourages us in dark days. The message is so relevant to
our world and our situation that it needs reading.

> A mighty fortress is our God,
> A bulwark never failing;
> Our helper He, amid the flood
> Of mortal ills prevailing.
> For still our ancient foe
> Doth seek to work us woe;
> His craft and power are great,
> And, armed with cruel hate,
> **On earth is not his equal.**
>
> Did we in our own strength confide,
> Our striving would be losing;
> Were not the right Man on our side,

The Man of God's own choosing.
Dost ask who that may be?
Christ Jesus, it is He;
Lord Sabaoth His name,
From age to age the same,
**And He must win the battle.**

And though this world, with devils filled,
Should threaten to undo us,
We will not fear, for God hath willed
His truth to triumph through us.
The Prince of Darkness grim—
We tremble not for him;
His rage we can endure,
For lo! his doom is sure,
**One little word shall fell him.**

That word above all earthly powers—
No thanks to them—abideth;
The Spirit and the gifts are ours
Through Him who with us sideth.
Let goods and kindred go,
This mortal life also;
The body they may kill:
God's truth abideth still,
**His Kingdom is forever.**[19]
(Emphasis added.)

## SURE WORD OF PROPHECY

God has not left us in the dark concerning His program.
The fascinating subject of Bible prophecy offers real hope and
assurance to followers of Christ. The student of the Bible can
look back through the centuries and note many fulfilled prophecies. Presently, the rise of spiritism, the falling away [apostasy],
and the seeming triumph of evil vindicate the prophecies of the

New Testament. Bible prophecy speaks specifically about the end times. This is called eschatology, the doctrine or study of last or final things.

The next great event on God's prophetic calendar is the rapture (catching away) of the Church.

> For the Lord himself shall descend from heaven with a shout, with the voice of the archangel, and with the trump of God: and the dead in Christ shall rise first: Then we which are alive and remain shall be caught up together with them in the clouds, to meet the Lord in the air: and so shall we ever be with the Lord. Wherefore comfort one another with these words (I Thessalonians 4:16-18).

> For God hath not appointed us to wrath, but to obtain salvation by our Lord Jesus Christ (I Thessalonians 5:9).

In no way is God going to forsake His own little flock.

Evangelism will not end after the Church is taken away. During the Tribulation Period (time of Jacob's Trouble) the missionary task will be committed to the 144,000 faithful men of Revelation 7 and 14. The success of their evangelistic endeavors is recorded in Revelation 7:13-14:

> And one of the elders answered, saying unto me, What are these which are arrayed in white robes? and whence came they? And I said unto him, Sir, thou knowest. And he said to me, These are they which came out of great tribulation, and have washed their robes, and made them white in the blood of the Lamb.

> At the end of the Tribulation Period, our Lord Jesus Christ

will come in power and glory. At this time there will be another ingathering.

> Immediately after the tribulation of those days shall the sun be darkened, and the moon shall not give her light, and the stars shall fall from heaven, and the powers of the heavens (Satan) shall be shaken: And then shall appear the sign of the Son of man in heaven: and then shall all the tribes of the earth mourn, and they shall see the Son of man coming in the clouds of heaven with power and great glory. And he shall send his angels with a great sound of a trumpet, and they shall gather together his elect from the four winds, from one end of heaven to the other (Matthew 24:29-31).

Christ will set up His millennial reign on earth. Toward the end of the Millennium, Satan will be loosed and permitted to deceive those that resent the restraints of righteousness. Once again Satan will lift his ugly head and lead his followers in a war against the saints (Revelation 20:7-9). Finally, the devil will be sent back to the Lake of Fire to join the Beast (Antichrist) and the False Prophet (v. 10). Peter in chapter 3, verses 10 and 13 of his second book describes this time as the Day of the Lord.

> But the day of the Lord will come as a thief in the night; in the which the heavens shall pass away with a great noise, and the elements shall melt with fervent heat, the earth also and the works that are therein shall be burned up. . . . Nevertheless we, according to his promise, look for new heavens and a new earth, wherein dwelleth righteousness.

The Holy Spirit gives us just a glimpse of what heaven

is going to be like in Revelation 5:9 and 5:12-14.

> And they sung a new song, saying, Thou art worthy. . . . Saying with a loud voice, Worthy is the Lamb that was slain to receive power, and riches, and wisdom, and strength, and honour and glory, and blessing. . . . saying, Blessing, and honour, and glory, and power, be unto him that sitteth upon the throne, and unto the Lamb. . . . And the four and twenty elders fell down and worshipped him that liveth for ever and ever.

The curtain comes down on the great task of bringing sinful, alienated people into a loving relationship with our great God. Evangelism ceases; glorious, eternal worship continues.

---

1. Bob Jones III, President of Bob Jones University (Greenville, South Carolina: Letter to the author, August 10, 1994).

2. Fred Moritz, General Director of Baptist World Mission (Decatur, Alabama: Letter to the author, March 7, 1994).

3. Bob Jones, Jr., Chancellor of Bob Jones University (Greenville, South Carolina: Letter to the author, March 10, 1994).

4. Dave Kistler, Evangelist (Hickory, North Carolina: Letter to the author, October 12, 1994).

5. Bob Shelton, Evangelist and Prophecy Conference speaker (Greenville, South Carolina: Letter to the author, October 9, 1994).

6. Rev. Paul Seger, General Director of Biblical Ministries Worldwide (Lawrenceville, Georgia: Letter to the author, November 11, 1994).

7. Texe Marrs, *Dark Secrets of the New Age* (Westchester, Illinois: Crossway Books, 1987) 98, 99.

8. Kroll, 31, 32.

9. Peter Jones, *The Gnostic Empire Strikes Back: an old heresy for the New Age* (Phillipsburg, New Jersey: Presbyterian and Reformed Publishing Company, 1992) ix, x.

10. Tal Brooke, "The Emerging Reality of a New World Order," *Spiritual Counterfeits Project Journal* (Berkley, California: Spiritual Counterfeits Project, Inc., 16:2, 1991) 17.

11. Referenced in Peter Jones, 96.

12. Peter Jones, 7-9.

13. Douglas R. McLachlan, *Reclaiming Authentic Fundamentalism* (Independence, Missouri: American Association of Christian Schools, 1993) 85.

14. Ibid., 86.

15. "First Things," A Monthly Journal of Religious and Public Life, Richard John Neuhaus, ed., Number 42, *Evangelicals & Catholics Together: The Christian Mission in the Third Millennium* (New York, May, 1994) 15-22.

16. Ibid.

17. Peter Jones, 21-22.

18. Helena Petrovna Blavatsky, *Isis Unveiled* (Wheaton: The Theosophical Publishing House, 1972) 184.

19. Nutter, Charles S., *The Hymns and Hymn Writers of the Church* (New York: The Methodist Book Concern, 1911) 56.

# Appendices

A. Operation Doorstep

B. Neighborhood Religious Survey

C. Visitation Record Sheet

D. Jerusalem Outreach Conference Profile

E. A Systematic Workable Plan for a Local Church to Reach its Jerusalem

F. Win Them One by One

# Appendix A

## OPERATION DOORSTEP

An old proverb says, "If everyone swept his own front yard, the world would be a cleaner place in which to live." With this proverb in mind, I would like to introduce a program that will help us evangelize our neighborhoods. Hence I have entitled this program: ***Operation Doorstep.*** We would all agree that if each family in your church put forth the effort to contact at least 10 neighbors, your city and your neighborhoods would be better evangelized.

There is no dearth of programs. One of the main problems with most programs is that they are complicated, requiring notebooks, seminars, training, and time away from home. As a result, good programs never get implemented.

Most of us have a desire to communicate the gospel to our neighbors, but find it difficult to make the approach. Without the proper tools, the successful completion of many tasks is impossible. Even the best craftsman is limited in what he can accomplish without the proper tools. To make the difficult task of evangelizing our neighborhoods easier, the use of a few basic tools is necessary. These tools are effective, easy to use, and will enable you to share the gospel more effectively with your neighbors.

TOOL 1   Neighborhood Religious Questionnaire
TOOL 2   Gospel Booklet, *Life's Most Important Question*
TOOL 3   New Testament
TOOL 4   Brochure from Your Church

The Neighborhood Religious Survey gives you a bona-fide reason to be at your neighbor's door. If you simply go to his door without the survey, there is a good possibility the conversation will take place on the porch. Unless your neighbor is interested in spiritual matters, he is likely to close the conversation as soon as possible.

With clipboard and pen in hand, introduce yourself as his neighbor and communicate that you are conducting a religious survey of the neighborhood and would like to ask a few questions. More than likely you will be invited into the house. If not, then suggest or ask if you could come inside. At this juncture, a little neighborly talk will break the ice. Let him know you are glad to meet him. You may inquire about his employment, children, and hobbies.

A gospel booklet is very helpful in giving a clear presentation of the gospel. If the interviewer feels more comfortable with the Romans Road or some other Bible presentation, that will be acceptable. People who are not experienced at sharing the gospel will gain confidence by using a gospel presentation in booklet form. Another advantage is that the booklet can be left for a further witness.

A New Testament should be in hand whether one uses a gospel presentation from a booklet or not. It may be that the conversation will require the use of the New Testament even though it is not being used in the gospel presentation. Its very presence gives authority to what is being presented.

After you have presented the gospel, you will want to give the church brochure and tell of the location and the ministries of your church. If there are children in the home, try to get permission to bring them to Sunday school, AWANA, or junior church. Also invite your neighbors to come to your church. In the event no one is home, leave a brochure so that the neighbors will know they have been visited and by whom.

## ADVANTAGES OF
## OPERATION DOORSTEP

In most church visitation programs much time is lost and gas is used trying to find someone to visit. Once you find the

PERSPECTIVES ON EVANGELISM

address, there is the possibility of no one being at home, or, if at home, otherwise occupied. In this program you can walk. You can go at the most convenient time when you know your neighbor is at home. Your witness in your neighborhood will become known and people with spiritual needs may come to you or refer others to you.

The fact that you are his neighbor will give credibility to your witness. In the event your neighbor is not open to the gospel, the visit has opened the door for future contacts. If your neighbor responds to the gospel, you are in a good position to follow up with frequent visits. Encourage him to come to your church and offer him a ride. By using this survey you can extend your neighborhood to cover hundreds of families. When you have evangelized your neighborhood, you may help another church member evangelize his. To avoid embarrassing and compromising situations, it is better to go out by twos—a couple, two men, or two women.

## RESULTS OF
## OPERATION DOORSTEP

The first good result—our fellow church members will be encouraged to witness to their neighbors. This method is a good way to help them begin to witness to their neighbors.

The second good result—a load of guilt will be released from church members who for years have wanted to witness to their neighbors but never knew how or never got around to it.

The third good result—some folks will start witnessing who have never done so before.

The fourth good result—many of your neighbors will hear the gospel, and some of them will be saved. The blood of those who reject the gospel will no longer be on your hands.

# Appendix B

## NEIGHBORHOOD RELIGIOUS SURVEY

INTRODUCTION:

Good morning, I am _____ and this is _____ .
We are your neighbors from_____ Church. We are visiting in your
neighborhood getting to know the people here. In order to get to know you we are
conducting a Neighborhood Religious Survey. May we have a few minutes of your
time to come in and ask you a few questions?

Names of visitor(s)
Date
Dr./Mr./Mrs./Miss
Age of children
Address

1. Do you own a Bible? Yes_____ No_____
2. Do you read your Bible daily?_____occasionally?_____ never?
3. What church do you attend?
4. Are you a member? Yes_____ No_____
5. Do you attend regularly?_____ occasionally?_____ never?_____
6. What do you expect from your church?
   a. Guidance in living a wholesome life?
      Yes_____ No_____
   b. Help in rearing your family?
      Yes_____ No_____
   c. Teaching the Bible way to go to heaven?
      Yes_____ No_____
7. Has anyone ever shown you from the Bible what you must do to go to heaven?
   Yes_____ No_____
8. Do you know for sure if you died today you would go to heaven?
   Yes_____ No_____
9. If someone could show you from the Bible how you could know that you would
   go to heaven if you died today, would you do what the Bible says or be willing
   to listen?
   Yes_____ No_____
10. May I take a few minutes to show you what the Bible says about this subject?
    Yes_____ No_____

# Appendix C

OPERATION DOORSTEP · VISITATION RECORD SHEET

Street: _____   Visitor (s): _____

| Date | House # | Last Name | At Home | Not at Home | Busy | Call Back | Church Member | Survey Conducted | Already Saved | Profession of Faith | Rededication | Prospect | Interest in Won by One Bible Study |
|---|---|---|---|---|---|---|---|---|---|---|---|---|---|
| | | | | | | | | | | | | | |
| | | | | | | | | | | | | | |
| | | | | | | | | | | | | | |
| | | | | | | | | | | | | | |
| | | | | | | | | | | | | | |
| | | | | | | | | | | | | | |
| | | | | | | | | | | | | | |
| | | | | | | | | | | | | | |
| | | | | | | | | | | | | | |
| | | | | | | | | | | | | | |

# Appendix D

For maximum success during and after the conference, careful attention must be given to these matters:

I. Preparation
   A. Prayer: Pray publicly and privately for the conference. Emphasize the conference in Wednesday night prayer meetings. If possible, organize special cottage prayer meetings to pray for an outpouring of God's power and direction.
   B. Promotion: Promote the conference orally in the church services, by radio, by newspaper article, and by invitation to sister churches to attend. Display posters on church bulletin boards. Create an awareness that something good and new is happening!
   C. Personnel: Prior to the conference, preach messages emphasizing witnessing, personal evangelism, and discipling. Keep the matter of human responsibility fresh (we are our brothers' keepers). Encourage as many as will, to make themselves available during the conference to be trained to reach neighbors with the gospel.
   D. Plan: Designate areas to be visited by the teams during the conference. Choose these areas so that every house in close proximity to the church will be visited. Trailer parks and apartment complexes afford prime areas for contacts.
   E. Program: Publish a complete conference schedule and have it available at the first service. This will prepare members to interact during the service.

F. Publications: A good supply of the following materials that will be used during and after the conference should be on hand.
   1. *Won By One* Bible Study Course, available from:
      Bible Press, Inc.
      6595 North West Sixth Drive
      Des Moines, IA 50313
   2. *Life's Most Important Question*, available from:
      BMH Tracts
      Box 544
      Winona Lake, IN 46590
   3. Neighborhood Religious Survey* (Appendix B)
   4. Visitation Record Sheet* (Appendix C)
   5. Church brochure with church's phone number, address, and schedule of services.
   6. Clipboards and pencils
   7. Jerusalem Outreach Conference bulletin* (A camera ready copy of the schedule will be provided for printing on bulletin covers.)
   * Photocopies may be made from forms which will be made available by this author.

II. Participation
   A. Wednesday
      1. Meet at the church Wednesday afternoon to pray, plan, and prepare materials for the conference.
      2. Decide what areas are to be visited. Arrange so teams will not overlap in their visitation.
      3. Meet at the church at 7 p.m. for public service. *Operation Doorstep* and *Won By One* will be introduced.
   B. Thursday
      1. Meet at the church at 9:30 a.m., at which time instructions in using Neighborhood Religious Survey, Visitation Record Sheet, and *Life's Most Important Question* will be given.
      2. Arrange teams, give assignments, and pray.

3. Visit target areas until 12 noon and return to church to report.
4. Meet at church at 2:45 p.m., pray, and visit until 5 p.m.
5. Evening service at 7 p.m.
C. Friday (same schedule as Thursday)
D. Saturday
  1. Meet at church at 9 a.m. for inspiration, instruction, assignments. Teams visit until 12 noon and return to church to report.
  2. Afternoon visitation from 3 p.m. until 5 p.m.
  3. Evening service at 7 p.m.
E. Sunday
  1. Sunday school: Combine the adult and young people's classes for an overview of *Operation Doorstep* and *Won By One*.
  2. Morning service: Statistical report of visitation and "Dynamics for Local Church Evangelism."
  3. Evening service: Guidelines for Teaching *Won By One* Bible Study and "Jesus' Prayer Request." At the close of the message, a commitment card is passed to those willing to work in Jerusalem Outreach. Those filling out a card are invited to come to the front for a prayer of dedication.

III. Perpetuation: On completion of the Jerusalem Outreach Conference, guidelines entitled, "Jerusalem Outreach Conference: A Systematic Workable Plan for the Local Church to Reach Its Jerusalem for Christ" is available. This resource will help in organizing *Operation Doorstep* and *Won By One,* and in continuing this vital ministry.

IV. Personnel
Gene Gurganus, a native of Rocky Mount, North Carolina, was saved in 1950 in an Oliver B. Greene tent crusade. A call to the ministry caused him to leave the study of Optometry to attend Bob Jones University and Seminary. After

graduation, Dr. Gurganus and his wife, the former Elizabeth English, served as pioneer church-planting missionaries in Bangladesh. Their ministry resulted in the formation of the Dampara Baptist Church and Chittagong Bible Correspondence School. The Gurganuses served with Association of Baptists for World Evangelism, (ABWE) for 40 years as missionaries and in the United States as Southeastern representatives. For more information write: 5 Woodleigh Drive, Taylors, SC 29687.

Mel Lacock is from Montana and was saved at nine years of age while attending a daily vacation Bible school. After graduating from Bob Jones University, Mr. Lacock served in the United States Air Force. He returned to complete graduate studies and married the former Julie Clinard. From 1965 until 1983 they served in Hong Kong as church-planting missionaries with Association of Baptists for World Evangelism (ABWE). Mr. Lacock developed the *Won By One* Bible Study program which has been translated into a dozen languages and is being used worldwide. For more information write: 114 Dalewood Drive, Simpsonville, SC 29681.

# Appendix E

The following are suggestions to help implement the programs taught during the Jerusalem Outreach Conference.

## JERUSALEM OUTREACH

### A SYSTEMATIC, WORKABLE PLAN
### FOR THE LOCAL CHURCH TO
### REACH ITS JERUSALEM

I.  Implement Operation Doorstep
    A.  Pray that the Lord will lead the right individual to assume the responsibility of Jerusalem Outreach Coordinator.
        1.  This material will serve as a guideline for what is to be done in carrying out his responsibilities in both *Operation Doorstep* and *Won By One*.
        2.  Once this individual has been designated, your responsibility as a pastor will be to encourage, help, and support him.
    B.  It will be his responsibility to carry out the following guidelines:
        1.  Meet with those who committed themselves to working in *Operation Doorstep*. Divide these people into teams of two persons per team.
        2.  It is suggested that these teams work together for at least six months. After that time, it may be necessary to team up with new members who wish to be trained. Working as teams will help in the area of accountability, mutually encouraging one another, and being consistent.
        3.  Ensure that team members practice the procedures of *Operation Doorstep*.

a.  The introduction should be memorized.

b.  Emphasis should be placed on the importance of getting into the house and going through the *Neighborhood Religious Survey.*

c.  Team members should thoroughly familiarize themselves with the gospel booklet, *Life's Most Important Question.*

d.  They should become skilled in using this important tool.

C.  The Jerusalem Outreach Coordinator should either assign areas for visitation or be made aware of areas in which the teams will be working. If teams are working in the neighborhoods of each team member, they should keep the Coordinator informed as to what these areas are.

D.  Teams should keep records of areas in which they visit. This is done by using *Visitation Record Sheets.*

1.  Use one sheet per street and if necessary to use more sheets for a street, number the pages.

2.  Do not record houses from different streets on same sheet.

3.  Team members should check with the Coordinator to make sure that their visitation area is not being duplicated by another team. People become irritated if two or three teams call on them.

E.  Team members should visit at least one hour per week (more if possible) reaching the neighborhood of each team member. This hour should be a set day of the week and hour of the day, and should not be changed from week to week unless absolutely necessary.

F.  Team members should covenant to pray for *Operation Doorstep* at least 10 minutes per day.

G.  Allow time in regular church services for testimonies from *Operation Doorstep* team members.

H.  A monthly report of visitation results should be given using the *Operation Doorstep Monthly Visitation Report.* This report should be given the first Sunday of each month in order to keep the church informed as to what is being accomplished.

II.  Implement *Won by Won*

    A.  Arrange a meeting with those who committed themselves to being *Won By One* instructors. At this meeting, the following is suggested:

        1.  Give each instructor a copy of the *Won By One Instructor's Checklist.*

        2.  Determine a schedule for weekly meetings to study together the *Won By One* Bible Study.

            a.  Because of busy schedules, it may be very difficult to find a time when all of the instructors can meet together. If possible, do so, as this can be a very profitable time when the lessons can be taught to prospective instructors.

            b.  It is not necessary to complete studying the entire *Won By One* Bible Study before instructors begin teaching other individuals.

        3.  Help instructors in finding students whom they can teach in *Won By One* Bible Study. Many contacts and hopefully prospective students will result from *Operation Doorstep.*

    B.  Follow the steps given in the *Jerusalem Outreach Coordinator's Checklist.*

# *Won By One*
# Instructor's Checklist

1.  Sign a *Jerusalem Outreach Commitment Card* indicating your availability to teach a *Won By One* Bible Study session.
2.  Make contact with a person whom you can teach.
3.  Give your student a *Bible Study Session Card.*

4.  Start a file of *Bible Study Session Cards*. Use these cards as daily prayer reminders to pray for your students.

5.  Inform the Jerusalem Outreach Coordinator about your new Bible Study session so he can enter this information on his *Bible Study Session Schedule Sheet*.

6.  Whenever additional Bible Studies are begun, inform the Jerusalem Outreach Coordinator so he can keep a record of each of them.

7.  At the end of each month, fill out a *Monthly Won By One Progress Report* and give it to your Jerusalem Outreach Coordinator. This information will be compiled to form his monthly report to the church.

8.  Give opportunities for students to give testimonies in the church services.

9.  Diplomas and Pins: arrange for diplomas to be awarded to those who complete the *Won By One* Bible Study and pins to those who taught the course. These should be given out on the first Sunday at the time the Jerusalem Outreach Coordinator's report is given.

# Appendix F

## WIN THEM ONE BY ONE

C. A. M.

C. Austin Miles

*In march time*

1. If to Christ our on-ly King Men re-deemed we strive to bring,
2. Side by side we stand each day Saved are we, but lost are they;
3. On-ly cow-ards dare re-fuse, Dare this gift of God mis-use;

Just one way may this be done—We must win them one by one.
They will come if we but dare Speak a word backed up by prayer.
Ere some friend goes to his grave, Speak a word his soul to save.

**CHORUS**

{ So, you bring the one next to you, And I'll bring the one next to me; In
{ If you'll bring the one next to you, And I bring the one next to me; In

1. all kinds of weather we'll all work to-geth-er, And see what can be done,

2. no time at all we'll have them all, So win them, win them one by one.

# Bibliography

Aldrich, Joseph C. *Life-Style Evangelism: Crossing Traditional Boundaries to Reach the Unbelieving World.* Portland, Oregon: Multnomah Press, 1981.

Allison, Mike. *Legalism: A Smokescreen.* Murfreesboro, Tennessee: Sword of the Lord Publishers, 1986.

Anderson, Courtney. *To the Golden Shore.* Grand Rapids: Zondervan Publishing House, 1977.

Anderson, Neil T. *Living Free in Christ: The Truth About Who You Are and How Christ Can Meet Your Deepest Needs.* Ventura, California: Regal Books, 1993.

Anderson, Sir Robert. *The Gospel and Its Ministry.* Grand Rapids: Kregel Publications, 1978.

Barlow, Fred. *Profiles In Evangelism.* Murfreesboro, Tennessee: Sword of the Lord Foundation, 1976.

Barnes, Albert. *Barnes' Notes on the New Testament.* Grand Rapids: Kregel Publications, 1962.

Bartlett, John. *Bartlett's Familiar Quotations.* Boston: Little, Brown and Company, 1955.

Baxter, J. Sidlow. *Explore The Book.* Vol. 3. London: Marshall, Morgan and Scott, Ltd., 1962.

Belk, Maynard H. *Discipleship, Studies for the Local*

*Church.* Elyria, Ohio: Baptist Mission of North America, 1987.

Blavatsky, Helena Petrovna. *Isis Unveiled.* Wheaton: The Theosophical Publishing House, 1972.

Blue, Ronald J. *Living Proof Evangelism as a Way of Life.* Dallas, Texas: Dallas Theological Seminary, 1984.

Bonar, Horatius. *Words to Winners of Souls.* Oradell, New Jersey: American Tract Society, 1950.

Bready, J. Wesley. *England Before and After Wesley.* London: Hodder and Stoughton Limited, 1939.

Brooke, Tal. "The Emerging Reality of a New World Order." Berkley, California: *Spiritual Counterfeits Project Journal,* Vol. 16.2, 1991.

Bruce, A. B. *The Training of the Twelve.* Grand Rapids: Kregel Publications, 1971.

Cairns, Earle E. *Christianity Through the Centuries: A History of the Christian Church.* Grand Rapids: Zondervan Publishing House, 1954.

Campolo, Tony and Gordon Aeschliman. *50 Ways You Can Share Your Faith.* Downers Grove, Illinois: Intervarsity Press, 1992.

Chafer, Lewis Sperry. *True Evangelism or Winning Souls By Prayer.* Chicago: The Bible Institute Colportage Ass'n, 1938.

Champion, John B. *The Living Atonement.* Philadelphia: Griffith & Rowland Press, n.d.

Chantry, Walter J. *Today's Gospel, Authentic or Synthetic.* London: Banner of Truth, 1970.

*Christian Century.* James Wall, ed. Chicago: Vol. 111, No. 18, June, 1994.

Coleman, Robert E. *The Master Plan of Discipleship.* Old Tappan, New Jersey: Fleming H. Revell Company, 1990.

_____.*The Master Plan of Evangelism.* Old Tappan, New Jersey: Fleming H. Revell Company, 1982.

_____. *The Mind of the Master.* Old Tappan, New Jersey: Fleming H. Revell Company, 1977.

Cosgrove, Francis. *Essentials of Discipleship: What It Takes To Follow Christ.* Dallas, Texas: Roper Press, 1988.

Crawford, Percy. *The Art of Fishing for Men.* Chicago: Moody Press, 1950.

Dean, Horace F. *Visitation Evangelism Made Practical: Reaching Your Community for Christ and the Church.* Grand Rapids: Zondervan Publishing House, 1957.

DeRidder, Richard R. and Roger S. Greenway. *Let the Whole World Know: Resources for Preaching on Missions.* Grand Rapids: Baker Book House, 1988.

Dobbins, Gaines S. *Evangelism According to Christ.* New York: Harper & Brothers Publishers, 1949.

Dodd, C. H. *The Apostolic Preaching and Its Development.*

New York: Harper & Brothers Publishers, 1951.

Dozier, Edwin B. *Christian Evangelism: Its Principles and Techniques.* Vol. 1. Tokyo, Japan: The Jordan Press, 1963.

Edwards, Gene. *How to Have a Soul-Winning Church.* Montrose, California: Rushtoi Publications, 1962.

Eims, Leroy. *Discipleship in Action: A Study of the Apostles' Ministry From Acts.* Wheaton: Victor Books, 1981.

_____.*The Lost Art of Disciple Making.* Grand Rapids: Zondervan Publishing House, 1979.

_____. *One to One Evangelism: Winning Ways in Personal Witnessing.* Wheaton: Victor books, 1990.

Ellis, Howard W. *Evangelism for Teen-Agers.* New York: Abingdon Press, 1958.

Ellis, William T. *"Billy" Sunday: The Man and His Message.* Swarthmore, Pennsylvania: L. T. Myers, 1914.

Engel, James F. and H. Wilbert Norton. *What's Gone Wrong with the Harvest? A Communication Strategy for the Church and World Evangelism.* Grand Rapids: Zondervan Publishing House, 1975.

Eusebius. *Dictionary of the Apostolic Church.* James Hastings, ed. New York: Charles Scribner's Sons, HE 3. 37, 1922.

Evans, Bergen. *Dictionary of Quotations.* New York: Delacorte Press, 1968.

Evans, William. *Personal Soul-Winning.* Chicago: Moody Press, 1910.

*First Things,* A Monthly Journal of Religious and Public Life. Richard John Neuhaus, ed. A Consultation, "Evangelicals & Catholics Together: The Christian Mission in the Third Millennium.*"* New York: Institute on Religion and Public Life, No. 42, May, 1994.

Fisk, Samuel. *Divine Sovereignty and Human Freedom: Seeing Both Sides.* Neptune, New Jersey: Loizeaux Brothers, 1973.

Flint, Annie Johnson. *Poems.* Vol. 1. Toronto, Canada: Evangelical Publishers, 1944.

*Focus on Missions.* Vol. 17, No. 1. "America–The Mission Field." The Win Arn Growth Report, 1986.

Foxe, John. *Foxe's Book of Martyrs.* Springdale, Pennsylvania: Whitaker House, 1981.

Gentry, Kenneth L. Jr. *Lord of the Saved: Getting to the Heart of the Lordship Debate.* Phillipsburg, New Jersey: Presbyterian and Reformed Publishing Company, 1992.

Goldberg, Louis. *Our Jewish Friends.* Chicago: Moody Press, 1977.

Green, Michael. *Evangelism in the Early Church.* Grand Rapids: Wm. B. Eerdmans Publishing Company, 1991.

_____. *Evangelism Through The Local Church: A Comprehensive Guide to All Aspects of Evangelism.* Nashville: Thomas Nelson Publishers, 1970.

Greene, Oliver B. *From Disgrace to Grace.* Revison with Part 2 by David B. Greene, 1984. Greenville, South Carolina: The Gospel Hour, Inc., 1991.

Greenway, Roger. *The Pastor-Evangelist, Preacher, Model and Mobilizer for Church Growth.* Phillipsburg, New Jersey: Presbyterian and Reformed Publishing Company, 1987.

Harrison, Eugene Myers. *How to Win Souls: A Manual of Personal Evangelism.* Wheaton: Van Kampen Press, 1952.

Henrichsen, Walter A. *Disciples are Made-Not Born.* Wheaton: Victor Books, 1979.

Hesselgrave, David J. *Communicating Christ Cross-Culturally.* Grand Rapids: Zondervan Publishing House, 1978.

Hutson, Curtis. *Lordship Salvation.* Murfreesboro, Tennessee: Sword of the Lord Publishers, 1986.

_____.*New Evangelicalism, An Enemy of Fundamentalism.* Murfreesboro, Tennessee: Sword of the Lord Publishers, 1984.

_____.*Repentance, What Does the Bible Teach?* Murfreesboro, Tennessee: Sword of the Lord Publishers, 1986.

Huxley, Aldous. *Ends & Means: An Inquiry into the Nature of Ideals and into the Methods Employed for Their Realization.* New York: Harper & Brothers

Publishers, 1937.

Hyatt, J. Philip. *Prophetic Religion.* Nashville: Abingdon-Cokesbury Press, 1947.

Jacobs, Charles M. *The Story of the Church.* Philadelphia: The United Lutheran Publishing House, 1925.

Jaffray, George R. Jr. *Explosive Evangelism.* MacDill Air Force Base, Florida: Tyndale Bible Society, 1972.

Jess, John D. *The Art of Fishing: Practical Hints on Soul Winning.* Wheaton: The Chapel of the Air, n.d.

Johnson, R. K. *Builder of Bridges.* Murfreesboro, Tennessee: Sword of the Lord, 1969.

Johnston, Julia H. *Missionary Annals: The Life of Adoniram Judson.* Chicago: Fleming H. Revell Company, 1887.

Jones, Bob Jr. Greenville, South Carolina: Chancellor of Bob Jones University, Personal letter dated March 10, 1994.

Jones, Bob III. Greenville, South Carolina: President of Bob Jones University, Personal letter dated August 10, 1994.

Jones, Peter. *The Gnostic Empire Strikes Back: an old heresy for the New Age.* Phillipsburg, New Jersey: Presbyterian and Reformed Publishing Company, 1992.

Judson, Edward. *The Life of Adoniram Judson.*

Philadelphia: American Baptist Publication Society, 1883.

Kempf, Charles A. *Let's Have An Evangelist: Preparing Your Church for Revival.* Greenville, South Carolina: Unusual Publications, 1987.

Kennedy, D. James. *Evangelism Explosion.* Wheaton: Tyndale House Publishers, 1970.

Kistler, David. Hickory, North Carolina: Evangelist, Personal letter dated October 12, 1994.

Kittel, Gerhard, ed. *Theological Dictionary of the New Testament.* Grand Rapids: Wm. B. Eerdmans Publishing Company, 1964.

Kroll, Woodrow. *The Vanishing Ministry: How Are We Doing? How Did We Get Where We Are? What Attitude Do We Need? Where Do We Go From Here?* Grand Rapids: Kregel Publications, 1991.

Kuhne, Gary W. *The Dynamics of Personal Follow Up: The Art of Making Disciples.* Grand Rapids: Zondervan Publishing House, 1973.

Kurt, Rudolph. *Gnosis: The Nature and History of an Ancient Religion.* Edinburgh, Scotland: T. and T. Clark, n.d.

Lacock, Melvin T. *Won By One Bible Study.* Des Moines, Iowa: Bible Press, Inc., 1978.

Leavell, Roland Q. *Evangelism: Christ's Imperative Commission.* Nashville: Broadman Press, 1979.

_____.*Romance of Evangelism*.  New York: Fleming H. Revell, 1942.

*Life's Most Important Question*.  Winona Lake, Indiana: Brethren Missionary Herald Tracts, n.d.

Lindsell, Harold. *Harper's Study Bible*.  Grand Rapids: Zondervan Bible Publishers, 1985.

Little, Paul E. *How to Give Away your Faith*.  Downers Grove, Illinois: Intervarsity Press, 1966.

Lovett, C. S. *Visitation Training Made Easy*.  Baldwin Park, California: Personal Christianity, 1961.

MacArthur, John F. Jr. *Ashamed of the Gospel: When the Church Becomes Like the World*.  Wheaton: Crossway Books, 1993.

_____. *Faith Works: The Gospel According to the Apostles*.  Dallas: Word Publishing, 1993.

_____.*The Gospel According to Jesus*.  Panorama City, California: Word of Grace, 1988.

MacDonald, William. *Winning Souls the Bible Way: A Twelve Lesson Self-Study Course on Personal Evangelism*.  Kansas City, Kansas: Walterick Publishers, n.d.

McDonald, Bruce. *Bridge Evangelism: The Art of Being a Witness Naturally*.  Cherry Hill, New Jersey: Association of Baptists for World Evangelism, 1984.

McGavran, Donald A. *Effective Evangelism: A Theological Mandate*.  Phillipsburg, New Jersey: Presbyterian and

Reformed Publishing Company, 1988.

_____.*Today's Task, Opportunity, and Imperative in the World Christian Movement.* Ralph D. Winter and Steven C. Hawthorne, eds. Pasadena, California, William Carey Library, 1981.

McGlothlin, W. J. *Baptist Confessions of Faith.* Philadelphia: American Baptist Publication Society, 1911.

McLachlan, Douglas R. *Reclaiming Authentic Fundamentalism.* Independence, Missouri: American Association of Christian Schools, 1993.

McIlwain, Trevor. *Firm Foundations: Creation to Christ.* Sanford, Florida: New Tribes Mission, 1991.

Malek, Sobhi Alam. *Islam: Introduction and Approach.* Irving, Texas: International Correspondence Institute, 1992.

Marrs, Texe. *Dark Secrets of the New Age.* Westchester, Illinois: Crossway Books, 1987.

Marsh, C. R. *Share Your Faith With a Muslim.* Chicago: Moody Press, 1975.

Marsh, F. E. *Discipler's Manual.* Grand Rapids: Kregel Publications, 1980.

Miles, C. Austin. "Win them One by One." *Christian Service Songs.* Chicago: Rodeheaver Hall - Mack Company, 1939.

Miller, Joe. *The Church Planter.* Vol. 8, No. 4. Lake

Worth, Florida: 1994.

Moody, Larry and Kenneth Boa. *I'm Glad You Asked–In-Depth Answers to Difficult Questions about Christianity.* United States: Victor Books, 1992.

Moore, Waylon B. *Multiplying Disciples: The New Testament Method for Church Growth.* Colorado Springs, Colorado: Navpress, 1981.

Morgan, G. Campbell. *The Great Physician.* New York: Fleming H. Revell Company, 1924.

Moritz, Fred. Decatur, Alabama: General Director of Baptist World Mission, Personal letter dated March 7, 1994.

Mullins, E. Y. *Christian Religion and Its Doctrinal Expression.* New York: Broadman Press, 1917.

_____.*Baptist Beliefs.* Louisville: Baptist World Publishing Company, 1913.

Nutter, Charles S. *The Hymns and Hymn Writers of the Church.* New York: The Methodist Book Concern, 1911.

Oates, Wallace and Charles Symonds. *What Baptists Believe: The New Hampshire Confession, an Exposition.* Nashville, Tennessee: Sunday School Board of Southern Baptist Convention, 1913.

Packer, J. I. *Evangelism and the Sovereignty of God.* Downers Grove, Illinois: Intervarsity Press, 1961.

Parker, Percy Livingstone, ed. *The Heart of John Wesley's*

*Journal.* Cincinnati, Ohio: Jennings & Graham, n.d.

Peters, George W. *A Biblical Theology of Missions,* Chicago: Moody Press, 1972.

Petersen, Jim. *Evangelism as a Lifestyle: Reaching into Your World with the Gospel.* Colorado Springs, Colorado: Navpress, 1980.

Pettingill, William. *Bible Questions Answered.* Finlay, Ohio: Fundamental Truth Publishers, n.d.

Phillips, John. *Exploring Genesis.* Chicago: Moody Press, 1980.

Pickering, Ernest. *The Theology of Evangelism.* Clarks Summit, Pennsylvania: Baptist Bible College Press, 1974.

Platt, Suzy, ed. *Respectfully Quoted, A Dictionary of Quotations from the Library of Congress.* Washington, D.C.: Congressional Research Service, Congressional Quarterly, Inc., 1992.

Reese, Ed. *The Life and Ministry of Adoniram Judson.* Glenwood, Illinois: Fundamental Publishers, 1975.

_____. *The Life and Ministry of Bob Jones Sr.* Glenwood, Illinois: Fundamental Publishers, 1975.

_____. *The Life and Ministry of John, R. Rice.* Glenwood, Illinois: Fundamental Publishers, 1975.

Reisinger, Ernest C. *Today's Evangelism: Its Message and Methods.* Phillipsburg, New Jersey: Craig Press, 1982.

Rice, John R. *The Golden Path to Successful Personal Soul-Winning.* Murfreesboro, Tennessee: Sword of the Lord Publishers, 1961.

_____.*Why Our Churches Do Not Win Souls.* Murfreesboro, Tennessee: Sword of the Lord Publishers, 1966.

Richardson, Don. *Eternity in Their Hearts: The Untold Story of Christianity Among Folk Religions of Ancient Peoples.* Ventura, California: Regal Books, 1981.

Roberts, Dayton W. *Revolution in Evangelism, The Story of Evangelism in-Depth in Latin America.* Chicago: Moody Press, 1967.

Sanders, J. O. *The Divine Art of Soul-Winning.* London: Pickering and Inglis Ltd., 1937.

Sauer, Eric H. *The Dawn of World Redemption: A Survey of Historical Revelation in the Old Testament.* Grand Rapids: Wm. B. Eerdmans Publishing Company, 1965.

_____.*From Eternity to Eternity: an Outline of the Divine Purposes.* London: Paternoster Press, 1934.

Scarborough, L. R. *With Christ After the Lost: A Search For Souls.* Nashville, Tennessee: Sunday School Board, Southern Baptist Convention, 1919.

Stott, John R. W. *Our Guilty Silence: The Church, the Gospel and the World.* Grand Rapids: Wm. B. Eerdmans Publishing Company, 1967.

Seger, Paul. Lawrenceville, Georgia: General Director of Biblical Ministries Worldwide, Personal letter dated November 11, 1994.

Sexton, Clarence. *Won By One: A Handbook on Personal Soul-Winning.* Murfreesboro, Tennessee: Sword of the Lord Publishers, 1980.

Shelton, Bob. Greenville, South Carolina: Evangelist and Prophecy Conference Speaker, Personal letter dated October 9, 1994.

Spurgeon, Charles Haddon. *The Soul-Winner.* Grand Rapids: Wm. B. Eerdmans Publishing Company, 1963.

Standford, Ray, Richard Seymour, and Carol Ann Steib. *Handbook of Personal Evangelism.* Florida Bible College, n.d.

Stewart, James A. *Evangelism.* Salem, Oregon: Schmul Publishing Company, Inc., 1955.

_____. *Evangelism Without Apology.* Lansdale, Pennsylvania: Revival Literature, 1967.

Strobel, Lee. *Inside the Mind of Unchurched Harry & Mary: How to Reach Friends and Family Who Avoid God and the Church.* Grand Rapids: Zondervan Publishing House, 1993.

Sumner, Robert. *Biblical Evangelism in Action, A Bible Manual on Personal Soul-Winning and Church Evangelism: Providing Instructions, Outlines, Illustrations and Inspiration.* Murfreesboro, Tennessee: Biblical Evangelism Press, 1966.

_____. *Evangelism: The Church on Fire.* Murfreesboro, Tennessee: Sword of the Lord Publishers, 1981.

Sweazy, Carl M. *Evangelism that Evangelizes.* Ventura, California: Clark's Printing Company, 1968.

Tam, Stanley. *Every Christian a Soul Winner.* New York: Thomas Nelson Publishers, 1975.

Taylor, Mendell. *Exploring Evangelism.* Kansas City, Missouri: Beacon Hill Press, 1954.

Thomas, W. H. Griffith. *St.Paul's Epistle to the Romans.* Grand Rapids, Michigan: Wm. B. Eerdmans Publishing Company, 1946.

Torrey, R.A. *How to Work for Christ: A Compendium of Effective Methods.* United States: Fleming H. Revell Company, n.d.

Verwer, George. *Literature Evangelism.* Chicago: Moody Press, 1963.

Wallace, O. C. S. *What Baptists Believe: The New Hampshire Confession, An Exposition.* Nashville, Tennessee: Sunday School Board Southern Baptist Convention, 1913.

Walvoord, John and Roy B. Zuck. *The Bible Knowledge Commentary.* United States of America: Victor Books, 1983.

Wile, Jerry. *How to Win Others To Christ: Your Personal, Practical Guide to Evangelism.* Nashville: Thomas Nelson Publishers, 1992.

Wilson, Erwin. *You Can Lead Roman Catholics to Christ.*
Nashua, New Hampshire: Bible Baptist Church,
1961.

Wimber, John and Kevin Springer. *Power Evangelism.*
New York: Harper Collins Publishers, 1992.

Winchester, C. T. *The Life of John Wesley.* New York: The
Macmillan Company, 1938.

*World Almanac and Book of Facts.* Mahwah, New Jersey:
Funk and Wagnalls Publishing Company, 1997.

Wright, Tom. *Bringing the Church to the World.*
Minneapolis, Minnesota: Bethany House Publishers,
1992.

# Scripture Index

# Person Index

# Subject Index

215, 245, 290

New Evangelicals . . . . . . 275

New Hampshire Confession
of Faith . . . . . . . . . . . . 201

New Park Street Baptist
Chapel in London, England
78

New Tribes Mission . . . . . 189

New World Order . . 285, 287

Nineveh . . . . . . . . . . . 37, 38

Northern Kingdom in Israel . .
249

Novatianism . . . . . . . . . . 67

Omission
Sin of . . . . . . . . . . . . . 176

Open air preacher . . . . . . . 74

Operation doorstep . 247, 254,
255, 256, 260, 261, 262, 263,
264, 300, 301, 302, 306, 307,
309, 310, 311

Orient . . . . . . . . . . . . . . . 76

Pacific Garden Rescue
Mission in Chicago . . . . . 79

Paganism . . . . . . . . . . 63, 291

Pakistan . . . . . . . . . . . . . 226

Panama City, Florida . . . . . 81

Pantheism . . . . . . . . . . . . 38

Parable of the soils . 117, 177

Parables . . . . . . . . . . . . . 118

Parachurch organizations 229,
230, 279

Pastor-evangelist . . . . . . . . 78

Pastors . . . . 71, 72, 81, 83, 207
250, 251, 287

Peaceful society . . . . . . . . 190

Pentecost . . . . 52, 54, 57, 136,
142, 145, 147, 230

Persecution 56, 63, 64, 67, 68,
117, 137, 146, 150, 153, 155,
156, 188, 208, 274, 287

Personal worker . . . . 204, 259

Philadelphia, church of . . 209

Philippi . . 158, 159, 160, 186,
188

Piedmont Bible College . . 226

Platonic wisdom . . . . . . . . 52

Pluralistic society . . 143, 191

Political treachery . . . . . . . 53

Politically correct . . . 63, 191

Pragmatism . . . . . . . . . . 224

Prayer . 57, 79, 83, 84, 85, 99,
113, 115, 116, 146, 148, 149,
153, 157, 169, 187, 189, 190,
198, 209, 221, 231, 232, 237,
248, 253, 263, 264, 265, 266,
271, 305, 307, 312

*Prayer–Asking and Receiving*
83

Preaching ix, 37, 45, 50, 162,
172, 181, 191, 193, 205, 219,
224, 231

Pre-tribulation rapturist . . 277

Pride of life . . . . . . . . . . . 93

Primitive tribes . . . . . . . . 26

Printing press . . . . . . . . . . 68

*Protevangelium* . . . . . . . . xv

*raison d'etre* . . . . . . . . . . 50

Rapture . . 230, 272, 276, 277,
278, 295

Rebellion against God . 15, 17,
55, 95

*Reclaiming Authentic
Fundamentalism* . . . . . . . 289

Reconciliation
Doctrine of . . . . . . 179, 180
Great work of . . . . . . . . 152
Message of . . . . . . 109, 179
Ministry of . . viii, 108, 109,
179, 246
Responsibility of . . . . . . 179
Word of . . viii, 91, 109, 179
Work of . . . . 108, 135, 152

Redemption